Cinnabaris
Series of Oriental Studies – V

Miyapma: Traditional Narratives of the Thulung Rai

MIYAPMA
Traditional Narratives of the Thulung Rai

N. J. Allen

Vajra Publications
www.vajrabooks.com.np

Cinnabaris
Series of Oriental Studies
Collection directed by Dr. Martino Nicoletti

Published by

Vajra Publications
Jyatha, Thamel, Kathmandu, Nepal
Tel.: 977-1-4220562, Fax: 977-1-4246536
e-mail: bidur_la@mos.com.np
www.vajrabooks.com.np

Distributed by

Vajra Books
Kathmandu, Nepal

ISBN No. 978-9937-506-82-3

Printed in Nepal

Contents

Photographs

Individuals and Domestic Life

Environment

Ritual

Foreword

The abundance of anthropological literature on Nepal produced in the past two decades stands in inverse proportion to its thematic range. The corpus has come to be dominated by two broad concerns: development and politics. Whatever the intellectual or humanitarian engagement of anthropologists with these domains, there can be little doubt about the motors that are primarily responsible for driving this production: funding opportunities in the first place and, in the second, the obviously topical character of all things political since the dissolution of the Partyless Panchayat System in 1990 and, more pertinently, the declaration of the Peoples' War in 1996. If it has seemed to some that attention to matters other than development and politics would have been inappropriate during this period, that is because anthropology as a whole has sought to preserve its existence by forging coalitions with more robust and confident disciplines – economics and political science, for example, or literary theory – and is obliged to follow the current interests of its senior partners.

Some arenas of interest that once stood at the very centre of the anthropological enterprise – such as kinship – have all but disappeared from writing about Nepal. One 'traditional' preoccupation that has, by contrast, proved to be more resilient is the study of myth. *Miyapma* was the first truly rigorous investigation of the mythic corpus of a Bodic language group in Nepal, and, in spite of the fact that it has never yet been published, it remains one of the most important. The years since it was first completed (as a doctoral thesis, in 1976) have seen a slow, but steady, increase in the appearance of works on related subjects: monographs by authors such as

Michael Oppitz and Anne de Sales on the Kham Magar, Martin Gaenszle on the Mewahang Rai, Simon Strickland on the Gurung and András Höfer on the Tamang have been joined by more recent studies of Himalayan populations outside Nepal: Anna Balikci and Heleen Plaisier on the Bhutias and Lepchas of Sikkim, and Stuart Blackburn among the Apa Tanis of Arunachal Pradesh are three recent examples. An important development from a comparative perspective is the renewed attention being paid by several authors to mythic traditions of Tibet itself, an undertaking that is already helping to advance the project, first articulated in the present work, of a closer rapprochement between the Himalayas and the Plateau.

For almost all the authors cited above, and several others besides, a major point of reference is provided by a handful of articles by Nick Allen (mainly 1974, 1978, 1980, 1997a; see the bibliography of this book). These articles are all substantially based on material that first appeared in *Miyapma*. As crucial as they may be for anyone working in the field of comparative mythology, their value is nevertheless compromised by their necessary brevity. As the author himself remarks in one of them, 'the material can only be compressed at the cost of considerable simplification' (1980: 2). But there are reasons other than the presentation of a great deal of material absent from the derivative articles that make this publication so welcome. One is the fact that the book is more than the sum of its parts. The subject of the Thulung mythic corpus extends from the Creation down to migration stories that have a plausible historical component, and this synoptic presentation makes possible a comparative cross-referencing of narrative motifs that a consideration of each episode in isolation does not.

There is another reason why the material is best served by a full-length monograph: the work sets an exemplary standard for how future students of Himalayan mythology might proceed. To begin with, it is based on a thorough understanding of the complexities of a hitherto undescribed language (itself the subject of a monograph by the author: 1975), the vector of a collection of disorganised narrative episodes recounted by often reluctant story-tellers. The lucid organisation of this material, in uncommonly limpid English, belies the fiendish difficulty of the task that must have confronted the ethnographer: *ars celandi artem*. This clarity has not been achieved by papering over the cracks. Indeed, the author is at pains to point out lacunae in the narratives (noises off, gremlins in the Uher), as well as inconsistencies in the narrations, probable lapses in his own interpretation, and so forth. The result is a body of material that, in spite of having been partially processed, preserves a vitality essential for its accessibility as raw material by future researchers: it has been presented in such a way as to make it more, not less, useable, avoiding the textual critic's cardinal sin of 'silent' editing. The wider Bodic context is provided by reference not only to other Tibeto-Burman (Lepcha, Gurung, Tamang) mythologies, but also to Tibetan literary material: the author is fully aware of all the relevant secondary literature in several European languages, and has mastered the rudiments of the Tibetan language itself.

The extensive commentary and reflection that follow the translated passages enliven an already rich narrative and facilitate a plausible traffic with this Tibetan repository, rather than – as happens so often – imprisoning it in a hypertrophied gall of theory. In this regard, we should be especially grateful to the author for his decision 'to err on the side of boldness than caution' (60) in pressing the case for areas of continuity between the Thulung and Tibetan mythic corpora.

The related field of Tibetan Studies is witnessing a depressing trend: the subscription by academics to influential Tibetans' sanitisation of their own culture, following the principle that a historical truth is established by its conformity to doctrinal orthodoxy. A corollary to this process of historical rectification is the pernicious notion of authenticity, according to which a given version of a myth is seen to be self-evidently genuine. The 'authentic' version is traceable to a valid source and is accordingly fenced off from the residue of folklorish material that is the only acceptable object for analytic scrutiny. *Miyapma* reminds us that nothing should be sacred, and that there is no such thing as authenticity; there is only selection, whether by the common consent of popular aesthetics or the efforts of a nation-building elite.

Let us take the example of the Tibetan myth of royal origins, a topic that receives considerable attention in this work. The version that seems to have dominated during the Imperial period has the first king (usually called Nyatri Tsenpo, the 'Neck-enthroned One') descending from heaven onto a Tibetan mountain-top. In the writings of the later period, which sought to establish Buddhism in the country by diffusing it as as widely as possible through all areas of Tibetan culture, the 'celestial origins' version is supplanted by one in which the first king is a refugee from India – the homeland of Buddhism, of course – who happens to be a member of the Shakya clan. These later claims notwithstanding, a short work from Dunhuang that can reasonably claim to be the earliest treatise on the subject (PT1038) adopts a completely disinterested position on the question of origins, indifferently presenting three versions, each prefaced by 'Some say that...'. Nowhere is there a mention of India, but according to one version the king 'originates from either the inferior caste of meat-eaters or the red-faced king of the *snod sbyin* [i.e. *yaksha*] Dza...'.[1]

Nick Allen is surely right to suggest that the Thulung anthropogonic cycle might profitably be compared with Tibetan stories of the origin of the first king. Parallels are discernable, but, by his own account, rather tenuous. The evidence of PT1038 hints that there may once have been a greater diversity of versions, most of which would have been weeded out by the process of official selection. As it happens, Allen's concluding argument that the Thulung and Tibetan cases share a common heritage prior to the rise of Bon and Buddhism is vindicated by a royal origin-myth that, to the best of my knowledge, does not appear in any secondary accounts. (The reader is referred to chapter 2, especially II and *Comparisons*, which include discussion of the motifs of the goitre, the wrapping up of an inchoate newborn to incubate it into a human form and, later, the importance of creatures associated with the *klu* category, that subsumes the Indic nagas.) The account in question appears in a fourteenth-century commentary, but was very probably current in other forms before being incorporated into this work.

To summarise, the princess Mucam Drama (dMu lcam Gra ma) develops a goitre the size of a stomach in a hollow at the nape of her neck. After nine months and ten days the goitre bursts, and from the interior there appear a crystal scorpion, a golden frog, a turquoise fish and a conch-shell tadpole. The parents wrap their strange progeny in a white cloth and keep them in a golden container as a support for their good fortune (*g.yang*). After three and a half days they open the wrapping and, to their amazement, find four men. The crystal scorpion has become a crystal man with turquoise hair, silken robes and a turban, who declares himself to be Nyatri Tsenpo, the first king: 'It is because I dwelt at the nape of my mother's neck for nine months and ten days that I am called the Neck-enthroned One'. The other three men are his priests.

This is just one of several cases in which the hypotheses proposed on the basis of this study can be validated by recent research on Tibetan written sources. Others – although there is insufficient space here to go into detail – include the practice of ultimogeniture and the absence of any marked unilineality. (As far as the latter is concerned, it may be noted that, for the

---

1   Karmay, Samten 1998. *The Arrow and the Spindle. Studies in History, Myths, Rituals and Belief in Tibet.* Kathmandu: Mandala Book Point. P. 286.

first seven generations that feature in the Tibetan royal genealogies, the name of each king is derived from that of his mother.)

Like *Miyapma*, some of the author's early essays have become the point of departure for more extensive exploration by subsequent writers. His discussion of verticality (1972), for example, provided the *notion clef* for the present writer's understanding of territorial rituals in highland Nepal, and inspired a collection of articles entitled *Himalayan Space*.[2] One article that I believe will be central to the future development of comparative studies on Bodic mythology is Allen's diachronic study of Sherpa kinship terminology (1976c; see also 1975), a work that has not yet been followed up in any significant way. Among the conclusions to the present volume is the suggestion that a shared language family may be less significant as a basis for valid comparison than a common alliance pattern: 'Perhaps...we should distinguish language families in which prescriptive alliance has been practised from those in which such an alliance pattern cannot be demonstrated. Ideologies associated with the former may have more in common with each other than they do with the latter' (234). While this observation is intended to encourage comparisons between Indo-European and Tibetan societies, *a fortiori* it offers a further explanation (in addition to the rise of Bon and Buddhism) for the widening gulf between Tibet and Himalayan groups such as the Thulung: the 1976 study of Sherpa kinship terminology argues that prescriptive alliance may once have been the norm in Tibet - another conclusion that has been supported by recent historical investigations. Keeping in mind the likelihood that Tibet was once characterised by a positive marriage rule will, I believe, be essential for the productive examination of archaic or provincial Tibetan mythic narratives.

Although the linguistic and cultural homogenisation of Nepal in the past generation has undoubtedly brought about the irretrievable loss of numerous narrative traditions, the publication of this volume is sure to stimulate a renewed interest in the comparative study of the mythology of Bodic peoples. And if researchers in this field who follow in the footsteps of Nick Allen apply exacting standards approaching those shown in *Miyapma*, then we, too, may earn the right to err in our conclusions on the side of boldness rather than of caution.

Charles Ramble

---

2 Bickel, Balthasar and Martin Gaenszle. 1999. *Himalayan Space: Cultural Horizons and Practices.* Zurich: Völkerkundemuseum Zürich.

Preface

This book is an edited version of a D.Phil. thesis submitted to the University of Oxford in 1976. The thesis was completed while I was a Lecturer in Anthropology at the University of Durham, just before I moved back to Oxford to teach.

My original plan was to undertake a thorough-going revision of the thesis before trying to publish it, and with this in view I began a series of articles. The first (Allen 1980) was an overview, while three others (1981, 1997a, 1997b) elaborated on particular narratives that were included in the thesis. One (1986) incorporated Thulung material but focused on a Newar narrative. However, with the passing years, it became ever clearer that the project of full-scale revision was unrealistic. Firstly, my rate of progress was totally inadequate – in the first twenty years the articles had covered only a minute proportion of the material included in the thesis. Secondly, my research and teaching interests gradually changed (in directions foreshadowed by the thesis – see Allen 2000, 2003; Onta 2004), so that I was no longer able to keep up with the rapidly growing literature on the Himalayas. Thirdly, I came to realise that my notion of revision had been incoherent. What I was doing in practice was expanding the geographical and historical range of material used for comparison with the Thulung narratives – but such expansion had no logical limit. The comparisons made in the thesis retained their value (I thought) and could not be pruned, and if the expansion continued indefinitely, the result would become both unpublishable as well as unreadable. I recalled Casaubon's failure to complete his *Key to all mythologies* in George Eliot's *Middlemarch*. I had to choose between publishing the thesis more or less as it stood and simply not publishing it.

As to how much I should revise, after considering various options, I settled on a policy of minimalism. I have often reworded to improve readability (but without trying to modernise the vocabulary); and I have inserted in square brackets a few annotations, most of which refer to subsequent work by myself or by linguists. On the other hand, I have made no systematic attempt to update the rest of the bibliography – any such effort could only have been patchy and half-hearted. This means for instance that, regrettably, no use has been made of some closely relevant work, for instance by Martin Gaenszle (1991, 2002; Ebert and Gaenszle 2004) or Charlotte Hardman (2000, esp. Ch. 5). Nor have I seriously tried to incorporate my own subsequent studies in Indo-European comparative mythology.

This study, then, is a historical document in two senses. It is an account of the oral heritage of the Thulung Rai as recorded in 1970-1, and it is a comparative study of that heritage on the basis of literature available to me at that time, using the conceptual tools and range of knowledge that I then possessed. I can only hope that the recording of the heritage and its comparativist elaboration will be carried further by others.

In the original thesis Appendix 2 contained 57 pages of transcribed Thulung texts with linguistic annotations. The present Appendix 2 only contains a short sample. The remainder has been placed on the internet so as to make it more conveniently accessible to electronic searching.[1] However I have retained the original Appendix 1.

All the photographs I took at the time have been digitally archived at the Pitt Rivers Museum in Oxford.

Acknowledgements. I should like first to thank the numerous Thulung who helped me while I lived among them, and particularly the narrators named in Appendix I. I had various supervisors at different times and places: Ravindra Jain, Maurice Freedman, Rodney Needham, all at Oxford, and Christoph von Fürer-Haimendorf at the School of Oriental and African Studies. I am grateful to all of them, especially the last two, who were most closely involved. I am indebted also to the authorities at Tribhuvan University, to the then Social Science Research Council for financial support (via a project organised by Fürer-Haimendorf), to Lyn Joiner (a

---

1   See: http://bit.ly/ThulungOnline

neighbouring fieldworker) for helpful conversations and correspondence and, most recently, to Charles Ramble and Mark Turin, for encouragement and advice. I thank also Vicky Dean for her hard work turning the antiquated typescript into electronic format.

Treatment of non-English vocabulary

Thulung. Apart from names, Thulung is written in the orthography discussed and used in Allen (1975a), with only one change: retroflexion of dentals is now shown by subdots rather than capitalisation. In the translations otherwise unexpected upper case initials indicate Thulung ritual vocabulary.

Nepali. Nepali words are identified as such on first mention by a following 'N' (e.g., *ghar* N). In their transliteration I have generally followed Turner (1931), replacing his *ṅ* by *ng* and his *ś* by *sh*. For the meanings I have regularly consulted both Turner and Sharma (1962), usually without mentioning the fact. I have anglicised proper names.

Tibetan. I have followed the Wylie system of transliteration.

Proper names have usually been anglicised.

Conventions

Abbreviations used to refer to Thulung individuals and to the texts they gave me are explained in Appendix 1. 'AS' refers to the book Rai (1944) and to its writer.

Cross-references. 5 VI Kam (b) refers to Chapter 5, section VI, text by Kamanjit, § b. Cross-references within a chapter sometimes omit the chapter number.

CHAPTER 1

Introduction

I. The Rai

Kathmandu is generally said to be situated in the Central Valley, an expression which implies a division of the country into eastern and western halves. In fact only about one third of the country lies to the east of Kathmandu and constitutes East Nepal. This area forms, roughly speaking, a rectangle 160 miles long from east to west and 100 miles from north to south. If one subtracts from the area a relatively narrow northern strip and a somewhat broader southern strip, there remains what may be called the middle hills. The traditional inhabitants of the middle hills of East Nepal have long been referred to as the Kiranti. Their domain in turn has sometimes been divided into Near, Middle and Far Kirant (as seen from the Central Valley), and the Rai, a subdivision of the Kiranti, are the traditional inhabitants of the second. A flight fifty miles due south from the summit of Mount Everest brings one to the middle of the Rai tract.

It has been conventional to refer to the Rai as a tribe, and I shall here follow this usage in spite of various objections that might be raised, both to the use of the term in general and to its application to the Rai. This means that the Limbu, the traditional inhabitants of Far Kirant will also be regarded as a tribe, and the term Kiranti itself will be taken to refer to a supra-tribal category. The category is certainly a vague one. Many use Kiranti to include traditional inhabitants of the southern strip of East Nepal, while some (such as Chemjong 1966) have extended it to certain peoples in West Nepal as well. On the other hand, one well-established usage (followed for instance by Bista 1972: 32ff) confines it to the Rai and Limbu.

If the Rai are a tribe, the Thulung are a subtribe. In the absence of adequate field research no one knows how many different Rai subtribes there are, nor even whether an exact figure would be meaningful. Bista lists eighteen subtribe names, and his list can be added to from various sources. So far as the Thulung are concerned, and the same seems to apply to their immediate neighbours, a subtribe can be defined quite precisely on linguistic criteria. The Thulung language is quite distinct from that of neighbouring subtribes and does not shade off into them through intermediate dialects. The Thulung themselves regard their language as separated from that of their neighbours by a barrier of mutual unintelligibility. Internally, the language is relatively uniform, and the only meaningful subdivision of the subtribe would seem to be the village. This may not apply in other areas, and some of the names in lists purportedly of Rai subtribes may in fact cover closely related groups which are currently differentiating one from another, or which are only distinguishable on very sensitive criteria.

The Rai languages, like the Limbu language, have generally been classified as Tibeto-Burman, e.g. in the *Linguistic Survey of India*. A more recent linguistic taxonomy can be found in Shafer (1974).[1] We shall take from him in particular the useful term 'Bodic' which he uses for a linguistic grouping of a rank that he calls a division. The Bodic division of Sino-Tibetan includes a Bodish section to which belongs Tibetan itself, an East Himalayish section consisting of the Rai languages, and a number of other sections represented on the borders of Tibet and in Assam.

The Rai are generally of Mongoloid appearance, and have sometimes been described as Palaeo-Mongoloid. Taken in conjunction with the linguistic evidence, this suggests that their cultural origins may also lie in the north, but of course this cannot be assumed. There is no reason to doubt that many, at least, of the ancestors of the present-day Rai must ultimately have come from the north, but we have no idea when, and can only speculate about possible routes of immigration. It cannot, for instance, be taken for granted that the ancestors of the Rai moved straight south from Tibet across the Himalayan passes to reach their present habitat.

---

1   [For more up-to-date work bearing on this and the next paragraph see van Driem 1998, 2003.]

Previous literature on the Rai is scanty. Generalised accounts of them can be found in the military handbooks and the more popular works written by officers in Gurkha regiments. Bista (1972), who covers the Rai in less than ten pages, shows a very similar approach. The standard bibliographies list a few articles mentioning or dealing with the Rai and deriving from enquiries made among emigré Rai in Darjeeling (in one instance from prisoners of war in Romania). Most of the earlier linguistic materials on the Rai were collected by Hodgson in the first half of the nineteenth century, and only small additional amounts were included in the *Linguistic Survey of India*. Shafer's taxonomy was based on this very imperfect material, supplemented by a handful of articles by Wolfenden from around 1930.

Only very recently has the situation begun to improve. We now have one article on the social structure of the Kulung subtribe (McDougal 1973), based on intensive fieldwork in 1964-5. Lyn Joiner was doing fieldwork among the Khaling subtribe while I was with the Thulung, and has kindly allowed me to use some personal communications. The Sunwar have generally been treated as a distinct tribe on the same taxonomic level as the Rai but of marginal Kiranti status. However, linguistically they are very close to neighbouring Rai subtribes, and from a historical point of view they should be included among them; so one should also cite Fournier (1974). The more relevant of my own contributions on the Thulung are listed in the bibliography below. Allen (1975a), an account of the Thulung language, refers to work by members of the Summer Institute of Linguistics on the languages of the Khaling, Kulung and Sunwar. It also describes the booklet on Thulung, written in Nepali and published in 1944, by Agam Sĩg Rai (henceforth AS), an emigré Thulung then living in the Darjeeling area.

II. Cultural Contacts

In spite of the great gaps in our knowledge, we need a general outline of the history and cultural contacts of the area. Nowadays the vast majority of Rai are sedentary agriculturalists, and there is no definite evidence pointing to a period when they might have been ignorant of agriculture. On the other hand, as we shall see, Thulung tradition clearly recalls a time when they were shifting agriculturalists without permanent villages, and since this has been the normal mode of subsistence for so many tribal peoples in the hill areas of south, east and south-east Asia, no doubt it was once shared by the Rai in general. No doubt too, as the traditions suggest, hunting and gathering were then major economic activities. I cannot say anything definite about the date when the Rai or their component subtribes began to form permanent villages, though for the Thulung my guess is that it was more than two centuries ago.

Until the public health campaigns of the 1950s and 1960s East Nepal was shut off from easy contact with the plains of India by the malarial forests of the Terai. The forests were inhabited by peoples believed to possess resistance to the disease, and although it was possible to cross this zone more or less safely at certain seasons, it seems certain that economic and cultural contacts between the middle hills and the plains were tenuous.

The area immediately north of the Rai tract is nowadays predominantly settled by Sherpas. Both linguistically and culturally Sherpas are closely related to Tibetans, and according to Oppitz (1968), they only began to immigrate into east Nepal shortly before the middle of the sixteenth century. We shall often mention their interaction with the Thulung, whose territory is located on the north-west edge of the Rai tract quite close to Sherpa settlements.

The most obvious source of outside influence on the Rai has been the Nepali-speaking peoples.[2] From at least the fourteenth century onwards, Hindus of non-Mongoloid stock have been spreading eastwards through the middle and lower hills of Nepal. A landmark in this mostly gradual process was the capture of the Newar city of Kathmandu by Prithvi Narayan Shah, the Raja of Gorkha, in 1768. Before his death seven years later, he had expanded his kingdom both east and west and laid the foundations for the present state of Nepal. For the first time the Rai definitely formed part of a larger political unit. A system of local government was set up under which responsibility for collecting taxes and maintaining law and order rested on local Rai headmen supervised, no doubt fairly loosely, from provincial capitals (Okhaldhunga, in the case of the Thulung). It is possible that even before the incorporation of the Rai area into Prithvi Narayan's kingdom, immigrant Nepali-speakers were already importing Hindu ideas. Certainly over the last two centuries Hindu influences on the Rai have been

---

2   The expression is less than satisfactory, but the alternatives are also clumsy or misleading. By 'Nepali-speakers' I mean peoples whose first and only language is Nepali. This category includes high-caste Hindus, but it also includes Untouchables, who are Hindus only under certain definitions of the term, and formerly tribal peoples who have lost their tribal language and culture (e.g., in east Nepal, the Gurung).

steadily increasing. In general, subtribes in the south have been more exposed to these influences than have subtribes in the north, since the immigrants were above all interested in growing rice and this cannot be done much above 6000 feet. But the degree of Hinduisation is greatly affected by local factors which may vary from village to village, and we do not know enough about the Rai to regard any subtribe as completely Hinduised.

If one wishes to periodise the history of the area, 1951 must be regarded as opening a new era. It was now that the 104-year rule of the Rana oligarchy came to an end, and the regimes that replaced it were keen to introduce modernising innovations. However the abruptness of the political change in the Central Valley is a little misleading. Since before the first World War many Rai had been enlisting in the Indian Army. Moreover many had also participated in the eastward movement of Nepali-speakers and emigrated over the previous century towards the employment opportunities available in the Darjeeling area. Links between emigrants and home village were sometimes maintained, constituting another channel for the spread of ideas. However, such ideas scarcely found institutional form until the 1960s, when government initiatives led to the founding of village primary schools, the multiplication of weekly markets, and the introduction of a form of democracy based on village committees or panchayats.

III. Circumstances and Orientation of Fieldwork

My reasons for choosing the Thulung rather than any other subtribe were various. Living towards the west end of the Rai tract, they are among the first groups one meets when travelling east. This was convenient for purposes of communication, but was not an important factor. Since I was interested in traditional Rai culture, it was important that their territory lay in the northern part of the Rai tract and hence they could be expected to be less Hinduised than many other subtribes. Of their more northerly neighbours, the Khaling and Kulung, both either had been or were being studied by ethnographers, as already noted. A more positive recommendation was the existence of the booklet mentioned above describing the language; I was lucky enough early on to meet the grandson of the author and via him to obtain a copy. I also had in mind Shafer's view that Thulung was the most archaic of the east Himalayish languages and that a study of it would be of particular value to the comparative grammar of Sino-Tibetan. Although I had no qualifications for such a study, it seemed that, if I was to learn any of the subtribal languages, this would be the obvious choice.

Arriving in the Rai area in early July 1969, at the beginning of the rains, I thought it impracticable to settle in a village straightaway, since the villagers were too busy with agricultural work to have time to spare for an outsider. My first two months were therefore spent improving my Nepali in bazaar towns, first in Okhaldhunga, then for a fortnight in Salleri. Early in September I moved to the small bazaar town of Nele in the Thulung area, and taught for a few weeks in the secondary school, attempting to expound in Nepali selections from English prose and poetry. Friendships and contacts with young Thulung schoolmasters made at this time were a great help subsequently, and it was the headmaster of a primary school in the village of Mukli who helped me move to lodgings there in early October. Mukli is by common consent the oldest Thulung village, the one from which the others were founded, and my lodgings were in the central and oldest part of the village. Though this was largely due to chance, it is worth mentioning since some types of historical information could perhaps not have been collected elsewhere.

The next eighteen months were spent among the Thulung with the exception of four three-week breaks. About every three weeks I made excursions of two or three days to the Tibetan refugee settlement of Chyalsa, which lay some four hours' walk to the north-west and where mail could most reliably be collected. For a few days each I briefly visited the Khaling village of Jubing and the Sunwar village of Sabra. Within the Thulung area, although Mukli remained my permanent base, I spent roughly a month each in Tingla and Lokhim, and ten days at Jubu. Short visits of a couple of days each were made to Panchen and Dewsa, but I never explored the south-east of the Thulung tract.

When asked to explain my presence, as I often was, I replied truthfully that I had come to learn about the history, customs and language of the Thulung. I tried to explain that, just as their children read about foreign countries in their geography class at primary school, so I was planning to write a sort of geography book, and had come from a higher sort of school called a university. I am unsure how many understood or believed this explanation, and I think I was widely thought to be some sort of a spy from the British Army. At first it was thought proper that I should employ a cook-boy, but after a matter of weeks this arrangement ended, and thereafter I always found it possible to arrange to eat in Thulung households. I was regularly treated with great kindness and hospitality, but it was not at all easy to collect the sort of information that I sought.

I have already noted that the Rai have long been involved in a process of Hinduisation.[3] This blanket term covers a large number of distinguishable changes, of which here is a list. (i) Demographic: the immigration of large numbers of Nepali-speakers.[4] (ii) Ecological: the consequent destruction of vast areas of jungle. (iii) Material culture: introduction of the plough. (iv) Politico-economic: change in land-ownership and the balance of power. (v) Kinship: change from prescriptive to non-prescriptive alliance system.[5] (vi) Social ideology: introduction of ideas of caste. (vii) Religion: employment of Brahman and Untouchable ritual specialists and celebration of Hindu festivals. (viii) Linguistic: development of bilingualism, with numerous borrowings from Nepali into the tribal language.

Other changes too might be mentioned, for there is probably no aspect of tribal life that has not been somehow influenced by the presence of the Nepali-speakers. Moreover the process of Hinduisation is in a sense continuous with the process of Sanskritisation (the imitation by lower castes of Brahmanical or high-caste life-styles), such as can be recognised, for instance, in changes in Thulung wedding practice and ceremonial. Related to Sanskritisation there is another process in operation that might be called neo-Hinduisation, with the development of sects of Thulung 'sadhus', whose worship is directed towards Bhagavan. This deity is conceived somewhat as is the Christian God, and is very different in 'feel' from the carnivorous deities more traditionally worshipped by hills Hindus.

---

3 For a description of a very highly Hinduised formerly tribal people see Hitchcock (1966), on a Magar group. Much of what he says would be applicable to the more Hinduised Rai. [For more on Hinduisation among the Thulung see Allen 1987 and 1997b.]

4 The national census of 1961 gave a total of 239,749 people who spoke Rai languages as their mother tongue; 90% of them live in the eastern hills. Unfortunately the census does not distinguish Rai subtribes. I guess that there are of the order of 10,000 Thulung, excluding those who have permanently emigrated; but no confidence can be placed in this estimate. Figures for the ratio of immigrants to Rai are available only at the district level: Okhaldhunga jilla has 61% Nepali speakers as against 11.6% Rai, and Majh Kirant jilla has respectively 56% and 36%. [Lahaussois (2003:1) estimates the number of Thulung speakers nowadays at about 1000, none of those under the age of 20 being fluent.]

5 In the Thulung case it is debatable how far this particular change is due to contact with Nepali-speakers, though such contact has certainly led to many other changes in the classification of relatives and their mutual behaviour.

This trend is itself closely related to the ideology of democratic social progress which is being spread through the schools and local government. Moreover there are younger Thulung who frequent bazaars and are not unaware of communist versions of the same secular world view.

If any sense is to be made of all this, we need to know as much as possible about the basal 'tribal' culture, on which the various processes have been operating. Of course it is unrealistic to imagine a tribal culture that was once static and changeless, and when we come to details no such postulate will be necessary. However, it is convenient to have a single term to refer to the non-Hindu components of contemporary Thulung culture. Diachronically, too, this tribal culture can be regarded as stretching backwards to the time when the Rai were sole inhabitants of the territory they now share with immigrants, and when contact with Nepali-speakers was negligible. At that time it constituted the totality of the Rai way of life. With increasing Hinduisation it was steadily displaced so that, to a first approximation, one can now envisage Thulung culture as composed of two parts, Thulung and non-Thulung, or tribal and borrowed. This will seem a crude dichotomy, and if it were our main subject it would call for further justification. For instance, one might argue that the model is excessively two-dimensional: contemporary Thulung tribal culture ought not to be seen simply as precontact culture with areas lopped off, for the remnants stand in a relationship to a whole body of borrowed Hindu culture and are qualitatively altered as a result. These are significant theoretical questions, but for now I would simply say that in practice one can classify a great many of the objects, actions and ideas of the Thulung into tribal and borrowed, and that such an analysis is generally less problematic than might be anticipated.

IV. Ritual and Ritual Specialists

The analysis of Thulung life into tribal and borrowed has little in common with the world-view of the Thulung themselves, who seldom have cause to think systematically about their society, and have little awareness of historical processes. Nevertheless, they do have a certain apprehension of what distinguishes them from the surrounding Nepali-speakers and Hindu populations. This sense of tribal identity and distinctness is closely associated with the concept of *ḍiumla*. The word is difficult to translate and I return to it in Ch. 6 when a good many instances of its use in the texts will be available for analysis. Provisionally, it can be rendered 'religion, tribal lore and custom'. If I hoped to record and understand the essence of the tribal culture, this had to be the main focus of attention. In other words I had to concentrate on myth and ritual. To explain the difficulties in doing so, I need to give a general picture of the tribal ritual organisation. The subject is complicated, and further details are given in Allen (1974, 1976a, b).

Within the general class of ritual officiants (*nokcho*), the Thulung contrast two main categories. The *dewa nokcho* can be conveniently referred to as the tribal priest, while the other type (*sele, seleme, bijuwā* N, or *jhãkri* N) will here be referred to, if less conveniently, as a medium. A single individual cannot be both priest and medium. A priest is always male and is the son or close agnate of a previous priest, from whom he learned the tribal ritual chants. In principle, a single line of priests serves a certain number of patrilineal clans within one village. When a person dies in the ordinary way from illness or old age, the priest acts as psychopomp: his chant accompanies the spirit of the deceased on its journey past named landmarks to the home of the ancestors, which lies some twenty miles south-west of Mukli. At fixed periods after a death, in fulfilment of a client's vow made during an illness, and perhaps for other reasons, the priest may be called on to perform one of a series of ancestral rites (*pitri* N). At a wedding he introduces the bride to the ancestors of her new family and invokes for the fertility of the match. In addition, he is responsible for collective agricultural rites, the *bhume pujā* N, or *tosi*. Unlike the rites already mentioned, the *bhume* rites take place at communal shrines located within the village on a fixed number of occasions per year related to the agricultural calendar.

In distinguishing between priest and medium, a difference emphasised by the Thulung themselves is that the priest lacks the relationship with a particular spirit that enables the medium to become possessed. The initiative in the recruitment of a medium is ascribed not to the humans involved but to the spirit. The typical sequence is for a young man (occasionally woman) to become possessed in the course of a seance. On receiving this sign of his (or her) vocation, he seeks instruction from another medium, his guru, who need not be of his own tribe or caste. At least twice a year, at full moon, he must worship the spirit or spirits who possess him. He commonly does so at large gatherings, where numerous mediums assemble from a wide area and dance at sacred spots situated usually on high ground and away from villages. This is the only occasion in which mediums participate communally, and nothing suggests that they do so in order to benefit the collectivity. The medium's main activity is as diviner and exorcist at nocturnal seances held in ordinary houses, and his services are obligatory in place of a priest's when a death is classified as bad, i.e., as unnatural or untimely. His gift is sometimes inherited from the father's or mother's side, but there is no regular link between medium and clan. A Thulung can call on a medium from any tribe or caste, his choice being influenced solely by the medium's reputation for success.

In broad terms, the priest deals with the orderly supernatural, the properly integrated ancestors, and the fertility of the village agricultural land, while the medium deals with the forces of chaos and disorder that afflict individual households. It is primarily the priest who is conceived of as guardian of the *ḍiumla*, maintainer of what is distinctive of the Thulung as opposed to outsiders. When I expressed an interest in the origins of the Thulung, I was always told to make enquiries from priests rather than mediums. The activities of mediums were sometimes loosely included under the term *ḍiumla*, but they are peripheral to the concept. The medium's activities were, in fact, one of the areas in which the analytical distinction of tribal and non-tribal is hardest to maintain.

V. The Study of Ritual

The rituals conducted by both types of officiant consist very largely of chants. On occasion, both practise symbolic behaviour such as dancing and certain gestures, and the medium may set up fairly elaborate material structures into which evil spirits can be lured for their destruction. On the whole, however, a typical Thulung rite consists of an individual officiant chanting in front of some offerings. The offerings have probably been contributed by members of the household, but neither they nor other members of the audience participate much in what is going on. An ethnographic account of a rite (and this applies even more to those of priests than of mediums) therefore consists very largely of a record of the chants used, and ideally an ethnographer would find officiants who were willing to dictate their chants and explain their meaning word by word.

This proved impossible for various reasons. One problem lay in geography, in settlement pattern. The term 'village' may suggest a fairly compact settlement with central meeting places and with inhabitants who are in fairly close touch with one another's doings; but Thulung villages are nothing like that. Mukli, in particular, sprawls vertically over more than three thousand feet of hillside, and one could easily take three hours to traverse it from end to end, never being more than ten minutes' walk from the nearest house. Most of the land is terraced, but the fields are interrupted by small patches of forest and by rocky areas too steep for anything but rough grazing. Here and there the houses cluster to form recognisable and named hamlets, but there is no regularity in this, and some houses stand alone amid their fields. The only way to view the village as a whole is to descend to the Dudh Kosi and climb up the hillside opposite – half a day's journey. There are of course no signposts of any kind, and simply to find one's way around is a challenge.

Nor is it particularly easy to expand one's range of social contacts. The exact population and ethnic composition of the village are unknown – to conduct a census would have been exceedingly time-consuming. At a conservative guess, Mukli may have some two hundred Rai households, averaging five members apiece, and about as many non-Thulung ones. The village has no central meeting place, and there are no shops; a villager who wishes to buy something visits the Tuesday bazaar at Nele. Nele lies a good hour and a half's walk from the oldest part of Mukli, and there must be many household heads who do not make the journey as often as twice a year. The village has numerous springs and streams, and the chances of meeting anyone washing or collecting water are not very high. There are three separate primary schools, which have no cause to interact. Admittedly, the panchayat house symbolises the whole village as a unit of local government, but it was built only within the last decade and stands alone, dank and unfurnished, used only a handful of times each year for sparsely-attended meetings. Two shrines in the oldest part of Mukli serve for the celebration of the *bhume* cult on behalf of the collectivity; but attendance at these ceremonies half a dozen times per year is even sparser than at the panchayat house. Most rituals take place on a relatively small scale within the house. In sum, the village has very limited significance as a social unit, and for many purposes the range of effective social contact is confined to the neighbourhood, i.e. roughly speaking, to the twenty or thirty houses within ten minutes' walk.

This meant that the Thulung themselves often had little idea of ceremonies being held outside their own hamlet, and it was harder still for the anthropologist to be well informed about what was going on and who was who. Thus it was not easy to locate and get to know really good informants. Moreover the period of the year when informants are most likely to be free from agricultural work is also the period when they are most likely to be away from home on trading trips, wedding processions, and the like.

In the whole village of Mukli there were only three full tribal priests. One was in his late seventies and failing in mental alertness (some thought that when he died his office would simply lapse). One lived at some distance from my lodgings in the oldest part of the village, and was regarded as not particularly knowledgeable. That left only one, DB, who was unwilling to be questioned or to give explanations of his work. He was an energetic and very busy man, and his attitude was understandable, however disappointing to the anthropologist. In fact priests were not the only people to have some knowledge of the tribal rites and traditions, and as I discovered rather late in the day, there existed a certain number of individuals who knew the chants and were able to stand in when priests were not available. Nonetheless, specialist knowledge was not widespread, I found it hard to contact the right individuals, and in the village where I stayed longest I never achieved a satisfactory relationship with an ideal informant.

One way round the problems was to tape-record and transcribe the chants, and then work at them with the aid of anyone willing to help. This was my main method, but it had severe limitations. It was particularly hard to obtain usable tapes of mediums at work. A close neighbour was a deaf and dumb medium who was supposed to be communing with his spirits but only emitted a sort of hum. This was an extreme case, but many other mediums enunciated very unclearly, and in any case their chants were normally drowned by drumming or by the beating of a brass plate. As for the priests, their chants at *bhume* rites were also regularly drowned by drumming, and in Tingla it was thought improper for an anthropologist to be present in the house during rites involving the ancestors. In Mukli and Lokhim there was no objection to the taping of rituals performed in the house, and when opportunities arose they were naturally taken.

In itself, the transcribed tape of a ritual may shed very little light on *diumla*, for the language used in chants diverges greatly from ordinary spoken Thulung. One thus has to master not only Nepali and Thulung, but what is virtually a third language. Allen (1975a: 168 ff.) gives a sample of ritual language, and discusses some of its peculiarities and particular difficulties. This particular sample was a dictated narrative, but most chants consist of lists of ritual names (*depcinəŋ*, from *dem-* 'invoke' and *nəŋ* 'name'). Examples of such lists are the offerings laid out for the ancestors, categories of people present at the ceremony, parts of the house and names of places visited in the course of verbal journeys, and types of illness and evil which the officiant hopes to ward off. Obviously, ritual names are artificial expressions specially devised for the sake of rituals and were never part of everyday speech, however archaic – as an example will show. The ordinary Thulung for 'eye' is *miksi*, but the ritual name for 'eye' is *loamiksi toamiksi*. One can distinguish analytically a number of types of ritual name, though the type illustrated is the commonest: its formula is XH YH, were the ordinary-language meaning of the repeated element H (the head) gives the meaning of the whole ritual name, and elements X and Y can be regarded as attributive to H. Very often one cannot determine the meaning of the attributes, and sometimes this applies to H as well. In the present example, X (*loa-*) is doubtless from *loas-* 'see', but the derivation of Y (*toa-*) is unclear. X and Y do not necessarily rhyme. Nothing quite like Thulung ritual language has been described so far from Nepal, nor so far as I know, from elsewhere in the Bodic-speaking area, and I hope to return to the topic elsewhere [see Allen 1978c]. In any case, the existence of a specialised ritual language raises a series of extra problems for the student of Thulung ritual.

VI. The Study of Myth and Oral Tradition

Chants in ritual language are only one of the verbal components of the *ḍiumla*. Another consists in the ceremonial dialogues that are delivered in a formal and rhetorical manner in the course of weddings. But this book deals chiefly with the last main component, the prose narratives. The distinction between myths and oral traditions is not intended to be sharp, and does not, I think, correspond to any explicit distinction drawn by the Thulung themselves. However, an obvious difference of atmosphere exists between the narratives of the next two chapters, which are frankly mythological, and those in Ch. 5, which are more like folk stories or legends, and are mostly at least pseudo-historical in character; and the Thulung would probably regard the former as more central to their notion of *ḍiumla* than the latter. Nearly all the narratives that I collected were related to me on non-ceremonial occasions and in ordinary language. However, there is good evidence that some were associated with rituals (see Ch. 3 Introduction), and many of them contain greater or lesser amounts of ritual language. My suspicion is that there was a time when all the more typically mythological of the narratives were chanted in ritual language during rituals, but whether they were then also told in other contexts I am not sure.

Although Thulung myths and traditions proved easier to study than the tribal rituals, this task too was not without problems. I distinguish problems of collecting, translating, and editing and annotating.

One aspect of Hinduisation is that most Thulung nowadays have very little interest in or knowledge of their tribal past, or of traditions concerning it. Although some of the narratives studied here were collected in half a dozen versions, they are by no means widely known. For instance, I estimate that Ramli, the mythical hero who figures so centrally in Ch. 5, is totally unknown, even by name, to at least half the Thulung population. When asked about traditions of the past, many informants simply replied that the men who knew those things had died. If they went further, it was often in purely Hindu terms. The birth of the Rai was ascribed to Shiva, or to Mahadev and Parbati, or was related to the events of the Mahabharata. Mention was often made of the tradition of Kiranti kings who reigned in the Central Valley of Nepal. Perhaps some who denied knowledge of the tribal traditions did so in order to present themselves as more Hindu than they really were, or to put off an inquisitive outsider whose interests they might have heard of. But I am sure that these were not the main factors.

It is natural that older men should know more about tribal lore and customs than younger ones, and in a Hinduising context this tendency is greatly strengthened. In practice, especially in Mukli and Tingla, informants under about the age of fifty could help me little either with narratives or with ritual language; and there were certainly some older men who were equally ignorant. The first problem in collecting narratives was thus to find people who knew them. Once located, by no means all were enthusiastic narrators. There could be various reasons for this, but many narrators, either in introducing or in closing their narratives, expressed one reason for their reluctance. Here is one of the very best and most knowledgeable narrators that I met, introducing the myth of Jaw and Khliw:

Karb What happened in the story of Jaw and Khliw, how things went, I'm afraid I don't know. I'll tell you the story that they used to tell, or parts of it; but as for whether it really happened, whether it is true or false, or what really happened...

Similarly he comments at the end of the Salewaceo story:

But these are not things that I know properly. Long ago, when I was a child, I heard people telling these stories – just a little – and

what I heard I have told you. Here and there, there must be wise
old men, and if they heard (my version)[6] it would be shameful
indeed. All the same, I've told you as much as I heard. There
must be a lot more to it, a whole sequence.

Not all the narrators were as modest or diffident as Karb, but most
were unwilling to put themselves forward as knowing correct and full
versions of stories; at the same time they felt there must be some people
alive who did know the full versions. This reluctance perhaps reflected the
belief that the stories, as *ḍiumla*, constituted a body of profound and ancient
truth. Although no one suggested to me that there were supernatural
sanctions on telling the stories incorrectly, such a feeling may have
influenced some narrators. On the other hand, the commentators showed no
particular inhibitions in discussing the stories.

After someone had been found who knew some stories and was willing
to tell them, there was still the problem of how many he knew. Thulung
narratives do not form a single unified sequence, such that a narrator asked
for stories about the past will begin at the beginning and go through to the
end. Only one narrator, Kam, came anywhere near to doing this. So far as I
could tell, the stories are very seldom told nowadays, and when they are,
very likely only one story will be told at a time. A narrator who has told one
story, say the Creation, may simply fail to recall that he knows some others,
and will only be reminded of them if the investigator prompts his memory
by mentioning the name of some character in another story. As my
knowledge of the narratives increased, it became more and more possible
to make positive enquiries in this way, but it was only in the last two or
three months that I was beginning to be in a strong position to collect a
broad spectrum of the stories.

The question thus arises how complete is the sample of Thulung oral
traditions presented here. A proper answer could only be given if attempts
were made to collect more of them, and this would be thoroughly desirable
– I should be sorry if the present collection were regarded as definitive.
Until further attempts are made, I can only offer the guess that, apart from
numerous variants of the episodes given here, probably a fair number of
stories would have to be recognised as different episodes. But perhaps the

---

6   In the translations of Thulung texts, brackets usually contain material that I
     understand to be implied by the original, but that is not actually present in it.

majority would resemble what is here included in Ch. 5, rather than Chs. 2-4.[7]

In order to understand the myths at all it was necessary undertake a fairly intensive study of ordinary spoken Thulung. For several months in the early part of my fieldwork I was assisted by an unemployed Thulung schoolmaster from Tingla (TR), who shared my lodgings and gave me regular daily lessons. Thereafter I found it more convenient and flexible to have regular two-hour sessions once or twice a day with another schoolmaster from Mukli (G). The main aim was to gain sufficient understanding of the language to give reliable translations of the myths. Fluency as a speaker of Thulung was never a high priority. Thulung were always pleased if I could answer in their own language the stock questions put to a stranger about his purposes, family, lodgings, destination, and so on, but it was only in the very last months that I could begin haltingly to collect information directly in Thulung rather than through Nepali. Nor can I claim much competence in understanding the language as it was actually spoken. I was very seldom able to learn much from conversations in Thulung between third parties, and although I could by the end follow the general drift of an uninterrupted narrative, I was never in a position to ask intelligent questions of a narrator immediately after he had finished speaking.[8] My procedure wherever possible was thus to tape-record myths, transcribe them myself, and then work through the transcripts with a commentator, returning to the tapes where necessary.

In ideal circumstances, the only barrier between the Thulung original and the present reader would then have been difficulties of translation – the difficulties of putting into English ideas that were expressed originally in alien categories with alien presuppositions. In practice, there were further difficulties at various levels. The narrators had no chance to edit their tapes or the transcripts from them, and they sometimes left loose ends and unclarities which do not represent their full knowledge. This was well illustrated when two versions of a single episode were given by one narrator (e.g. Ch. 5 II Ant). Technically, the recordings are sometimes imperfect, with passages inaudible for one reason or another – coughing, for instance, is very common in the smoke-filled atmosphere of the chimneyless Thulung house. For reasons already touched on, much material was collected only

---

7   Cf. the list in Appendix 1 of episodes narrated by Kam, but not used in this study.

8   As a result of many hours listening to my tapes, I now understand the language rather better than when it was being spoken around me all day.

in the last few months, and there was limited time for thinking it through and inquiring about the problems it raised. In the last ten days a minor mechanical fault in the apparatus (an Uher 4000 Report-L) unfortunately prevented me from working through with local informants large parts of the tapes made in Lokhim. Although, with this exception, tapes were transcribed and roughly translated in Nepal, further ambiguities or uncertainties only came to light when careful translations were written out after return from fieldwork. I have tried to minimise the various potential sources of error by giving the annotated texts in Appendix 2. Question marks only appear in the translations at points where I am particularly unsure of the meaning, but it would be naive to imagine that transcriptions and translations are elsewhere error-free.

The commentators were usually my schoolmaster assistants. All schoolmasters in the area were relatively young, in their twenties or less, for the obvious reason that schools had only opened a few years before my visit. As teachers of the language, they had several advantages. They were of above average intelligence; they were accustomed to explaining things in Nepali to those with less understanding than themselves; they had at least an elementary acquaintance with grammatical concepts and terminology; they were flexible; and they were used to ordering their lives by the clock and working for a salary. Being only the first generation to have had schooling, they were not entirely out of touch with the traditional life that went on in their families, and only on fairly rare occasions could one detect a nascent aspiration towards a sort of middle-class distinctness from their peasant and ex-military relatives and contemporaries. On the other hand, there was much that they did not know about the more traditional aspects of their culture, and they could not always clarify questions of language or substance arising from the tapes. The obvious solution, namely to turn to the older men and, in particular, to the narrators themselves, was often impossible, for a variety of reasons. For instance, older men often disliked being cross-questioned on matters of detail, especially if the result was sometimes – inevitably – to show that they did not know the answer. Many loose ends in the stories will have to be left dangling.

The more detailed problems of editing are considered in Appendix 1. It seems that Thulung narratives do not have generally recognised titles, and all titles and subtitles are my own. In some cases the breakdown of narratives into shorter episodes was obvious, but in others it was a matter of judgement or arbitrary decision. For convenience, I sometimes extend the term 'episode' to stretches of text that are purely descriptive and do not narrate events. Generally it is obvious when two narrators are giving different versions of the same story, rather than different stories, but there are a few debatable instances. In order to compare different narrators' versions of particular episodes, I have quite often had to ignore the order in which they were told. Appendix 1, Table I, shows the extent of such editorial intervention, and should allow the reader to reconstitute the material on the tapes in all relevant respects.[9] As regards the order of presentation of texts by different narrators, I have not been very systematic, but tend to put first the narrator who gives the fullest version of the chapter as a whole.

There are several different levels of annotation and commentary. Comments that are more or less purely linguistic are relegated to the footnotes accompanying the texts in Thulung; footnotes to the translated texts have been kept to a minimum, and many points of detail are dealt with immediately after the translation. Further comments will often be found in the discussion of an episode that follows presentation of all the versions, less often in the general discussion of the whole chapter, and occasionally in Ch. 6, which draws on the whole corpus presented. The material is intrinsically complicated.

Much of the commentary relates different versions of the same episode, or different episodes. Apart from these purely internal aspects of the narratives, comments may also link the myths to contemporary or recent Thulung life. As should already be clear, there is not much scope for the second approach. In a society that is so far Hinduised, the half-forgotten tribal myths cannot be expected to act as charters for, or symbolic statements of, many contemporary attitudes or practices. Nevertheless, it would have been possible to confine the study to material collected from the Thulung in the course of fieldwork. More attention could have been paid to the stylistic properties of the narratives, and an attempt could have been made to study the chants, in spite of their difficulty. However, I have preferred to pursue another type of inquiry, and it is to this that much of the commentary is devoted.

---

9 Of course a transcription inevitably omits some information present on the tape and relevant to its interpretation. Matters of tempo, tone of voice and intonation can be only imperfectly conveyed by means of punctuation and footnoting.

VII. Comparison within the Bodic-speaking area

One of the traditional purposes of ethnography is to record for posterity the ideas and creations of societies that do not produce their own written documents, and this is intrinsically worthwhile. But social anthropologists have generally aspired to go further than this and to formulate ideas whose scope or implications extend beyond the group studied at first hand. Thus the Thulung might have been compared with other peoples who have recently been exposed to Hindu influence, or with others sharing the same ecology, or with other 'tribal' peoples who have recently come in contact with a literate civilisation, and so on. In fact comparison is here limited almost entirely to those who speak genetically related languages, and more particularly, to those who speak Bodic languages.[10] Perhaps a special case could be made for the value of this approach in the study of mythology, but I limit myself to a few more general remarks.

Language family based comparativism has undoubtedly made most progress within the domain of Indo-European speakers. There are several reasons for this. The native languages of most scholars have been Indo-European, and much more attention has been paid to this family than to any other. Many branches of the family possessed large and ancient literatures that have been intensively studied from various points of view. The complex morphology of Indo-European languages makes them peculiarly suitable for diachronic linguistic study. For reasons such as these, those undertaking comparative study of the cultures of Indo-European speakers can build on the work of generations of previous scholars. I am thinking here particularly of the achievements of Benveniste and Dumézil.

I cannot comment on the Sino-Tibetan area as a whole, but in the Bodic-speaking area the situation is certainly very different. There may well be some Bodic languages whose very existence has not yet been recorded, e.g. in Bhutan. For the majority of them our linguistic knowledge is exiguous. Even if adequate descriptions were available, the tendency towards monosyllabism and a relatively simple morphology would tend to make comparison harder than in Indo-European. Only a handful of the Bodic languages have an indigenous literature, and when they do it may be of difficult access and little known (as Newari or Limbu). Ethnographically, our ignorance is no doubt even greater. For many areas reports are

---

10   A certain number of references are made to the Lepcha of Sikkim whose language was classified by Shafer as Burmic, but the literature on them is relatively large and has been studied only in part.

superficial, and for others completely lacking. These considerations apply *a fortiori* to our knowledge of Bodic mythology.

In this situation it might be argued that the first task was description, and that comparison was premature. There is something to be said for this view, especially since with every passing year less and less of the culture of the Bodic-speaking tribes remains to be recorded. On the other hand, as in most areas of knowledge, collection of materials and their theoretical elaboration should proceed hand in hand. The work of the Indo-Europeanists suggests that a comparative approach will eventually prove fruitful, and even if some of the results of the present study are dubious, hopefully they will stimulate further work in the same direction.

A more serious objection is that, while comparison of the sort attempted is desirable, it ought to be based on thorough knowledge of all the available material. In contrasting the materials available for Bodic comparativism with those available to the Indo-Europeanist, one stresses the relative paucity of the former both in quality and quantity. This does not mean – far from it – that the quantity is such as can be readily mastered by a single part-time student within a period of three or four years. Just as my corpus of Thulung myths partly depends on the particular narrators whom I happened to meet, so I well know that the comparisons I have drawn are limited by the sources that were available in accessible libraries and happened to come to my attention. I do not know how much relevant material may exist written in Nepali on peoples such as the Magar and Gurung. Of all the Bodic-speakers, by far the greatest amount of scholarly attention has been devoted to the Tibetans, and they are the obvious focus for a comparativist; but Tibetology is a large subject and not of easy access. The indigenous literature is itself vast, starting from the Tun-Huang documents,[11] and so is the western literature of the last century and a half. An outsider who ventures into such a specialised field, without knowing the language and armed only with Das's dictionary (whose shortcomings have often been noted), risks charges of naivety and misunderstanding; all one can do is to proceed cautiously, relying on acknowledged experts. So far as this study is concerned, the most relevant aspect of Tibetology has been pre-Buddhist mythology, and without claiming exhaustiveness, I have tried to consult the main sources.

---

11   These documents were written between the introduction of writing to Tibet, generally believed to have taken place under the great king Srong-btsan sgam-po (died 649 AD), and the sealing of the Tun-Huang grotto in 1035.

In any case, a start has to be made somewhere, and the importance of including all possible evidence is greater for some undertakings than for others. One of my aims here is simply to show that certain sorts of question can be posed and are worth posing; and this argument would not necessarily be strengthened by increasing the quantity of material considered. Moreover this study is conceived as part of a wider comparative investigation of the Bodic-speaking area which is still in progress. Reference will occasionally be made to preliminary results arrived at in this wider field, in particular to some hypotheses on quadripartite classifications current in early Bodic societies; these are in part based on, in part have still to be related to, comparative studies of the kinship terminologies of the area.[12]

---

12   [For quadripartition see Allen 1978a & b; for kinship Allen 1975b & 1976c.]

CHAPTER 2

The Creation

Introduction

Thulung tradition contains only one myth that clearly describes the birth of mankind, and there is no serious competitor for the title of the chapter. The story centres on a female being called Miyapma, who woos one star but is impregnated by another. As a result, she gives birth to various species, among which mankind is the last. Eventually she is killed and buried.

Four main versions of the story were recorded, together with a number of fragmentary versions which contain useful additional details. All the main versions have the core episodes concerning Miyapma's wooing and giving birth, but three of them break off at that point. In the remaining main version I have distinguished two further episodes, and for analytical convenience I have also recognised a preliminary episode dealing with the origin of Miyapma herself. In general, the characters in the Creation are seldom mentioned elsewhere in Thulung ritual or mythology; but there are two exceptions, both of which concern Miyapma's youngest son, Mini, the First Man. Mini appears briefly in a story about the origin of death which is narrated during the funeral ritual. Ritual is not treated in any detail in this study, but for reasons given later, the story is excerpted and included here as episode VI. Mini appears also in a story I have called the Sandalwood Tree, which was told as part of the Migration of the Ancestors (Ch. 4), but is not entirely appropriate there. It is not very closely linked to the main story of the Creation either, but has been appended here as episode VII.

I. Origin of Creatrix

Ph   As to the Primal Lake[1] – long ago, at the time of the creation, Heaven rained, Earth opened (?). The Heavens formed a Lake here below, and into it the Wind swept together fallen leaves. From the moistened mass there sprang up a plant called the *wadakhor*, and in the plant Namprəngma was created. In Namprəngma's body Miyapma was born.

On a previous occasion Ph had mentioned that the fallen leaves were, or included, those of a sandalwood tree. Actually, the emphasis is not on leaves as such: the Thulung term (rendered as *sotar-kasingar* N) would cover any miscellaneous loose vegetable matter lying on the earth. The image is apparently of spontaneous generation in a rotting vegetable mass. The *wadakhor* was thought to be a lotus. The narrator was not entirely certain of the story, for on earlier occasions he either gave Namprəngma as Miyapma's father, or thought that Miyapma was born directly from the leaves, without parents.

The very fragmentary version of the Creation embedded in the funeral oration mentions no named creators:

DB   Originally, who was it that instituted dying for us humans? It was Lizard. Because of the primal Fire, because of the Wind, the fallen leaves were swept together. Within the leaves, down there, everything was created:

Ant   Regarding the origin of us Kiranti – a certain woman had emerged from the earth. When she grew up, she could not find a husband, so all

---

1   Capitalisation will be used for various purposes. Here, as often, it tries to convey the solemnity imparted to the original by the use of ritual expressions or other non-everyday vocabulary. I shall also use it for individual characters in the stories who, in the original, are referred to only by their species name (as one might write of Reynard or Bruin). Thirdly, I use it in expressions such as First Man or First King, to refer to mythological roles which are performed by characters whose names are variable and/or unimportant in the context.

around the hills she gave herself to the Wind. That is how Miyapma gave birth to a daughter Ninamtho.

Ninamtho is the name used in mythological contexts for the village of Ribdung (as in 5 VII), and it may here be a slip for some other name beginning with N. Although Ant II continues to tell of the doings of Ninamtho, there is an abrupt change of name to Miyapma at the start of Ant III, and this makes it virtually certain that, whether or not the name beginning with N is a slip, it ought to come before Miyapma's in the story, and not after it. The expression rendered 'gave herself to the Wind' literally means 'caused the Wind to eat or consume her', and like the Nepali equivalent (*hāwā khuwāyo*) is to be understood in a sexual sense, as referring to female masturbation.

Mj Long ago, among us, first of all Miyapma was created. After her, Nayapma was created, then Namprang,[2] then Khakcilik, with Jaw and Khliw.

In spite of this opening, which gives the sequence Miyapma, Nayapma, Namprang, Mj later goes on to recount how Miyapma gave birth to Mini. Again one wonders whether the names beginning with N should not precede Miyapma's, as they do in the following brief versions.

PB Miyapma's mother was Nayapma... Miyapma's youngest son was Mini, and it was from him that we originated.

CP Miyapma's father was Ninamrangma, child of the Wind.

Dim's version (not on tape) started with mention of Namprekma and Mayekma, before coming to Miyapma. Two other versions open without mention of a name in N-.

SSJ Kuwekma had a daughter Miyakma.
Kam First of all, our creator was Miyapma, the creator of Mini.

---

2   = Ph's Namprɔngma. The final -ma in a name is quite commonly present in one narrator's version and not another's.

In general there is little agreement between the various versions. At most one can say that Miyapma probably had at least one forebear, a female whose name began with N. Otherwise, particularly in the longer versions, two traditions can be distinguished. Ph describes, partly in ritual language, how the interaction of Heaven and Earth, Wind and Water led to the germination of a primal lotus, while another Mukli version (DB) mentions fire as taking part in the same process, albeit obscurely. I leave till later the question whether this tradition implies the notion of four or five elements. These Mukli versions give an essential role to the wind, which sweeps together the leaves in which the next stage of creation occurs. Ant I represents the other tradition, in which the wind is directly creative and fertilises the first woman.

II. Wooing and Impregnation

Ph   In time, Miyapma grew to be a young maid. Seeking a husband, she decided to woo Ruwasila. So she sent two birds, Jigengma and Kekuwa, to arrange the match. Actually she sent Jigengma, and on his way Jigengma met Kekuwa, greeted him, explained his mission and sought his company. The two of them journeyed up to Ruwasila's abode. But learning that they were coming, Ruwasila hid, leaving Khomda in his place.[3] Khomda asked the two birds where they were going and where they were from. They explained that Miyapma was wooing and they had come on her behalf. 'But what was it you saw in me that made you come with a proposal of marriage?' 'She saw Ruwasila shining and fell in love and sent us. That's why we've come.' 'It is not me that shines, it is my goitre,' he said, and showed it to them.

The two birds brought Khomda down to earth. But when they arrived, as soon as Miyapma saw the goitre, she cried out in horror. 'Alas, not someone like this, not for me, not someone with a goitre. I am not going off with this goitrous fellow.' So saying, she hid herself away. Khomda was furious. He urinated into the hollow of a *cɔsa* tree and departed. With him he took the grandmothers of the waters, and all the springs and rivers ran dry.

Miyapma was parched with thirst and lost consciousness. Jigengma went and dipped his wing in the water in the hollow trunk, and came

---

3   On another occasion Ph explained that Ruwasila hid because he was afraid.

and sprinkled her with it. 'Who are you, taking pity on my hunger and thirst?'[4] she exclaimed. 'Grandmother, it is I, will you drink this water?' said Jigengma. 'I will indeed. I was fainting for lack of it.' Jigengma brought the urine from the hollow tree in a *pĩḍālu* N leaf, and gave it to Miyapma to drink.

Rolasila[5] was glossed as *shukra* N, i.e. Venus, and Khomda as *brihaspati* N, i.e. Jupiter. Khomda's name echoes *khomjeol* 'goitre', a condition that is relatively common in the Himalaya owing to the deficiency of iodine in the drinking water. Apart from the present myth, I know nothing of local systems of astronomy: nowadays Thulung ideas about the heavens derive entirely from Hinduism.

Jigiyom is the name of the Brown Hill Prinia, a small variety of bird, now rare in the Thulung area. Like a sparrow in colour, it waves its tail up and down in a characteristic manner. Kekuwa is a hawk (*bāj* N), and was hovering when Jigiyom met him. The Thulung original never indicates the sex of birds (except of cocks). The English term 'woo' usually applies to a male who pursues a female, rather than vice versa, but I cannot think of a less inept rendering of the Thulung expression. The phrase translated 'grandmothers of the waters' is a little obscure. Some informants thought that in the context the reference was to serpents (*nāg* N), but others who understood the phrase as referring to water insects were perhaps closer to tribal tradition. The word for grandmother (*mim*) in fact also applies to a small insect that eats cloth (*māu* N, ? 'silverfish').[6] Grammatically, one could translate 'grandmother of the waters' in the singular.

---

4   The reference to hunger is not particularly appropriate. The whole phrase occurs appropriately in several versions of the Jaw-Khliw myth (Ch. 3 IV), and the narrator has perhaps taken it from there.

5   Some names are given different forms by different narrators, and it is convenient to fix on a standard form. I shall thus replace Ph's Jigengma with the commoner Jigiyom, and Ruwasila (etc.) with Rolasila, which is used by Kam. Rolasila is preferred partly because four-syllable names of the form XH YH are so characteristic of archaic contexts in the area. A few examples are: from Tibet, Bya-sgong nu-sgong, Mo-bya btsun-bya, Ming-dgu sring-dgu, Mi-bon lha-bon rgyal-khrims sngar-ba, 'O-de bed-de ring-mo; from the Gurung, Sildo naldo, from the Lepcha, Rilbu shingbu. Cf. also Ch. 1 V on the structure of Thulung ritual names, and Allen 1978c.

6   The explanation of the Mongolian black spot (*koṭhi* N) is *u miŋka yalliu*, literally 'his grandmother has struck him'.

The Thulung word for 'water' (*ku*) does have a slightly broader range than the English word, being used to cover other types of fluid such as sap and juice. However the words for 'urinating' and 'urine' cannot ordinarily be used to refer to ejaculating or semen. The *pīḍālu* is a tuber (*Colocasia esculenta*), whose shiny leaf makes a suitable container for fluids; to this day Thulung women are supposed to avoid using it for that purpose because of what happened in the Creation story.

Ant (As previously noted, in this episode the expected name Miyapma is replaced by Ninamtho). Mother and daughter lived together for some years. When Ninamtho grew up, she began wondering who her father had been, and asked her mother about it. At first the mother refused to say, but eventually she was wearied by her daughter's questioning and told her that her father had been the wind. 'I'll go and live with him (as wife),' said Ninamtho; but her mother would not allow it. 'Then whom shall I go and live with?' Her mother showed her Shukra, so she sent the Jigiyom bird, Kekuwa and Koṭera to go and fetch him. But Shukra had set in the west, and in his place was Brihaspati, that is Rowa or Rowasila. So the birds brought him down instead and took him to Ninamtho. The girl was horrified. 'I'm not living with *this* sort of man,' she said obstinately. Thereupon Rowasila cursed the three birds. 'I had decided not to go down among the mortals, I knew they would not like me – and then you went and brought me down here.' So saying, Rowa laid a curse on them. He told Jigiyom to go and look for a large hole in a tree and spread out a *pīḍālu* leaf in the bottom of it. Jigiyom went and did this, and came back to say that it was ready. Rowasila went there, urinated into the hole, and departed; but as he went, he dried up all the water upon the earth. Ninantho became desperate with thirst. 'Quickly, quickly, get me some water!' Rowa had left instructions with Jigiyom that later, when she asked for water, he was to give her the urine to drink. So Jigiyom brought the urine and splashed it over her. 'Here you are, drink it!' After she drank, all things had their origin from her.

Ant is the only narrator who makes Rolasila descend to earth rather than Khomda, and since in any case he muddles Miyapma and Ninamtho, on this point I shall henceforth ignore him. No other version mentions the despatch of as many as three birds, and I can suggest an explanation for the presence of the extra bird, Koṭera. Koṭera is the Nepali for *pojiu*, a variety of small bird which forms flocks, but the same syllables appear in certain astronomical terms. AS gives *pojiuchium* = *bagale tārā* N, which Ph understood as a constellation of five or seven stars near Orion's belt. SSJ gave *pojiuche* as the Milky Way, which is mentioned in his version of the episode. So the third bird in Ant's version might derive from the astronomical formations (which in turn may be named after the bird).[7]

The star could reasonably curse the birds for having brought him down in vain in spite of his reluctance. However, since there is no mention of the terms or results of the curse so far as the birds are concerned, perhaps it served merely to reinforce his instructions to Jigiyom.

Mj Miyapma chose Ruwa in the sky to be her husband, but it was Khomda who came down. The creation followed from there, and Mini was born. Is that the story he is thinking of?…

Miyapma chose Ruwa, but in his place – she actually sent Kekuwa, but Kekuwa hung around hovering, so then she sent Jigiyom. Jigiyom went to Ruwa's dwelling place, and found Khomda weaving a basket. He urged Khomda to come down with him to Miyapma, but he refused. They got hold of a ginger root and Khomda sliced it (as a divinatory procedure). 'I'm not to go,' he said. 'You must go, grandfather.' In the end they went. When he reached earth he scarcely fitted in the doorway. Miyapma had everything ready, the vessels for beer and all the preparations. But it was all in vain (?). 'I said as much to Jigiyom at the start; but he would not believe me.' Taking the mothers of the waters,[8] he returned to the sky. When he had gone, there was not a drop of water to drink. But he had left behind his seed in a *pǐḍālu* leaf, as water, and had told Jigiyom to give it to Miyapma to drink when she became thirsty. When the bird gave it to her all the creatures were formed in her womb.

No explicit reference is here made to Khomda's goitre, but presumably it was because of its size that he almost failed to fit in the doorway.

SSJ Miyakma decided to marry Shukra. She sent Kekuwa as marriage intermediary, to carry her invitation. But the vultures ate the food

---

7   It may also be relevant that three emissaries are despatched in connection with a wedding in Ch. 3 VII.

8   Apparently the expressions 'grandmothers of the waters' and 'mothers of the waters' mean the same in this context.

Kekuwa had taken for his journey, and he only managed to reach the Milky Way, to whom he delivered the invitation. The invitation was accepted, but when Miyakma saw the Milky Way's large goitre she sent him packing; but with him he took the water insects. On the way back to heaven he urinated in a large hole in a tree. A great drought ensued, and Miyakma became faint from thirst and fell to the ground. When Jigiyom came and asked what was the matter, she explained that she was faint from lack of water. Jigiyom flew off and found the hollow tree containing the urine. Dipping his tail in it, he flew back and sprinkled Miyakma's lips. Slightly revived, she asked where the water had come from, and went and drank it.

CP's version referred to Ruwapa silapa, to the spirits of the waters (*chekureni bayureni*), and to a hole in a tree.

CP   In the drought Miyapma fell to the ground and lay spread-eagled on her back.[9] She was helped by a bird called Jirkili porokta, and drank the seed.

Kam   Up in heaven there was a being called Khomtang, a man, while Miyapma was a woman...[10] Miyapma's first periods came, and she fell ill. Up in Heaven was Rolasila, who was truly handsome, and immortal. They performed a divination to see who could help, and the omens directed them to the Cetla bird, who was an officiant.[11] Miyapma gave Cetla her instructions: 'Perform a divination for me. I am ill and suffering from pain. What is wrong with me?' Cetla came and had a look, and sliced the root. Then he advised her: 'If you can associate with Rolasila up in Heaven, you will get well again' – it was like when one is ploughing and the rain comes.[12] 'But he is up in

---

9   The word *phenderere* used here also implies (like *phandalala*) untidiness and immodesty: 'any old how, showing everything'. For the -pa in Rolasila's name, cf. AS *shukra* N (Venus) = *miksipa*, from *miksi* 'eye'.

10   Kam apologises for not telling the whole story, pointing out that his young female relatives are present. He is urged to do so, and apparently tells all he knows or remembers.

11   This is Ph's interpretation. As I understand it, the sentence more naturally means: 'They performed a divination at the house of Cetla, who was an officiant.'

12   The implication of this aside is perhaps that Miyapma is suffering from being too dry.

Heaven. Who will seek him on my behalf? Who will tell me what to do?' 'I'll do the sending,' said Cetla, and he despatched Jigiyom.

Off flew the bird with a quick burst of movement, then a rest, then another burst, and so on – you know how the Jigiyom moves its tail even nowadays – that's how it went on its journey. Khomtang was busy making a bamboo basket. 'Greetings, Jigiyom pareakma, where are you going? Your home is down in the Lower World. What have you come up here to Heaven for?' 'Grandfather, Miyapma is ill, and sent me up here for Rolasila.' 'But what can Rolasila do about it?' If he had gone up to Rolasila, how happy and long-lived we humans would have been!' But that Khomtang did not allow him to proceed to Rolasila. Khomtang was goitrous, and also suffered from leprosy. It was he who sent (his semen?) as a gift in Jigiyom's tail, splashing the fluid on it. Jigiyom flew down as he had flown up, resting from time to time on the way, and found Miyapma comatose from her illness. She was sprinkled with water from the bird's tail, and half of it fell into her mouth. So she became pregnant, and was cured of her illness.

When she was better, Cetla came and asked after her. 'Yes, I'm better now.' 'Where has Jigiyom gone?' 'He is over there on the ridge.' Cetla summoned him and asked what report he brought with him from Heaven. 'I was not told anything new. Rolasila is up there in Heaven.' 'Yes, go on.' 'Khomtang splashed my tail with water and told me to go and sprinkle Miyapma with it.' 'Oh dear! If you had gone up to Rolasila, splendid human beings would have been born, with eternal life and happiness. But that Khomtang, oh dear, he is a leper, and goitrous as well. I don't know what will come of it.' Rolasila went on living in the sky – they still call him Rolasila. (If only we were?) his family. If only he had come down, what a splendid race humanity would have been, with eternal life and happiness! But Jigiyom did not reach him, and it was Khomtang who sent him back.

This version departs from the others in several ways. Firstly it adds leprosy (which is not uncommon in Nepal) to Khomda's defects. More importantly, it omits his descent to earth, and hence his removal of the spirits of the waters and his use of the hole in the tree. Thirdly, it introduces the diviner Cetla in episode II (rather than, like the others, in III), and thereby removes from Miyapma responsibility for initiating the marriage. The version is particularly interesting for its presentation of the myth as an explanation for the ills of humanity. It is also worth noting the mode of flight of Jigiyom: when a shaman undertakes a journey to the other world, he too intersperses his progression with pauses or rests (*ŋeluŋ*). The quick bursts of movement (*pareak*) are the source of the Bird's ritual name Jigiyom pareakma.

In spite of detailed variations, the general outline of the other versions is pretty uniform. Miyapma wishes to marry Rolasila, and sends one or more birds as marriage intermediaries. For one reason or another their mission goes astray, and they bring down the goitrous Khomda in error. He is rejected by Miyapma and departs in anger, leaving his urine[13] in the hollow of a tree. He causes a drought and leaves instructions with the Jigiyom bird so as to ensure that Miyapma is impregnated willy-nilly. Either the bird sprinkles the seed on her lips from his feathers as she lies comatose, or she is made to drink it from a *pĩḍālu* leaf; or else both methods are used. If one takes at face value the sex of the stolen waters, there is a certain symmetry in the story: Miyapma gets Khomda instead of Rolasila, Khomda gets the (grand)mothers of the waters instead of Miyapma.

Nowadays at a wedding two marriage intermediaries or negotiators are involved from each side. According to Ph, the two birds in this episode were the archetypal precedents for the two negotiators from the bride's side. If this were the general view, one might expect a reference to the creation episode in the course of the wedding ritual, but there does not appear to be one. All the same, it is worth noting certain other features of the episode which relate it to contemporary or recent Thulung weddings. The *layemokchium*, the basket Khomda was weaving when the birds arrived (Mj), is of a type formerly used specially for marriage prestations. The same version mentions Khomda as performing divination before deciding whether to descend; nowadays too, no prudent parent would omit to compare the horoscopes of the prospective couple. It is also conventional for the side which is approached to demur at first, rather than accept with enthusiasm.

It is interesting that one tradition of episode I (Ph and DB) foreshadows the framework of episode II. Let us call the two traditions respectively A and B. (i) In both A and B, sky fertilises earth. The stars in B are explicitly located in heaven, and Miyapma not only lives on earth but, according to CP II, is lying back on it in an abandoned posture at the moment of

---

13   The substitution of semen for urine is no doubt a rationalisation, while the converse shift would be surprising. If I often follow the rationalisers and talk of Khomda's 'seed', it is because it is so much more natural in English.

impregnation. In Ant I she or her mother emerges from earth. (ii) In both cases the fertilisation takes place by means of 'water': in A it is rain, in sufficient quantity to form a primal lake, while in B it is no more than can be carried in a leaf cup, or on the tail of a small bird. (iii) In both cases leaves are important. In A the fallen leaves form the moist mass in which germination occurs, while in B the *pĩḍālu* leaf contains the germinal water. (iv) Both traditions involve trees: in A the sandalwood tree from which the leaves fall, in B the *cəsa* tree which provides the hole where the seed is deposited.

On the other hand one should note the contrasts. (i) In A the germination occurs in the context of a primal lake, i.e. of a copious supply of water, while in B it occurs in the context of a drought. (ii) In A the sky acts first, and apparently on its own initiative, while in B it is very definitely the earthlings who take the first step and the stars who hang back reluctantly. Since nowadays it is the groom's side that takes the initiative in marriage negotiations, it is perhaps odd that this primal mating is still regarded as a precedent for marriages – the sexual politics of the Creation mythology will recur more than once in this study. (iii) More generally, where A is abstract and depersonalised, B is concrete and personalised. Again, discussion is deferred.

III. Birth of the species

Ph   Thereafter in Miyapma's body all the natural species were created: the mountain thorny creeper, the valley thorny creeper, Tiger Rai, Bear Rai, the monkey, and Mini Rai. After the creation, all the species – the two types of creeper, the tigers, bears and monkeys went off to the jungle.

The word *sabdiuma* (elsewhere *sabdiri*), translated 'all the natural species', is used only in mythological contexts and was thought by the narrator to connote an uncountable multitude of beings. Logically it should not include species such as Jigiyom, who have intervened earlier in the story. I do not know whether it is significant that the narrator avoids calling the monkey 'Rai'. The term serves to add a note of respect and individuation to the bare names, at least as much as it relates them to the Rai people of the present day. Many other versions will also distinguish between Miyapma's last-born, who stays at home, and her other progeny, who depart.

Ant The tiger, the bear, and all the various species she created, and last of all Mimmilim Miyapma gave birth to a male child. As the infant was about to be born, her labour pains became so severe that she went to the river, intending to jump in. The branch of a sandalwood tree stretched out over the water, and on it a platform had been put up, with the river flowing beneath. 'Next time I have a contraction I shall jump in,' she said. But upstream and downstream the water suddenly all dried up, and the wind brought the fallen leaves and swept them together. As she jumped, her son was born on a pile of leaves. She found to her astonishment that she had been delivered of a son. She gathered him up in a cloth, made the *roko-roko poak-poak*, and took him up. Uttering some invocations, she brought him home. And that is how we Kiranti originated.

The *roko-roko poak-poak* is a method of calling the soul to join the body. It can be used by officiants in rituals, but also by laymen, for instance when a companion is dazed by a fall and his soul (or consciousness) has flown off ('like a fly'). The word *roko* is probably an altered imperative of *rok-* 'come'. The *poak* is a vigorous sucking noise. Meanwhile one should tap on stone with a metal object, preferably a sickle (*hãsiyā* N).

The birth of Mini here strongly resembles that of Namprəngma in Ph I. In both cases the birth is associated with a pile of leaves from a sandalwood tree swept together by wind into a place where water is or has been.

Mj After the creation of everything there were twelve officiants: Cetla, the grasshopper – I can't think of them all – anyway a large number of them. It was Cetla who identified Miyapma's condition. 'In Miyapma's womb all species are being born – that is how the slices of the root have fallen.' The place where they sliced the root was way up at Surke, by the spring, or some place beginning with Ser- or Seor- (unclear discussion of the name, mentioning Nagira, Bipara Neorima, Payya). What was that place called – with the *pheaklim* tree?[14] Anyway his divination showed that here was the creation... Her labour dragged on without success, until all at once... The *reopceo* plant was born first, then the *proakceo* plant, then the mountain thorny creeper, then

---

14 He is no doubt thinking of the Surke and Puiyan (or Poyan) that stand on the east bank of the Dudh Kosi a little south of Chaurikharka, though there are also villages called Surke and Sherka between Salleri and Chiwong Gompa. For the *pheaklim* tree see Ch. 4 VI.

the valley thorny creeper, all of which went off to the jungle. Then came the tiger (*rodhero*), the bear (*buwam*), then Chiuniu, then Mini, a human like us.

Kam   After Khomtang's return Jigiyom came again to Miyapma and prophesied: 'Grandmother, in your body, first *boakpa* will be born, that is to say the tiger, then *buwam*, then the mountain thorny creeper, then the monkeys. Up to this point you will not pick them up in a cloth. They will be born by themselves, they should go off by themselves; let them get born in their own way, and let them run off to the jungle. Then Mini will be born. As he is born, you will pick him up in a cloth, pick him up in cotton wool' – this was what he said, you understand. 'Mini will be born with arms and legs normal, and similarly his head, and with a cry coming from his mouth. This one you will pick up and hold in a cloth. Put a layer of cotton wool on the cloth and pick him up in that, and keep him carefully.'

This is what Miyapma did. His name was Khakcilik. The bear went off to the jungle. Yes (to interlocutor) Mini's son was called Khakcilik. The bear went off to the jungle, and so did the tiger and the mountain thorny creeper – the thorny creeper still likes really fertile earth. The monkey also went off to the jungle. Mini alone, her youngest, she picked up and kept. He was Khakcilik.

In the first line Jigiyom is no doubt a slip for Cetla, who acts as diviner both in the previous episode as told by the same narrator and in other versions. In the last paragraph too, when he talks of Mini's son being called Khakcilik, the narrator evidently intended to refer to Miyapma's son. The relationship between Mini and Khakcilik in Thulung mythology is unclear, but Kam was the only narrator to identify them.

SSJ   Now she became pregnant and gave birth to nine plants and animals, including the wild boar, the bear, the tiger, the mountain thorny creeper and finally the first man (or first Kiranti). Only the last stayed with his mother. The others went off to the jungle.

DB   the tiger, the bear, the valley thorny creeper, the mountain thorny creeper, all the various birds, and our own kind, Mini.

So far none of the Mukli versions has mentioned a divination in this episode, but certainly it is part of the tradition, there as elsewhere. On a previous occasion Ph had mentioned Miyapma's recourse to Cetla at the start of III in order to find out what was happening in her belly, and the following fragmentary exchange is also between Miyapma and a diviner.

Dim 'In your body has been created Mini, the mountain thorny creeper, the valley thorny creeper, *buwam*, and the tiger,' whose ritual name is Lolomi tolomi. Miyapma was indignant (because she had not made love with anybody). 'What is this shameful thing you are saying of me? I sent Jigepca and Kekuwa heleku to heaven on an errand of love, but... Bring it, I am dying of thirst.'

PB From him we were created, more and more of us, all gradually branching in different directions – isn't that so?... Boakpa the tiger, Buwam the bear, Mini the youngest, the three of us share this descent; the monkey... We were born in the womb of Miyapma. Cetla was the priest, Jigiyom was the one sent to look at the omens.

The mention of *three* 'brothers' can probably be ignored, since the customary fourth, the monkey, is added immediately as an afterthought.

In CP's version, the list of diviners consulted by Miyapma included the *toŋtimi* bird, and rice grains were used for divination. Miyapma gave birth not only to the usual thorny creepers, but also to a plant called *rebuceo* or *repciu* (cf. *reopceo* in Mj); also to wasps (*supel hoapel*), as well as to the four brothers, the tiger (*gupsiupa toŋdebupa*) the eldest, the bear, Chiuni, and Kolatiup, who was born with ornaments and a bow.

Looking at this episode as a whole, we may distinguish two aspects, the general nature of Miyapma's creative activity, and the particular species to which she gives birth. We have already noted that Miyapma does not create the whole universe. Before she gives birth, the tradition has already mentioned (in its various versions) her own forbears, elemental constituents such as wind and earth, planets, birds having social functions, bamboo-working, trees. On the origin of all of these, and other objects, Thulung tradition is silent. Three different verbs are used for originating, being created and being born (*prə(ŋ)-, mun-, gəks-*) and one could add two composite expressions involving Nepali *utpanna* and *paidā*; but I cannot detect any systematic differences in their meaning. At least three of the versions state that the creation took place in Miyapma's *body*, rather than (as one might expect) in her *womb*. Does this hint that the species originated from different parts of her body?

Only one version (SSJ) gives a figure for the total number of species created, namely nine. Moreover, although others emphasise that large numbers of species were created, the lists they give cover a rather restricted range, none including more than eight species. From the vegetable kingdom, the two species of thorny creeper are regularly coupled, only two narrators omitting the (second) lowland variety. Mj mentions two further species which are bushes or plants rather than trees. Both are edible to cattle but are of no great significance nowadays. Three of the species (not *proakceo*) appear among many other plant species in certain ritual chants, but the contexts give no clue as to why they are mentioned in the creation myth.

In many of the versions the order in which the species are born appears unsystematic, but three of them (Ph, Mj, CP) agree in listing the vegetable members before the animal ones. Broadly, the lists seem to progress from species less like Mini to those more like him. This encourages one to accept the Tingla insertion of insects, represented by wasps, between the vegetable and animal members. In any case, the sequence tiger, bear, monkey, man is well established, and here the progressive trend is obvious. A definite conceptual gap separates the vegetable and animal members. Though Kam differs, Mj clearly notes that the vegetable members depart for the jungle, presumably leaving the subsequent members where they are born, and it is only they who play any part in later episodes. A Tingla man once told me casually, while we were watching a ceremony, that the various human races descended from four brothers: the Russians from the eldest, a tiger, the Bhotes from the bear, the Europeans (*gorā*) from the cliff monkey, the Kiranti from Mini napca. Possibly Europeans, vaguely thought of by many as inhabiting India, have here replaced the people of the Plains, but the point of repeating the anecdote is to emphasise that the four animals in the creation myth constitute a definite schema.

All four species have special names in the creation narrative. Presumably they are ritual names, though the monkey's, Chiuniukepciu or the like, was not encountered elsewhere. The special names of the tiger and bear are coupled, in the usual order, in the common ritual expression *bakpaceo* (or *bakwamceo*) *buwamceo*, said to mean 'male children'. The identity of Mini as First Man is made abundantly clear. Kolatiup, an alternative name used in Tingla and meaning 'the naked one', relates to the details of his birth, which in several versions is more typically human than the births of the other species. Thus the references to his wrappings emphasise his nakedness, in contrast to the other animals who need no special covering. Unfortunately I know nothing about delivery among present-day Thulung.

IV. Quarrel between Mini and Tiger

Ph   Mini Rai possessed magic powers, and was a skilled bowman. When the brothers all grew up and went off to live by themselves, there was enmity between Tiger and Mini Rai. All the time Tiger was watching for an opportunity to eat his younger brother. 'One day I'm going to shoot him, that elder brother of mine,' said Mini. 'No, my son,' said his mother, 'what, shoot him! No, you must not do it.' One day Mini and Tiger Rai both went off hunting. 'I wonder if elder brother wants to eat me,' thought Mini Rai. He climbed into a tree and waited there in hiding. In the course of his day's hunting, Tiger Rai arrived at the base of the tree. 'Will he eat me?' wondered Mini, and he made a slight movement. Down below, seeing the shadow of his younger brother, Tiger pounced. At that moment, Mini shot him. He had been warned that if he was not careful he would shoot his brother, and in fact one day that is what he did.

On another telling, Ph mentioned that Mini was born with a bow in his hand, and with the power to steer and call back arrows. This time it was not Mini's shadow but his reflection in water that the tiger mistakenly attacked. But Ph omitted the end of the episode as given by Dim.

Dim Tiger threatens to kill Mini and crunch him up. 'What is my elder brother saying?' Mini asks his mother. (Passage concerning Tiger and shadow).

Miyapma gives Mini warning or instruction. Next day, Mini shoots Tiger with his bow. On his return Miyapma is suspicious and questions him, but he denies his deed. Miyapma resurrects Tiger with the aid of a *hadibom* (a variety of gourd). On coming to life, Tiger exclaims what a nice sleep he has had. 'No,' explains Miyapma, 'Your younger brother killed you.'

CP   The movement of Mini that made Tiger pounce was the shaking of his feathered headdress. Miyapma went looking for her son blowing a horn and beating a metal vessel to make a noise. She revived him by blowing through his penis (?) 'as if through a bamboo tube'. He exclaims how well he has slept. 'Henceforth...'

Mj   Mini was armed with a bow, and later on he killed Tiger. That is why tigers are afraid of us (?). That's all I know.

The notion that Kiranti are essentially and traditionally bowmen is very widespread, though bows are nowadays only used in rituals. It is not clear in detail how the resurrection was performed, but such an undertaking is commonly a matter of sprinkling or splashing with fluid (cf. Jigiyom's resuscitation of Miyapma, or the use of the gourd in 5 IV). Tigers may be afraid of the Rai, but the Rai nowadays are by no means unafraid of tigers.

V. Death of Miyapma and dispersal of brothers

Ph   Before all this, Tiger had one day said to his mother: 'Mother, what shall I give you? Where will you go, and what will you have to eat? When I go off hunting, if you hear me roar in the valleys, look for me on the high ground; if I roar on the high ground, look for me in the valleys.' In spite of his words, his mother went straight over to where he roared, so his hunting was ruined and he caught nothing. His anger welled up, and he blamed his bad luck on her (?). And so he killed her, his own mother.

Wondering where his mother had gone and what had become of her, Mini found out that his brother had killed her. He sent off Bear and Monkey – who is also called Chiuniukepciu – telling them to bury her and perform proper obsequies. Instead they went off and ate her. Mini Rai asked them if they had really buried her or not, and they said they had. 'I wonder. Are you sure you did not eat her instead?' They denied it. 'Open your mouth and say Ah!' On Bear's teeth he saw his mother's hair. Now he knew that they had eaten their mother instead of performing her obsequies, and he sent the two of them off into the jungle. We humans are the descendants of Mini Rai. We are the descendants of the god (*deutā* N).

In untaped versions it is Miyapma who asks who is going to support her. Tiger claims there is not enough food for both of them, though it is unclear whether this explains his departure or his refusal to let his mother approach when he is hunting. When Mini finds that his brothers have eaten Miyapma, he hammers a piece of wood up Bear's anus. The narrator added sceptically that this was said to be an explanation for the fact that bears have loose stools. His wife added that Mini also hammered an axe handle up Monkey's anus. Thereafter an officiant (*seleme*) came to perform the mortuary rites.

At the start of the episode Ph appears to suggest that episode V should precede episode IV, as happens in Tingla. This would introduce a contradiction, since the resuscitation of Tiger in IV was carried out by Miyapma, who dies in the course of V. Perhaps Ph only meant that Tiger's decision to become a hunter should have been mentioned earlier.

Dim   Tiger refuses to eat grain. 'You are purely a grain-eater, I am purely a meat-eater.' He decides to go away and live in the jungle. He warns his mother that when he roars in the west she should go east, and so on; if she comes near him while he is hunting he will kill her. One day Miyapma forgets; she disobeys the instructions and is killed. The second and third brothers are sent to perform the obsequies. There should be different kinds of tomb for different parts of Miyapma's body. Instead of doing what they are told, the brothers eat her flesh, leaving only the bones. They are told to grin, to make the sound 'ee'. Mini sees the blood and hair on the second brother's teeth. Bear and Monkey are sent off to make their homes elsewhere. The former goes uphill, the latter down; but Monkey *(sokse)* comes back after a few years. He is nowadays worshipped as Rangkime Deu.[15] Ritual practitioners (*dhāmi* N) were instituted.

The following notes on types of tomb (*siulium*) were either part of Dim's Creation narrative or comments occasioned by it. A *serepmalium* is thatched, high, with a wall round it. A *bukumalium* is low, earthen, with a low roof. A *yawlium* is seven-storeyed for a priest, and eight-storeyed for a *muliu* or advisor/councillor (the latter type ? also being called a *parilium*). Reference was made also to the *caŋmahəp liblihəp*, spirits of the earth associated with the tombs.

CP   The question arises how Miyapma is to be supported. Monkey drops some faeces, and offers them to Miyapma, who refuses to eat them.

---

15   Cf. Allen 1976a: 534-6.

A member of the audience suggests that Miyapma ignored Tiger's instructions because of her love for him. An evil force *(samse kuyya)* is born. Bear laughs and shows his teeth.

The 'evil force' is one generated by killing in anger,[16] and must here refer to Tiger's killing of Miyapma.

This episode is particularly rich, and it is especially unfortunate that the material is so sparse. Dim's version opens with an opposition between two types of diet, meat for the tiger, and grain, which may stand for vegetables generally. The intermediate brothers, but more especially Monkey, are associated with the anus and faeces. The latter is suggested as a food in CP's version, and can perhaps be taken as intermediate between the carnivorous and vegetarian diets. The same two brothers, though more especially the bear, are associated with cannibalism, another presumably abnormal type of diet.

Whatever Miyapma's reasons for disobeying Tiger's instructions, it is not surprising that he was angry since her action resulted in his 'bad luck' (*broal*). Like the English expression, *broal* does not simply describe or refer to a hunter's lack of success: the relationship of *broal* to lack of success is partly that of cause to effect. Another shade of meaning is suggested by the Nepali translations *narāmro sāyat*, *ashubh*, *lodar,* which denote or connote evil omens. The term can be applied to any undertaking involving a journey, but perhaps especially to hunting expeditions. It is *broal* to see a Blacksmith, snake, *malsãpri* (pine-marten?), or an empty metal water pot, as one sets out while, conversely, it is good luck to see a full water pot, someone milking, or a Tailor. You will catch nothing if anyone you meet on the way asks you where you are going; so you should avoid meetings. Most relevant here, it is *broal* to go where someone else is hunting. Miyapma is emphatically told to go in the opposite direction from the one where the tiger is hunting, and she brings her fate on herself. It may perhaps be particularly wrong for Miyapma, a female, to become involved in the male world of hunting. In any case, killing in anger gives rise to a negative force which, as I understand it, is altogether more serious than a *broal*, and unlike it, is often deprecated in rituals.

The death of Miyapma introduces for the first time in the Creation narrative the problem of corpse disposal; it does not arise in episode IV because Tiger is resuscitated. If different parts of the body require different

16   Cf. Ch. 6 III (ii).

tombs, this implies that the corpse is dismembered. In any case, there is a distinction between the fate of flesh and bones. The flesh is disposed of first, by being eaten; the bones are disposed of subsequently, apparently by burial. Presumably the dismemberment is performed by Tiger, who anyway is not implicated further. Bear and Monkey, who together dispose of the flesh, form a couple in other respects too: they are uninvolved in the quarrel of Mini and Tiger in episode IV, they alone have wooden objects hammered up their anuses, and they are banished along the uphill-downhill axis. Mini's role is to champion the proper human or civilised disposal of corpses. We are not told that he participated directly in the disposal, but apparently he summoned the priests who did.

Out of the list of species created by Miyapma the vegetable members have already left her to make their own homes in the jungle, and the present episode completes the process of dispersal – compare the brief allusion to everyone 'gradually branching in different directions' in PB III. The episode opens with the departure of the eldest of the animal brothers to the jungle, thus emphasising the distinction between domestic space and wild space. It is because she does not fully accept or respect this distinction that Miyapma is killed. The tiger's departure is described as *ano*, i.e. 'across', implying neither uphill nor downhill. The next two brothers are banished uphill and downhill respectively, i.e. to the north and south; this accords with the ecological fact that the favoured habitat of monkeys in this region is lower than that of bears. Mini presumably stays where he is, since we are not told otherwise. As a human, he is the natural successor to his mother, whose marriage and childbirth were conceived in such very human terms.

VI. Origin of death

DB Our elders,[17] without mother or father, went through the jungles, between the vast trees, among the huge boulders. We too... mankind, without mother or father, incapable (...) without the lap of mother or father (to turn to for comfort ?) – as to this dying, it was the lizard who was filled with envy and wickedness. 'Come, Mini, let us go and die, the two of us.' Mini agreed – until just yesterday humanity was foolish and ignorant indeed. So they went off to die. They collected supplies of stone and wood, and built tombs, the *parilium*, the *somolium*, the

---

17 Usually *ŋaceo* refers to respected elders in a community, but may it here refer to the elder brothers, whose association with the jungle has been so often emphasised?

bukumalium. After this, Lizard invited Mini to die first; but Mini did not know how to. So Lizard cast his slough, telling Mini to watch. 'Is that how it is, Lizard?' So Mini departed this life (by imitating Lizard).[18]

There are several justifications for including the passage here. The text follows directly after very summary versions of episodes I and III, and apart from VII it is the only other narrative recorded that tells of Mini. If Mini is the First Man, it is not inappropriate that the creation myth should include an account of his death, the death of his mother being an event of a different character, a matricide and a dismemberment. Moreover the list of types of tomb recalls Dim V.[19]

It is interesting that Mini's death is associated with an unwrapping: Lizard casts his slough, and apparently Mini sheds his own skin. Mini's birth in III was associated with wrapping, and at that point his nakedness was stressed. No doubt the cloth in which he is wrapped at birth relates to the skin he sheds at death.

VII. The Sandalwood Tree

CP Then Night fell. 'Oh Mother Sandalwood tree, I am benighted. Where shall I go? What will become of me? Alas, good Mother!,' he cried. 'What's this, Mini? Where have you got to, what are you doing? You cannot stay here,' replied Mother Sandalwood Tree. 'Alas, what is to become of me? I am benighted. The tigers and bears, the wild animals and jungle spirits will eat me,' he cried in distress. He was in despair. 'Come inside my body. Here, take shelter then.' And so he spent the night. Her womb suddenly opened and he stayed inside. Night had fallen, and in the darkness the jungle animals[20] and spirits, the bear, the tiger, all the wild things pressed threateningly around the tree on all sides. 'Where are you off to? What's up?' 'We've smelled the

---

18 The oration goes on to tell how Lizard informs the relatives, who then celebrate Mini's death ritual. This continuation belongs in a treatment of Thulung death ritual rather than here.

19 The fragmentary CP version leads on from episode IV (which follows what I call episode V) by telling how Mini *jasta*, which usually means 'broke', but may here mean 'died'. Or might it be an error for *jeasta* – cf. *jeaksi bomu* 'die badly'? A suicide is of course regularly considered a bad death, but it is not clear that this applies to Mini.

20 The narrator's gloss for *sabdiuma*, for which cf. comment to Ph II.

scent of a man.' 'He is not inside me. There is nothing here, neither a man nor anything else.' 'Yes, there is,' they shouted, jumping up and down on all sides around the tree, raging and threatening. But Mother Sandalwood Tree continued to deny it, and put them off till dawn came. The sun rose and suddenly the womb of the tree gaped open again. She spoke again to Mini napceo: 'Well then, now you have had your lodging in my womb. Now go and wash. But make sure you wash in still water, not in running water.' So he went over and washed at Ghumne Pani, at Bange Pani.[21]

This episode has been extracted from the Migration of the Ancestors (Ch. 4) and inserted here for several reasons. In its original position the episodes that precede and follow it make no mention of Mini. The immediately preceding one is expressed entirely with plural verbs, the following one predominantly so. Both of them relate journeys, and the geographical location of this intervening episode introduces a southerly diversion for which I see no motive. So the episode does not fit well in Ch. 4. Conversely, several of its themes tie in with the present chapter. Indeed, since it apparently deals with Mini's *birth*, it could well have been treated before episode VI, which recounts his *death*.

The sandalwood tree has already appeared in connection with the births of Namprəngma in Ph I and of Mini in Ant III. It is sometimes said by Thulung to be king among trees. In one wedding ceremonial dialogue the bride's party compared themselves to a *githo* N creeper and compared the groom's side to a sandalwood tree. Some say, too, that the tree cannot be cut down: it becomes invisible and communicates its smell to surrounding trees, which are cut down instead.

In this episode the sandalwood tree is clearly not a king but a female being. The word translated 'Mother' is not the ordinary term for mother (*mam*), but the uncommon word Mamaciuniu. It appears here and there in invocations but is not very clear to present-day informants. According to some, it is the Thulung equivalent of Nepali *bhagawān* or *isor*, i.e. 'God'. One said that Mamaciuniu learned all knowledge from the thunder. The name seems to be linked with death: *mamahami* or *mamame* means the evil spirit of a woman who dies in childbirth, and such a woman may be said to

---

21 Both names refer to some rather striking meanderings of the Siku Khola (or possibly one of its tributaries) quite close to its origins above Nele. The water would have moved very slowly in this part of the stream.

be 'taken by *mama*'. Similarly, *mamalapter*, pieces of banana leaf, are placed in the armpits of a corpse when it is laid out.[22]

However, Mamaciuniu is here no doubt concerned rather with birth. We have already seen links between sandalwood trees and birth in the creation mythology, and the tree's protective cavity here recalls the hollow in which Khomda left his seed. Indeed, Mini spends the night, not only inside the tree, but explicitly in its womb (*ŋele*). Moreover, although the earlier episodes do not mention it, one expects a new-born baby to be washed, and it makes sense that this be done in still water – otherwise the infant's spirit, as yet insecurely attached to its body, might be carried off by the current. As it stands, the text gives no motivation for the washing, let alone for the opposition of still and flowing water.

Thus the episode was perhaps originally a variant account of the birth of the First Man, with Mamaciuniu replacing Miyapma. The tree from which Mini emerges recalls the tree from which Jigiyom takes the fertilising seed. One might also detect a slight echo of episode IV. In both cases a mother figure gives advice to Mini when a tiger is threatening to eat him. In both cases Mini is in the tree – whether in its trunk (as no doubt in VII) or in its branches – and the tiger is raging outside or below.

The division into episodes is only a device to aid comparison of variant versions, and we can now attempt a global view. It is widely recognised that no single answer can be given to the question of what a myth is about – one expects to find indefinitely many layers of meaning, or levels of interpretation. But the approach taken here is to summarise the Thulung material under headings derived from the life cycle: impregnation (or fertilisation, coming together, marriage), birth, differentiation, death. Here, each is of course primal or cosmogonic. Regarding the relative order of the first two, impregnation and birth, the old conundrum arises: which came first, the chicken or the egg? I opt for the egg.

We have encountered many types of birth. (i) According to Ant I the first woman simply emerges from the earth (a motif which recurs in 4 II). (ii) The wind creates a germinal mass by sweeping together leaves or dead

---

22   Perhaps Mamaciuniu is related etymologically to Chiuniukepciu the monkey – aspiration is often lost in non-initial syllables.

vegetable matter.[23] (iii) A lotus arises from the mass, and in or on it a woman is created. (iv) Possibly, though not certainly, the different species originate from different body parts of the Creatrix. (v) The First Man is born from a woman after a difficult labour during which she locates herself on a platform. (vi) If episode VII was rightly interpreted, the First Man was also born from a tree.

Under the heading of impregnation we have: (i) the Wind fertilises a primal woman; (ii) Heaven sends Rain upon Earth; (iii) Khomda sends his seed to earth and impregnates Miyapma via a bird (Kam); (iv) Khomda descends to earth in person and performs the impregnation via a tree and a bird. Perhaps (iv) is an elaboration of (iii).

As children grow up, they have to find their own place in life: they may have to leave the parental home, or become initiated into some distinct role. One way or another they become socially differentiated from the previous generation, and independent of them. At the same time the siblings diverge from each other. Inside the womb each is equally closely associated with adults; in time each will be equally differentiated. The point of these commonplaces is that differentiation is a part of life no less basic than the familiar triad of birth, impregnation and death. That may be why initiation is often as important a rite of passage as those marking the more abrupt biological events.

Anyway, to return to the Thulung, the theme of differentiation has already been touched on under the heading of 'dispersal' (episodes III and V). Some of the discriminations introduced by the dispersal may have a bearing on social organisation, e.g. hunter's sphere versus woman's sphere or carnivore versus vegetarian, but does the myth contain any more direct reference to social structure? Allen (1978a, b) argues that among the tribal and outlying Bodic speakers a fourfold organisation of society was once widely prevalent, and that traces of the same pattern can be found in early Tibet. According to this theory, each of the four components of society had, either absolutely or relative to a given component, one of four functions: king, priest, minister, and (standing slightly apart and on a lower level) priest's servant. If the theory is right, the four Thulung brothers might correspond to the four functions. Perhaps one could even justify the following equations: Mini = king (associated with war), Bear = priest (most closely linked with disposal of corpse), Monkey = minister (associated

---

23   If the wind is a whirlwind, the implied circular motion might recall the theme of churning in Sanskrit mythology.

with wealth?), Tiger = priest's servant (associated with butchery). However, the arguments are less than conclusive and will not be presented here. If the comparative framework is one day established, then will be the time to return to this issue.

Three sorts of death have appeared in the chapter. (i) Tiger was shot by Mini, but resurrected by his mother with the aid of a gourd. (ii) Miyapma was killed and dismembered by one of her own sons. Her corpse was disposed of by a combination of endocannibalism and burial. (iii) The First Man was tricked into dying by Lizard. Although (iii) might be seen as a suicide, the context of the narration suggests it was a good death, i.e. a natural one, for the funeral oration occurred at a ceremony held for a lady who died quite normally at a ripe old age. (iv) Possibly too, Miyapma had earlier been 'killed' by the drought, and resurrected by Jigiyom's sprinkling.

Comparisons

For reasons discussed in Ch. 1 VII, the main comparative emphasis will be on Tibet. Both here and in later chapters, we shall meet a number of instances where Tibetan and Thulung narratives have so much in common that some historical link is likely. That being so, it is sensible to look for as many links as possible between the two bodies of material. Some of the rapprochements proposed may seem bold – more a matter of similar situations within a context than of intrinsic resemblances of substance. However, I prefer to err on the side of boldness than caution. Little is lost if a few of the parallels are rejected as forced, while something is gained if attention is drawn to relationships that may be substantiated by further work. Much of the Tibetan narrative matter is well known and comes from Macdonald (1959) or Haarh (1969) without detailed references being given.

One of the few features of episode I shared by most versions was that the name of Miyapma's parent began with N. So it may not be coincidental that the Khaling recognise a progenetrix called Ninamridam, whose children were the Rai ancestor, the bear, the tiger and other animals (Joiner). I heard also that the Chamling[24] equivalent of Miyapma was Nayma. The names are variable, but a significant subset contain the syllable *nam* (Thulung Namprəngma, Namprekma, Ninamrangma, Ninamtho(?)). A Dewsa sadhu gave me the ritual name of the sun as Ninamma laditma, and

---

24 [I follow the conventional spelling, even though the initial is not aspirated.]

in such a cosmogonic context one might also cite Limbu *nam* or Khaling *nwaam* meaning 'sun', and Tib *gnam* 'sky, air' (as in gNam-gyi Gung-rgyal, who is mentioned below). However comparable names occur in other religious contexts in the area. Namrung siuciu was the name of a minor spirit addressed in a cattle-shelter ritual in Lokhim. Namrung ('chef des Limbus') comes in a list of the *sikāri* spirits who may possess mediums in Darjeeling (Macdonald 1962: 139), and in agricultural or pastoral contexts the Gurung worship a deity called Namru (Pignède 1966: 290, 308).

In discussing Ph I, I raised the possibility of a reference to elements. After presenting a number of creation myths, some written, some taken from oral tradition in north-eastern Tibet, Hermanns (1949: 832) notes that the Tibetan sequence of elements is wind, fire, water, earth, with heaven or the ether often added as the fifth. Ph I mentions heaven, earth, water and wind, and DB's parallel version mentions fire. Thulung has no indigenous term for 'element', and I never met with evidence of the concept in other tribal contexts. One might compare the lotus, and birth within it (Ph I). These motifs too are prominent in the literate traditions of the area, and were not found elsewhere in the tribal tradition. I have already noted Ph I as being in part parallel to episode II, but expressed in abstract and depersonalised form. The contrast with the main body of Thulung creation myth suggests the influence of a literate tradition and, as we shall see, the suggestion is strengthened by the fact that the initiative is taken by the sky.

In contrast, Ant I, which emphasises the fertilising role of the wind, has a more typically tribal character. The Idu Mishmis of Arunachal Pradesh tell how the first woman sat with legs apart on the wind god's hill, and the god entered her and made her pregnant (Baruah 1960: 7). Closer at hand, a Limbu myth tells how 'the first woman Tapunama-Wahinama out of loneliness sought a child... was impregnated by the storm and gave birth to a male child' (Jones 1974: 259f).[25]

Reduced to essentials, episodes II-III of the Thulung myth tell how an earthly female is fertilised by a male from heaven, and how she then gives birth to various creatures including the First Man. At this level of generality, one can compare what is probably the best known of all Tibetan creation

---

25 Perhaps the impregnator was 'wind' rather than 'storm' – Nep *ādhi* has both meanings. Note again the element *nam* in the name of a creator being. Another Limbu myth (ibid) attaches the name Tapunama Wahinama to the First Man, created by Brahmā from the four elements.

stories. The story goes that the first humans in Tibet were four (sometimes six or seven) brothers or clans, who were the offspring of a male monkey and a female rock demon. The monkey was an emanation of the Bodhisattva Avalokiteshvara, formed by a ray of light projected from his left hand as the holy one surveyed Tibet from a mountain summit. The demoness, an incarnation of the Goddess Tara, burned with desire for the monkey, and while he was meditating in a forest repeatedly approached him in the form of a strumpet. At last he took pity on her and asked Avalokiteshvara how to answer her importunities. He was told to live with her and engender humans who would become Buddhists.

Comparing the Thulung myth, one notes the following points. (i) Two male figures from above are involved, (ignoring the role sometimes given to a third, Amitabha, in initiating the whole episode) – cf. Rolasila and Khomda. (ii) Of the males it is the subordinate one (monkey, Khomda) who physically impregnates the single female in the story. (iii) The monkey is presumably ugly, as Khomda is. (iv) The demoness burns with sexual desire, as Miyapma is parched with a thirst only assuaged by the seed of the god. (v) Only after importunities from the demoness is the monkey induced to act – cf. the importunity of Miyapma's emissaries. (vi) In Hindu tradition Tara is the wife of Brihaspati (O'Flaherty 1975: 299), and Brihaspati, like Khomda, is identified with Jupiter.[26]

An important difference is that in Tibet the whole episode is initiated by the heavenly beings, whereas for the Thulung the initiative is taken by the female throughout – in emitting attractive light the Evening star is expressing its ordinary nature, not taking an initiative. Since the Tibetan story is very much part of Buddhist tradition, the centrality of the Buddhist gods is unsurprising, but one should note the greater emphasis on the male – a point that will recur.

Although the motif of descent-from-heaven is clear enough in the story of the monkey and the rock-demon, it is even more prominent in the Tibetan myth of the First King. Tibetan writers recognise three versions of the story, each with its own variants: a Buddhist version, a Bon one, and the least known, 'most secret' one, which is probably pre-Bon and to which we shall return. The first two differ mainly in the ancestry of the king: the Buddhists make him the son of an Indian king, while according to Bon he is a *lha*, the general term for celestial god. In either case he regularly appears in Tibet on the summit of a mountain, from which he descends. The

---

26   However Tara's name means 'star'.

motive for his coming varies. Some accounts, including the orthodox Buddhist one, ascribe it to divine providence (cf. the coming of the monkey), while others mention a prophecy; in others again the earthlings take the initiative because of the prevailing distress in their country (Haarh 1969: 234). On the advice of a 'voice', the earthlings' request is addressed in the first instance to a deity called sKar-ma yol-sde (*skar-ma* means 'star'), and it is he who transmits the request to the future king. The latter demurs at first: the Land of Men below is a world of unhappiness, and he lists the evils to which it is liable. However sKar-ma renews his request, and the king is persuaded to go, once he has received certain requisites to protect him against the evils. Several versions mention the king descending a 'ladder' of nine steps. This is normally taken as referring to nine cosmic levels, but may refer to descent through nine generations (ibid: 264).

The 'most secret' version of the King's descent makes him the youngest of nine Beings called the The'u brang. Usually the First King is called gNya'-khri btsan-po.[27] The name is generally explained by the story that when he arrived on earth the representatives of the Tibetan people who welcomed him carried him on their necks (*gnya'*). Often they do so in response to his gesture pointing upwards towards the heaven from which he came, but other explanations refer to the neck of his mother or of himself at his birth.

Here again, as in the Monkey-Rock Demon story, two male heavenly figures are involved, one of them in some way stellar. Often the initiative comes from earth, and the one who descends demurs at first. The requisites he takes with him might recall the basket suitable for marriage gifts which is woven by Khomda for no clear reason. One Tibetan account has the First King descending as a 'substitute' for the god of heaven (Hoffmann 1950: 156, 245)[28] – cf. Khomda, the substitute for Rolasila. The focus on the neck of the First King recalls Khomda's goitre (albeit *gnya'* applies more to the nape or back of the neck than to the front). Finally, the nine steps in the descent of the king recall SSJ's statement that Miyapma had nine successive offspring, of whom Mini was the last. If there is anything in this last point,

---

27   There are many variants: e.g. a Tun-Huang fragment mentions one Khri Bar-la bdun-tshig descending from the thirteenth storey of heaven to become First King.

28   Another manuscript of the same version (Haarh 1969: 449 n.7) reads *bod* 'Tibet' rather than *dod* 'substitute'. However the scribe is more likely to have amended a word unintelligible to him in the context than to have introduced the *lectio difficilior*.

it implies that the Tibetan First King conflates features that in Thulung tradition belong separately to Khomda and to Mini.

Tibetan mythology contains several versions of the First Man, as distinct from the First King. The best known is Ye-smon or Yid-smon rgyal-po (*rgyal-po* = king); another is Sangs-po 'bum-khri. In one source Ye-smon is born by breaking out from an egg, and has 'eighteen sons and daughters' (Hermanns 1946: 276f). But mostly these First Men are just names, rather than characters in narratives.

However, we can extend the comparison to other mythic humans – let us call them Founders – who are the First Men of their religious groups, rather than of humanity in general. One example is Padmasambhava, founder of the rNying-ma-pa order, and famous for bringing Tantric teachings to Tibet. His miraculous birth from a lotus in a lake or in the Indus river recalls that of Namprəngma from the same plant in the Thulung primal lake (Ph I). A richer example for us is gShen-rab(s) mi-bo, mythical founder of the Bon religion. His name has been variously rendered 'Man of the lineage of gShen' or 'Best of sacrificial priests' (Stein 1972: 236, Snellgrove and Richardson 1968: 96), but the element *mi* 'man' is no doubt cognate with the same element in Mini's name. Similarities exist between traditions of the First King and of these two Founders, especially between the King's journey from heaven and the triumphant, demon-subduing journeys (*digvijaya*) of the Founders (Haarh 1969: 238, 319), but I shall focus on gShen-rab's birth.

Two main accounts exist of this birth.[29] According to the older source, the diversity of creation arose from the Grandmother of the world, Ming-dgu sring-dgu ('The nine brothers and sisters'), and an obscure figure, King Khugs-kyi-thugs. The text passes abruptly to gShen-rab, who when he came from the eastern heaven radiated light in all directions. The five-coloured rays penetrated the spheres of the cosmos and reached the summit of a certain willow or poplar tree. There the blue cuckoo, the turquoise bird, king of birds, rejoiced all beings with his song. The bird descended onto the crown of the head of heavenly mother Gung-rgyal,[30] lover of wisdom, and beat its wings. When it had shaken them three times, a white and red ray of light came from the bird's sexual organs and passed down the mother's

---

29   The one generally recognised as older is given in Hoffmann (1950: 250 translation, 200 commentary), while the *gZer-myig* version was translated by Francke (1924: 332-7). The two are briefly compared by Stein (1972: 242).

30   In spite of the epithet 'heavenly', the story clearly suggests that she lives on earth. Her relationship to the Grandmother of the World is left unclear.

body. When gShen-rab issued from his mother's body his melodious voice rang forth as had the cuckoo's.

Hackin (1923: 117), citing a similar account from another text, describes a Tibetan painting of the episode. gShen-rab is shown leaving paradise in human form, but beside him is the blue bird into which he mutates to enter his mother's body. The magic bird descends from heaven, and eventually gShen-rab is born from his mother's right armpit.

In the later *gZer-myig*, gShen-rab chooses his two parents. A white light like an arrow enters the crest of his father's head and passes to his sexual organs, while a red light like a spindle or distaff enters the crest of his mother's head and passes to her womb. There follows a long description of the pregnancy. When the Founder is born, he coos like a turquoise bird and rejoices all creatures. His mother lifts him up in a silk napkin and says to his father: 'This son is like unto a jewel wrapped in silk.'

As regards the conception, two motifs merit note. Firstly, the gShen-rab traditions greatly emphasise rays of light: in the earlier version the light passes from gShen-rab to an earthly tree, and perhaps on to the cuckoo, and in both versions rays are also direct precursors to the conception.[31] Though the Thulung material does not feature rays as such, stars are necessarily emitters of light; Miyapma fell in love when she saw Rolasila *shining*, and Khomda's goitre was *luminous* (II Ph). Secondly, both traditions involve birds and trees. Khomda's fertilising seed passes from him to the mother figure via a bird as intermediary, and usually the bird brings it from a tree, albeit from a hole in the tree rather than from its top. Perhaps events at the mother's head provide a third rapprochement. Jigiyom does not explicitly stand on Miyapma's head, but to convey seed from his tail or wings into her mouth he might well need to do so. In any case, to 'sprinkle' her, he must have waved his wings or tail, just as in the Tibetan, for no evident reason, the cuckoo beats or shakes its wings.

As regards the birth, firstly, immediately on being born, gShen-rab emits a melodious sound, but the link between birth and sounds will be discussed in the next chapter. Secondly, the double mention of the newborn infant being wrapped recalls Thulung emphasis on this motif (III Kam, Ant).

One tradition claims that gShen-rab was an incarnation of the Buddha, and appeared at the same time as he did (Haarh 1969: 111). Moreover the

---

31   Cf. also the ray of light that emanated from Avalokiteshvara on the summit of the mountain and issued in his earthly counterpart, the monkey.

story of his birth and life, certainly the *gZer-myig* version, has been understood as modelled on that of the Buddha Shakyamuni (Stein 1972: 242, cf. also Snellgrove and Richardson 1968: 99). The Buddha descends from the heavens into the womb of Queen Mahamaya, who gives birth while she stands in the grove at Lumbini, holding a branch of a great *sāl* tree. The Buddha comes from her 'like a man descending stairs… shining like a jewel laid on Benares cloth', and being born from her right side (Thomas 1927: 33f). We note again familiar themes: descent from heaven, a tree, stairs, cloth (for wrapping the infant).

The historical interpretation of such similarities between Thulung and Indian Buddhist traditions is not obvious, and I cannot discuss it at length. The Thulung narratives constitute a reasonably coherent tribal mythology in which elements clearly marked by the influence of the literate traditions are (at least sometimes) detectable as such, as I hope to have shown regarding Ph I. One cannot take for granted then that all such similarities are due to the influence of the literate tradition on the non-literate. Perhaps the reality is almost the reverse: a story like Ant III may be representative of stories that were current when the Indian Buddhist tradition was developing. But this is speculation.

A stronger historical claim can be made linking the Thulung with Tibet. The tribal mythology does explain details in Hoffmann's account of the birth of gShen-rab that are not clear from the Tibetan text as we have it, in particular the nature of the cuckoo and its movements. Stein explains the bird as being apparently gShen-rab himself in another form. Perhaps this is somehow related to the shamanistic tendencies of Bon and the interest it took in birds and magical flight (e.g. Hoffmann 1950: 145). But why should gShen-rab transform himself into a cuckoo in order to emit the fertilising rays that will enable him to be born from his earthly mother? In demoting the cuckoo from the prenatal period to the status of simile for the birth cry, the *gZer-myig* removes a needless complication and improves the narrative line, but the Thulung material offers a possible starting point for the motif. Although in most Thulung versions all the bird does is transfer the star's seed from the hole in the tree to the woman, in Kam II its role is the wholly logical one of linking heavenly male and earthly female by carrying seed from one to the other.

In the birth of gShen-rab the bird can be seen either as transferring the rays from the top of the tree to the mother's head (Hoffmann), or as being the form taken by the heavenly being in order to enter the mother (Hackin, Stein). In the *gZer-myig* the bird is almost eliminated. We have already suggested that the Tibetan First King conflates features of a god who descends from heaven with features of a human being born on earth who initiates a line, and in this story the bird (and indeed the earthly mother) is entirely eliminated. The five stories form a sequence leading from a situation in which the heavenly and earthly males are related only by the most tenuous and distant link, to a situation in which they are identified; correspondingly, the role of the bird in ensuring the link is progressively reduced. Whether one supposes that the sequence is purely typological, or that it bears some resemblance to the actual history of the stories, it does offer a possible interpretation for the Tibetan bird, namely as mediator between heaven and earth.

In discussing birds, we have so far been concerned on the Thulung side only with Jigiyom, and particularly with his return journey, and we should also look for any Tibetan parallels for Cetla. The Tibetan Gesar Epic refers to several fragmentary creation stories not otherwise incorporated in the written tradition. In particular, it mentions a wise old man contemporary with the creation of the world, who knows how the world was born, how living beings are formed, and perhaps how birth occurs in the human body (Stein 1959: 464f). The name of this figure varies: the commonest name is sPyi-dpon khra-rgan, but in Ladakh he is called dPal-le rgod-po. *Khra-rgan* means 'old falcon', while *rgod-po* means either 'the Wild', as Stein takes it (ibid: 470, 514), or else 'the eagle'. One of his acts is to procure a chieftain for his country. He thus combines the traits of being contemporary with the creation, of knowing about the birth of things, of being related to birds, and of playing a part in inducing heaven to send a ruler. The last trait recalls Mj II, where it is Cetla who despatches Jigiyom.[32]

The Nakhi [or Naxi] are a people living on the south-east border of Tibet, about whom considerably more literature exists than I have been able to use here. Nevertheless, they merit mention in connection with the curious fluid used by Khomda to fertilise Miyapma.

> A male being dwelt on the top of Mount Sumeru, and a female called Mimakhomima dwelt in Lake Manasarowara. As they could never meet, the male spat from the mountain top into the lake. The female caught the spittle in her hand, swallowed it, was impregnated, and gave birth to nine demon-planets.

---

32 Mj III makes Cetla one of twelve officiants. The old man in the epic is sometimes one of eighteen 'father's brothers', but the number twelve is often given for the vassals who welcomed the first king.

In another myth, the 'father of the human race' saw his reflection in a white lake, felt lonely, and threw into it his tears and the foam from his mouth. A water maid arose, and there were born nine sons and nine (or seven) daughters (Rock 1937: 13ff).

An occasional feature of the Tibetan First King is that he possesses physical signs such as turquoise eyebrows and webbed hands and feet. The relationship between these signs and the *mahāpuruṣa-lakṣana* shown by the Buddha at birth is discussed by Haarh (1969: 197ff). They do not seem to be reported of gShen-rab, but is there any trace of them in Mini? Three accounts mention his bow, which some say was present at birth, and one mentions ornaments; but these are accoutrements, not physical signs. Apart from a mention of 'magical powers', the only other attribute ascribed to him at birth is that he will have hands, feet and head (Kam III). These are such banal human attributes – moreover, ones shared with monkeys – that they might be hints of a more interesting physical description missing from the available versions. But nothing conclusive can be said.

In looking for Tibetan parallels to episodes IV and V of the Thulung tradition, one focus would be the four brothers. Different animals are sometimes associated with the four cardinal points (e.g. Stein 1959: 456), but what we are looking for in the present context is a set of four brothers of whom the eldest is definitely animal and the youngest definitely human. These do not seem to be common, and the nearest parallel to the Thulung motif that I have met so far is the 'very well known tradition, frequently included in the introduction to historical works in Tibetan', to the effect that Tibet was once inhabited by the following animals: the elephant and deer in Upper Tibet, the deer and monkey in Central Tibet, and the monkey and rock demon in Lower Tibet (Haarh 1969: 449). Such pairing evidently enables the four beings to be accommodated within a three-fold spatial classification. From a Thulung point of view this schema replaces Tiger by the elephant, Bear by the deer, and Mini by the species who in the best-known Tibetan creation myth corresponds to his mother.

As for the eating of Miyapma by her children, I have failed to find any compilation or analysis of Tibetan material bearing on cannibalism. A key term would be Tib *sha-za*, literally 'flesh-eater'. In its general sense it signifies mammals including man (ibid: 160). More specifically it can apply to humans with the connotation 'uncivilised', and to a class of demons who eat human flesh (Das).[33] In speaking of their own history Tibetans use it both of the prehuman inhabitants of the country and of those whom the first king came to rule, and perhaps only a western mentality would wish to distinguish clearly between such related meanings as cannibal demons (who could not 'really' exist) and uncivilised savages (who could). Doubtless too, the exact indigenous interpretation of *sha-za* varied with date and context. However, the salience of the term in descriptions of early Tibet might imply a tradition that the early inhabitants of the country ate human flesh. However, even if this could be proved, the question would remain whether the flesh eaten was that of relatives.

After the descent of the first king, Tibetan tradition moves rapidly through his immediate successors. A well-known fact about the first seven kings (sometimes six) is that they left no corpses; nor did the first twenty-four (or twenty-three) queens. The explanation given is that, being gods, the first kings were able to return to heaven at their death by means of the *dmu* rope. 'His (the king's) body dissolved into the rope which resembled a kind of rainbow extending from his head into the sky' (Stein 1972: 48). The first tomb was that of King Gri-gum, who cut through his own *dmu* rope during a fight. Before coming to detailed rapprochements between Tibetan and Thulung accounts of this primal death and burial, we may note the overall similarity of pattern. In both cases stories of a descent from heaven lead on to stories of the first mortuary rite. Admittedly, in the Tibetan myth a number of generations intervene, but the intervening kings are shadowy figures named after cosmological entities. As Haarh argues, and as Thulung material considered later seems to confirm, Gri-gum forms an alternative start to the royal dynasty, i.e. an alternative version of the creation.

Tibetan traditions about Gri-gum are quite complex and exist in various versions, while the Thulung material on episodes IV-VI is relatively scanty and particularly incomplete. Thus there is little point in pressing the comparison to the smallest details, and we need not distinguish the different Tibetan versions (for the full data plus analysis see Haarh, esp. Chs. 4-9). The following seem to be the main points.

---

33 Human flesh is the 'great flesh', *sha-chen* – clearly a loan translation from Sk *mahāmāṃsa;* it is much used, in real or symbolic form, in Tantric ritual (Haarh 1969: 346). The epithet *sha-za* is often coupled with *gdong-dmar* 'red-faced' (e.g. Macdonald 1959: 438), which might recall the blood Mini sees on Bear's teeth.

(i) Like Miyapma, Gri-gum died through his own fault in spite of warnings (by challenging one Lo-ngam to combat). (ii) In one version, his corpse was placed in 'one hundred copper vessels', which implies dismemberment. (iii) After his death his two or three sons disperse to become rulers of kingdoms, but one of them later returns to continue the line and displace the usurping Lo-ngam. The death of Miyapma was followed by the banishment of the bear and monkey, but the latter subsequently returned as a god. (iv) The wife of Gri-gum, taken as queen by the usurper, is once called 'The mother of the four brothers' (Haarh 1969: 145). (v) The fourth son is supernaturally conceived and has an abnormal birth. (vi) It is this last son, who stays where he is, who with some difficulty recovers the corpse of his parent and summons the priests to perform the First Burial.

The youngest son in the story is an interesting and complex figure. His exiled half-brothers are rather clearly linked with the animal kingdom, for their names contain the elements Nya 'fish', Sha or Sha-za 'flesh eaters', and Bya 'bird'.[34] In lacking such zoological characteristics the youngest son, Ru-la-skyes, comes closer to ordinary humanity, and he can also be related to the First Man or First King. In some versions he becomes First Minister, while in others he becomes King himself. Among his various names is Ru-pa-skyes, which echoes the name Rupati given by some Buddhist sources to the First King, who came from India to Tibet.

The conception of this being was unusual. His mother dreamed that she copulated with a beautiful white man, and when she awoke, she saw a white yak rise from the pillow and go away. The white man was an incarnation of Yar-lha sham-po (elsewhere identified as the sacred mountain onto which the First King descended). After eight months she gave birth to a lump of steaming and quivering blood, which she placed in the warm horn of a wild yak and rolled up in a pair of clean trousers. 'It boiled by the heat, and out of it came a beautiful baby.' The nocturnal visitor must be a heavenly figure, not only because of his link with the mountain, but also because of the regular association of whiteness with gods (*lha*) and heaven. The lump of blood is presumably more or less skinless (as well as, in one account, lacking eyes and mouth). Like Mini and gShen-rab, it needed at birth to be wrapped in a cloth. The motif of heating a baby appears in

---

34   The triadic grouping probably corresponds to that of the first three kings in the official list, and to the three cosmic spheres of Underworld, Earth and Heaven (Haarh 1969: 142).

Thulung tradition (5 VI), but also in the infancy of the Founder among the Nakhi. Nakhi religion is closely related to later Tibetan Bon, and its Founder, Dtomba Shilo, is recognisably related to gShen-rab: *dtomba* means priest, and Shi-lo is merely the Nakhi pronunciation of the Tibetan name. In one account, soon after his birth from his mother's armpit, he is carried off by demons, who boil him in an eight-handled pot; on the third day he rises from the vessel, takes a sword and kills them (Rock 1937: 48).[35] Thus the youngest son of Gri-gum's wife belongs in the same group of representations as Mini and the other Founders.

Although a number of rapprochements have been made between Thulung and Tibetan traditions of the First Burial, one obvious difference is that for the Thulung the first corpse is female while for the Tibetans it is male. This is not an isolated difference, but one aspect of a pervasive contrast between the two mythologies, to which we shall revert in the final section of the chapter.

In Thulung episode VI the death of Mini follows the removal of his skin. Some Chinese sources (apparently all deriving from an unknown original) discuss the mortuary customs of the Sum-pa or Su-pli, who lived in two groups, one towards the northeast of Central Tibet, one to its west. Though spoken of as foreign by the Central Tibetans (Stein 1972: 46), they were apparently closely related to them, but were ruled not by kings but queens, the succession passing through the female line. When a queen died or, according to other versions, when a person of rank died, the skin was peeled off the corpse and treated specially (Haarh 1969: 348f). Traces of similar practices are found in Tibet proper. 'From the Buddhist and Bon iconography it appears that it has been no unique occurrence to peel off the human skin and a certain religious significance must of ancient time have been ascribed to the human skins which serve as attributes to many deities in the later Tibetan Buddhism' (ibid). Human skins appear to be especially often associated with dPal-ldan lha-mo (Nebesky-Wojkowitz 1956: 32f, 35), a goddess we shall meet again shortly. Ekvall (1964: 29) mentions human as well as animal skins being hung up as offerings to the guardian deities of monasteries.

---

35   Rock (ibid) cites a similar episode from the childhood of the epic hero Gesar. Stein (1959: 302 n.22) notes that Gesar also resembles Ru-la-skyes in his miraculous birth. Gesar's celestial father takes the form of a white yak, though Gesar is actually procreated by a sacred mountain. He is born, in some accounts, as a ball or sack of flesh.

Thulung episode VII finds an interesting comparison in a text reported by Hermanns (1946: 288), which describes four types of men associated with worlds at the four cardinal points. The first three types differ as regards food, height, length of life and mode of birth. The fourth, whose nature is formulated slightly differently, live in the north, eat one measure of food, are seven fathoms tall, and kill by means of words rather than weapons; when such a man is born it is from a tree. A disagreeable noise comes from the tree, and at the same time a man descends; the birth is supernatural, not warm. The text lists the other sorts of birth as from warmth, from the womb and from eggs. Hermanns notes that Buddhist lists give the following: from an egg, from the soil like flowers, from warmth and moisture (also putrefaction), and from the womb. The Buddhists thus omit the tree-birth to which Hermanns' text gives prominence both by its position and its special wording. The existence of such a notion in north-east Tibet is confirmed by a briefly reported oral tradition (ibid: 290): mankind was created when Heaven made two humans, later man and wife, who emerged from a tree or piece of wood. Neither of these Tibetan tree-births mentions the species of tree. Presumably they too are female, like Mamaciuniu, and like the tree in whose hole Khomda deposited his seed.

Female Creator Deities

We have already seen several times that where Thulung emphasise the creative activity of females, Tibetans emphasise that of males. In the Monkey and Rock Demon story it was the male gods in heaven who took the initiative. In the descent of the First King, no human mother was involved at all. The Tibetan first corpse was a male. Where women are mentioned in the Tibetan stories, they are seldom more than names. In contrast, Thulung tradition gives Miyapma (or Mamaciuniu) the central role. We shall meet the same difference in relative emphasis in the next chapter too. I have little information about other Bodic tribal mythologies in Nepal, but in Lepcha mythology the creator Itpomu is definitely female, her husband Debu being 'merely a name, without personality or independent existence' (Gorer 1967: 225).

Apparently however, the emphasis on the male is a relatively recent feature of Tibetan mythology, and the further back one goes the greater the importance of female deities. Although Buddhism has relatively little interest in any creator deity, it brought with it from India a predominantly male pantheon but, as is well known, it also incorporated many preexisting deities into its pantheon, especially in the form of 'guardian deities'; and it is suspected that the preceding Bon religion did likewise. Bon certainly recognised a Great Mother goddess (*yum chen-mo*) Sa-trig er-sangs, mother of space and the female component of the supreme god-head (*dharmakāya*) (Hoffmann 1950: 334, 340); however I know little else about her.[36] It is not easy to interpret the hints in surviving Tibetan literature concerning the pre-literate past, and the subject is really one for specialists. Nevertheless, I venture a brief look.

The most prominent of guardian deities in Tibetan Buddhism is dPal-ldan lha-mo, who is also described as 'the most important among the aboriginal female deities adopted by Buddhism'. The Fifth Dalai Lama identified her with A-phyi ('grandmother') gNam-gyi gung-rgyal; the latter is taken by Tucci (1949: 719) to be the consort of a supreme celestial god, and may also be identical with the Mo-bya btsun-bya or Mo-btsun gung-rgyal who is mother of the First King in the 'most secret' version of his origin. In several contexts dPal-ldan lha-mo is definitely associated with the creation (Tib *srid-pa*). In reviewing these facts and suppositions, Haarh (1969: 221 ff.) associates her also with the mother of gShen-rab and the mother of the First King, and concludes that:

> in all these cases we are dealing with various versions of the same fundamental idea of a primary couple of celestial deities, the female party of which has survived in the general aspect of dPal-ldan lha-mo... It seems as though the goddess, the female party of the couples, is the superior party... with regard to offspring, the role of the god is quite inferior. We have to consider not a genitor but a genetrix... an ancient matriarchal system of theogony.

But dPal-ldan lha-mo is not only associated with creation and giving birth. We have met her already as – in her various forms – clad in skin stripped from a human body. In a study of her iconography Róna-Tas (1956: 168) remarks that she is 'repeatedly...a goddess of death', often being the wife of Yama. Das (1881: 178f) equates her with the Hindu Kālī.

Before leaving the topic of female creator deities in Tibet I should mention briefly the two versions of a cosmogony given by Tucci (1949: 712). In one version, from the vacuum arose a Queen of the serpents (*klu*)

---

36   There is only one reference in Nebesky-Wojkowitz (1956: 317): Sa-trig er-sangs rgyal-mo dbyings-kyi-yum is the first of the six names of rNgam-mo yum-chen srid-pa'i bde-sgrol-ma, where the last two syllables are the ordinary name for Tara.

who arrayed existence. From the summit of her head came the heavens, from her eyes came the sun and moon, from her voice came the thunder, from her bones the mountains, and so on. In the other version, the components of the cosmos arose from a nine-headed female serpent born of an egg. Neither goddess is actually stated to be sacrificed in the process of creation, but Tucci compares them with a nine-headed male demon or monster in the Ladakhi version of the Gesar saga: the monster is killed, and from the different parts of its body the kingdom of Gling is constructed (summary in Stein 1959: 461ff). It is in the light of such accounts that one should view the fragmentary material on the dismemberment of Miyapma.

I cannot here explore further the nature of ancient Tibetan goddesses or their relationship to Miyapma. The question needs to be tackled systematically, taking into account not only the Tibetan material but also that from surrounding peoples, of whom the Nakhi are only one. Such an investigation could reasonably hope to throw light on the relationship between Bon and the pre-Bon stratum of beliefs. The matter is complex, but Bon is widely considered to have been introduced from outside, from the south-west. Stein (1972: 236) remarks that 'Bon may have done more than has hitherto been supposed towards preparing the ground for the adoption of Buddhism, by assimilating Indo-Iranian elements before Lamaism did so.' One element it may have assimilated is suggested by the Buddhist source which states that 'Heaven was much beloved by the Bon-po' (Hoffmann 1950: 324). In similar vein Haarh (1969: 317) postulates that 'the idea of a celestial world of lHa has been introduced by the Bon-po', in basic contrast to previously prevailing ideas of existence which focused on the chthonic. From a Thulung point of view, what the Bon-po would have done was to shift the emphasis from the female creator towards the male creator, from Miyapma to Khomda. Such an attitude would be understandable since Bon was the official state religion of the Yarlung dynasty in historical times, and according to the ideology the legitimacy of the dynasty was founded on the descent from Heaven of the First King (Macdonald 1971). Highly comparable myths in fact supported divine kingship among a number of East and Central Asian peoples (Waida 1973).

Though much remains to be explored, the Thulung material already seems to support those Tibetologists who suspect that Tibet has experienced a shift in the balance of sexes within the pantheon. If this could be established, the finding would be interesting in its own right, but would also have implications stretching beyond the history of religion, even if that term be taken to include divine kingship. The Yarlung dynasty, both in its historical and mythological portions, was undoubtedly patrilineal, and even if nowadays Tibetan society often reckons descent bilaterally, the reckoning in the conservative aristocratic families and in the outlying Himalayan tribes is still patrilineal. But it has already been mentioned that the Sum-pa were ruled by a matriline of queens (according to an eighth century Chinese source), and the Nakhi (for one) continued to reckon descent matrilineally until the Chinese take-over of 1723 (Jackson 1971).[37] Thulung creation mythology contains no evidence of patriliny: the parents of the stars are not given, and the relationship between Khomda and Mini is about as tenuous as a relationship could be. We are not told of Mini having a named son. It cannot be said that the evidence for matriliny is particularly strong, but the named forbears of Miyapma are almost always female, when there is evidence bearing on their sex. Interestingly, though the Nakhi text gives both a matriline and a patriline leading up to Dtomba Shi-lo, it gives the matriline first. The connection between a female creator goddess and matriliny is not a logically necessary one, but it seems that in investigating the culture history of the area, it might be profitable to look at the two questions in conjunction.

---

37 [See now Oppitz and Hsu 1998.]

The Jaw-khliw Cycle

Introduction

This chapter concerns two sisters, Jaw and Khliw, their younger brother, Khakcilik, and his wife, Wayelungma. The sisters try to kill their younger brother, leave home, quarrel and are reconciled. By her persistence Wayelungma persuades Khakcilik to take her as wife, and she then instructs him how to build a house and perform other tasks of a householder. Finally the sisters are induced to return home for a large ceremony to which they contribute gifts.

Although not all versions collected contain all episodes, the story gives a relatively clear sense of unity and distinctness, and the problem that arose in the last chapter – whether to include extraneous traditions about Mini – has no counterpart here, since none of the characters appear in other narratives.

I am not sure on what occasions the Jaw-Khliw cycle is or was told. Internal evidence suggests that it would be appropriate to a wedding, and I heard that it was in fact recited at the wedding of a Mukli man now in his early fifties. Nowadays however, so far as I could discover, only an extremely fragmentary reference is made to it in the wedding ritual, even more fragmentary than DB's reference to the Creation in his lead-up to the Origin of Death. The only version I have in ritual language was given me

as being part of the Nagi Ancestor rite in Tingla, and I heard fragments of
the story chanted at a Nagi rite in Jubu.

I. Jaw and Khliw leave Khakcilik

Ph   Jaw, Khliw and Khakcilik were living together, just the three of them.
Jaw and Khliw decided to kill their brother and leave home. So they
made an effigy of him out of a gourd and stamped on it and killed
him.

Karb   Khakcilik was an orphan. His mother had died, his father was not
around. His father was Pacoksi, his mother Dilangju, or rather his
mother Dilangju, his father Pacoksi. There were also two orphan
sisters, Jaw and Khliw, Khakcilik being their only brother. He was
just a young child, Jaw and Khliw being pretty much grown women.
They had to feed the child on rice, which they cooked and gave him
in little earthenware bowls. According to their *ḍiumla* [1] long faggots
were not to be collected and brought home. Anyway, realising that the
boy was hungry, they put on his rice to cook. When he saw this, he
started dancing and, not noticing the faggot, he knocked over the little
pot and the rice spilled. 'Look, Khakcilik, we were cooking your rice,
and now it is all spilled. Now what are you going to eat?' They were
angry with him and refused to start cooking again. Soon he went to
Jaw and complained of being hungry. She sent him to Khliw. He ran
over to her, but she sent him back to Jaw. Both of them refused to cook
for him, and he languished from starvation. The sisters decided to kill
this little brother of theirs. They stripped an *allo* N plant [2] and made an
effigy of Khakcilik. They knocked the effigy down and trod on it, and
it gave way with a loud crack. 'Good, now we've broken his bones,'
said one of them. Actually Khakcilik himself had simply gone off and
hidden, and their operations on the effigy were quite ineffectual. 'Now
let's break his skull,' they said. They stamped where the head was, and
the wood gave way with another crack. 'That's his skull broken,' they
said. 'Now he is well and truly dead.' They got together a few things
and decided to fly off and leave home.

---

1   Here the term *ḍiumla* means less 'tribal religion' than 'tribal custom'.
2   The Thulung term is *jakhli*. None of my informants pointed out the similarity
to the names Jaw and Khliw, but could it be accidental? The plant is a type of
nettle (*Girardinia diversifolia*) whose fibres were formerly used for weaving.

Kam So Khakcilik stayed there and the years passed. Later, at Miyapma's home, Jawma and Khlewma were born – or rather they were born first and Khakcilik later. Their mother Miyapma died, and just the three of them were left, the two elder sisters and Khakcilik.

There was no agriculture, so food was scarce, but somehow or other they survived. Day after day the sisters brought home something to eat, but eventually they noticed that Khakcilik was not growing. Two or three years passed, but he was still not getting any bigger. 'Our little brother just won't grow. Why do we waste our time like this, staying here and trying to support him? Let's kill him and go somewhere else.' So they stripped the outer fibers from some *allo* plants – you know the sort – boiled them, made an effigy of a man with head and legs to represent their brother, and carried it away from the house. 'First let's break his head,' they said. They had made his head from a gourd and it burst with a loud crack. 'Now we've done that, let's stave in his ribs.' (All of this was not on his real body of course, they were destroying him in effigy.) Down by his belly they had made his ribs out of something and now they cracked them. 'That's done for his ribs,' they said; 'now for his arms'. They broke the arms that they had made. 'Now it's time for the legs.' These too they broke.

TR There were once two sisters called Jawa and Khliw who had a younger brother called Khakcilik. Each day the sisters searched around the village and prepared a meal of rice to give to their brother. One day the sisters got hold of some rice, brought it home and put it on the fire to cook. On seeing it Khakcilik began jumping with joy. Carelessly he caught his foot on a faggot and the boiling rice was all spilled. This infuriated the sisters. 'What a lot of trouble we go to looking for food for this tiny brother of ours!' they exclaimed. 'And then you go and spill it.' Thereupon they decided to kill him, and so they kicked in a gourd.

Ant The mother was Dilamjung, the father Pacoksi, and the children were two sisters and one brother. This story comes later on. They say they were birds – but the creation was from birds (?). The mother was Dilamjung, the father Pacoksi, and as for the daughters, the elder was called Jawma and the younger Khlewma; their brother was Khakcilik. They lived just wandering about through the jungle. When Jawma and

Khlewma grew up they went off on their own. Jawma to the north and
Khlewma to the south. They went off to look for husbands.

Mj   Jaw and Khliw killed Khakcilik, then flew away to seek husbands.

PB   Jawma the elder sister, Khlew the younger and Khakcilik their brother
...Jaw and Khlew flew away leaving Khakcilik behind.

Only Kam attempts to knit the Jaw-Khliw cycle into a continuous
narrative starting from the Creation and leading on to the Migrations of the
Ancestors. As for the former link, hesitations on the tape suggest that he
was uncertain of his ground. He embarks on a statement that Miyapma, the
mother of the siblings, died, interrupts himself with the more neutral
statement that it was their mother who died, then repeats the original
formulation on prompting from the audience. I think that his attempt is an
ad hoc or idiosyncratic development, rather than an established variant of
Thulung tradition. Much the same applies to Mj (Creation episode I), when
he places Khakcilik fourth in the sequence Miyapma, Nayapma, Namprəng.
The narrator was trying at that point to discourage the ethnographer with
curt replies, and this introductory list of his simply omits Mini, about whom
he afterwards told more or less the standard story. Otherwise, those who
name the parents of the siblings give the names Dilamju or Dilangjung for
the mother and Pacoksi for the father. These names, or variants of them
such as Tingla Dilimjumi, are not uncommonly mentioned in the course of
wedding rituals, apparently in allusion to the present story. The two names
always appear in that order, which explains the wording at the opening of
Karb. Nothing further is known about them. The mother's name bears a
curious but perhaps coincidental resemblance to Diliju, the Primal Wind,
while the father's resembles many names for types of tree ending in *-si* (e.g.
kicaksi, toploksi).

As is stated most clearly in Ant, and will be obvious later, Jaw and
Khliw or Khlew are definitely conceived of as birds. Jaw is the name for the
species Greater Hornbill (*hongrāyo* N), while Khliw is that of another
species of hornbill (*dhanes* N). It is curious that *khakcilik* is the name for a
species of tree (*khiruwā* N); but this fact seems to play no part in the story,
and I do not know whether it is recognised or commented on by Thulung.

II. Jaw and Khliw quarrel

Ph   As they were setting off, Jaw told her younger sister to go first. 'No, you go first,' said Khliw. As she would not give in, Jaw flew off and left her. Later she came back to look for her sister, but Khliw had mocked an owl and the owl had pecked her to death. Now she was nowhere to be found. 'Brother-in-law,' Jaw addressed the owl, 'Have you not seen my sister?' 'No,' said he. 'But as you have been here, you must have.' 'Go over there and look in the hole in the tree.' Jaw searched all around, but after pecking her to death, the owl had eaten all the flesh on her, and there was nothing left but bones. Jaw collected up the remnants, invoked over them, and splashed them with libations from a gourd (*hadibom*). Her sister awoke: 'What a nice sleep I've had!' 'That's what you think, is it? Actually the owl pecked you to death and ate you. I have just brought you to life again. You're one of those people who don't do what they are told. You remember when I told you to go first and you wouldn't? Well that's why the owl killed you and I've had to resuscitate you. Now will you go?' 'Yes,' she said. Jaw had previously gone to Luwale, and now Khliw went south to Wayecaptiu. So the two of them flew off. Later Jaw came south again bringing with her all sorts of mountain flowers. From the south Khliw brought cotton and beans and the like, and they met at Jawaji. Thinking that they had killed their brother, they met and set up a loom.

Karb. Before going, they decided to leave something as an omen. One of the sisters, I think it was Khliw, planted a *singauṭo* N, and Jaw planted a *salisi*, as omens. Jaw told her younger sister to set off first. Khliw refused, telling Jaw to go first. 'No, I'll see you off.' 'No, I'll see *you* off.' So they argue. In the end, Jaw flew off first and Khliw watched her go. But when she tried to set off herself she found that her sister had laid a curse on her. Scarcely was she off the ground when bump, down she fell. She tried again, and bump, she fell. Progressing slowly in this manner she met an owl, who was either her mother's brother or her brother-in-law – I've forgotten which. When she met him – I think it was mother's brother – Khliw's trail disappeared. When planting the two omen plants, they had agreed that later, when they came back to the same place, the plants would serve as omens to show whether the other was alive or dead. 'If I die, then my plant will die. If you die, that will happen to yours.' When Jaw came back and looked at the plants, she found that Khliw's was dead, so she followed the trail. This led her as far as the owl, and there it stopped. 'Oh brother-in-law,' she said, 'Surely you have seen my sister?' 'No, sister-in-law, I have not.' Again she followed the trail and it came to a dead stop just by the owl. 'My sister must have come this far. Are you sure you did not eat her?' 'What do you think would make me eat her? Have I gone mad?' There was no way of proving the charge. Yet again she followed the tracks, searching uphill and down. There was nothing to be found, nothing but the owl. 'You must have eaten her,' she said. At last he admitted it, 'Oh sister-in-law, how you keep on at me. Yes, I did eat Khliw. It was because she kept mocking me. I told her not to, and threatened to eat her if she didn't stop. "*You* eat *me*," she laughed, 'A little thing like you eat someone like me! That's a likely story!"' The owl simply told her to open her mouth, and when she did so he leaped into it in a flash and clawed her to death from inside. Once she was dead, he ate all the flesh, and put aside the bones. Later on, Jaw came and questioned him, and conducted a full examination. 'Oh brother-in-law, you certainly have eaten my sister. What did you do with the bones?' 'I put them away over there in a hollow bamboo.' 'Fetch them,' she told him. He went and got them and gave them to her... and she invoked and splashed them from a gourd (*hadibom*). She joined them all up, and when she splashed them: 'Ah sister, what a lovely sleep I've had!' said Khliw. 'Huh! a sleep was it? Your father, the owl, ate you, don't you realise? A nice sleep, was it?' Then, getting ready for a journey, the two of them flew off in different directions.

Kam Jawma the elder and Khliwma the younger now began to argue over which should go north and which south. 'You go first, and I'll watch you,' said the elder. 'No, you fly first, and I'll watch,' said the younger. Eventually Jaw became angry and flew off first towards the north. The younger flew south towards Chamling territory, the elder went north to the Nachiring, the Dumi, the Khaling – or rather just to the Nachiring and Dumi, those were all she had as family. Meanwhile our Forefather Khakcilik stayed on where he was – the story returns to them later. So the two sisters flew away, agreeing with each other to go off and get married.

TR Then the two of them went off to the south. At a point where the path split they could not agree which sister was to go by the upper path and which by the lower, and an argument developed. They decided to plant two flowers. 'If we are both alive, the flowers will not die, but if one of us dies, one plant will necessarily die also.' So one sister went on the lower road and one on the upper. After wandering through the whole world, the elder one, called Jawa, came again to the spot where they had planted the flowers. She searched in all directions, but could not find Khliw anywhere. Seeing a *bobo* bird she asked him: 'Grandfather, perhaps you have seen my sister?' 'I don't know anything about it,' he replied. Not satisfied, she asked again. 'No, surely you saw her. Tell me about it.' Eventually the crane (*bakullo* N) gave in and told her to look up in a hole in a tree. When she looked, all she could find was Khliw's bones and skin. She wrapped the remnants in a cloth and made a parcel of them. Coming to the place where the flowers had been planted, she found that her sister's flower was dead. Using threads of hair she began to weave. Assembling various ritual requisites, she invoked, and eventually Khliw came to life again. The flower that had been planted in her name also recovered. In this way the two sisters met up and settled down to live together.

Mj What happened down at Jawaji? The two sisters Jaw and Khlew parted company there, and planted a *samse* flower to serve as omen and reflect their subsequent fortunes. Then they flew off in search of husbands. Later on, Khlew was eaten by an owl, who threw her bones into a piece of stony waste ground. Jaw came and looked for her sister's flower, and asked her brother-in-law what he had done with her – the two were relatives by marriage. He told her he had thrown the remnants far away in the waste ground... Jaw searched the stony waste and the swamp, and began a long and elaborate invocation over the remnants. For a long time she rubbed the bones with fat and invoked over them, and eventually she brought her sister to life; but Khlew's skin remained delicate. Nepali-speakers call that kind of bird a *hongrāyo*, and the other one a... *das* – Oh, what's the word?[3] Anyway at long last she resurrected her. It had happened because of a curse on the two Hunmarāni sisters.[4] 'You fly off first,' said the younger to the elder. 'No...,' said the elder. They argued, and before flying off the elder uttered a curse. Khlew then found herself unable to fly, which

---

3   The narrator is searching for the word *dhanes*.
4   Hunmarāni, ? from *hunmu* 'to fly,' and *rāni* N 'queen'.

is why the owl ate her. Their flower was at Jawaji, the flower which was to tell one sister about the fortunes of the other. When Jaw came and looked at Khlew's flower, it was dead. Wondering if her sister was really dead, she kept on pressing the owl with questions, and eventually he told her. So she joined up the bones, but Khlew's skin remained thin.

Two of the versions definitely mention the planting of 'flowers', but the fullest version gives one of the plants as a *singauto*, a large climber with edible fruit. Although the translation once refers to them as 'omens,' the word is not ideal for plants whose condition magically reflects the fortunes of the absent person in whose name they have been planted. I do not know of an ideal abstract term in Thulung either. Karb simply has the ordinary word *cino* N, which can generally be translated 'sign'.

Most sources agree that the bird who killed Khliw was an owl (*lāṭokosero* N), and it is only the youngest narrator (TR) who states that it was a crane. Most sources agree too that the bird was related to Jaw and Khliw as *riw* to *rime*, that is to say as the male sibling of one partner to a marriage is to the female sibling of the other partner.[5] One version (Karb) begins by suggesting that the owl was mother's brother to the sisters, but eventually reverts to the former relationship, except for the one reference to the owl as father. The version that diverged on the species of the killer bird diverges here too and makes it a grandfather. The events in the story suggest that the owl is a same-generation affine to the hornbills. Two versions agree that Khliw 'teased' him, and even nowadays *rime* and *riw* stand in a joking relationship to each other. Such joking typically involves sexual innuendo, and this could be taken as support for a sexual interpretation of the owl's assault. Certainly he 'penetrates' her, whether by pecking or through her open mouth. The oral penetration might remind one of how Khomda's seed entered Miyapma.

Two versions describe how Khliw's remnants were deposited in a hole in a tree, while the fullest version puts them in the hollow of a bamboo. Similar motifs appear in certain death rituals. For instance among the Gurung a tube of bamboo containing hair and nails of the deceased is used to render as concrete as possible the association between the effigy of the dead man and the true presence of his spirit (Pignède 1966: 348). There is possibly too a curious echo of the hole in the tree in which Khomda's seed

---

5   *Riw* can also mean 'husband's brother'.

was deposited. Khliw's words on being resuscitated, as well as the means of resuscitation, echo those used in the quarrel between Tiger and Mini in the Creation; Tiger too was killed by a male using a penetrating pointed object.[6]

Jawaji was located by Ph near Halesi, twenty miles to the south of Mukli. Another informant mentioned it as 'the place where everyone met', and it appears below in Karb VII as the place where the sisters set up their looms side by side (or in conjunction). It can hardly be coincidence that the name begins with Jaw-.

III. Wayelungma becomes a Stone

Ph   Later, Wayelungma's mother, whose name I don't know, said to her daughter: 'You don't listen to what I say, you take no notice. Go and jump in the water.' So she went and jumped in the water and became a stone.

The Tingla version of this episode included a dialogue between Wayelungma and her mother. The daughter says she wants to visit the home of her mother's brother, and is told that it is down in the primal Lake (*agidin*). She is instructed to throw various things in the water, including apparently part of a loom. She has to throw three times before jumping.

The name Wayelungma can be decomposed into *waye* meaning 'valley bottom, lowlands', *luŋ*, the ordinary word for 'stone', and the optional -*ma*. Otherwise, my only comment on this scanty material concerns Wayelungma's mother's original home. If she originally lived in the primal Lake, then when Wayelungma leaves the river to live with a landsman, she is repeating her mother's emergence from water.

IV. Wayelungma becomes wife to Khakcilik

Ph   Meanwhile Khakcilik had become a fisherman. One day he cast his net and in it he brought up that stone. He picked it out and threw it back in the water. He cast again, again he brought it up, and again he threw it back. The same thing happened a third time, and this time he said: 'Well, I'd better take it and use it as a stone to crush salt and

---

6   For another instance of a bird resuscitated from its bones after its flesh has been eaten see the story of Baginanda in Allen (1976b).

chilli.' He slipped it in his bag, took it back to his home, and put it in a storage basket (of the type that hangs from the beams).

When he went off fishing again, during his absence Wayelungma came out of the basket, swept the house and prepared a proper meal. Then she went back and hid in the basket. When Khakcilik returned he found his meal already prepared, and the house all neat and tidy. 'Who is this,' he cried, 'who has been looking after a poor orphan like me? Come, and we'll eat together.' One of his neighbours was an old woman. 'It was me, good Sir, who took pity on you.' 'Come on up, grandmother,' he invited her, and they ate together. The same thing happened two or three times.

Then someone else from the neighbourhood – people began to say: 'This old woman of yours, all she does for you is eat your food. The person who looks after your meals, who sweeps the house and lays out the bedding, that's someone quite different, who lives in your storage basket. Pick up your net as if to go fishing. Then take a winnowing fan and broom, and hide in the corner by the doorway. When your helper comes to get the broom, grab hold of her. "So it's you who has taken pity on a poor orphan." That's what you should say.'

So he took the broom, covered himself with the winnowing fan, and hid in the corner. Down she came from the basket and went to get the broom. Casting aside his cover, he caught her and clasped her tightly. 'Ouch! Who are you?' she exclaimed. 'It's me, Khakcilik. So it was you who has been doing all the cooking and sweeping, and laying out the bedding.' 'No, no! It was when you went fishing. When I came up in your net, you threw me back in, and gave me a bruise on the body, just here. The same thing happened a second time. The third time you put me in your bag, brought me up here and left me in the storage basket. I could see you did not love me. Do you love me now?' 'No, no. I truly love you. It's you who have been looking after me.' And so they settled down.

Karb Meanwhile Khakcilik the orphan was still at home. One of his sisters flew south, the other north, while he stayed put. Right from the earliest times hunting has been part of the *ɖiumla* of the Kiranti. So the orphan went down to the river and supported himself by catching fish with his net. He would bring them home, cook and eat them, spend the night, then pick up his net and set off in just the same way the next day, and the day after. One day he set off as usual, but it was to be a fateful day (*karmu*) for Wayelung, who was waiting down there in the water all ready for him. He cast his net, and up came the stone. He picked it out with an exclamation. 'Normally I can catch fish;[7] what's gone wrong today?' He took the stone out of the net, threw it back, and moved a bit upstream on his beat. Again the stone came up. 'This cursed stone! Where can it come from? I am catching no fish today. What shall I have to eat? All I can catch is this stone.' Again he threw it in, this time breaking her skull (for the stone was his wife). He moved upstream, but the same thing happened. This time he broke her leg. Next time it was her arm. 'Drat it! What a nuisance this stone is being today, keeping on finding its way into my net. What I'll do is take it and use it for grinding chilli for my meals.' So he put it in his bag and took it home. Moving upstream again he cast his net, and this time he was successful. He took the fish home and cooked them for his meal.

He spent the night and did what had to be done around the place; and next day he went off as usual. In his house there was rubbish all over the place, and the floor was unswept. But after the day when he brought home the stone, his sweeping was always done. The next day he went fishing again, and when he returned from the river with his catch, he found the house swept and the meal ready cooked. Everything was perfect, and he had nothing to do but eat it. 'Who is this' he cried out, 'that has taken pity on a poor orphan and prepared a meal for him? Whoever you are, come and share it!'

Among his neighbours there was a certain old woman. 'Oh Prince,' she said, 'you come back exhausted. It is I who cooked the meal and did the sweeping.' 'So it was you who took pity on me,' said Khakcilik. 'Come and eat.' She accepted his invitation and thereafter for month after month the old woman stayed around eating vast amounts of Khakcilik's food. One day however, her wrong-doing[8] was unmasked; for she had really been gobbling away. 'Don't give anything to that old woman' said his Fate (?, *karmu*). Recently you have been returning exhausted from your fishing, finding your meal ready, and sharing it with that old crone. Today don't give it to her. The person who has cooked for you and taken pity on you is actually

---

7   Literally, 'Normally the fish die', an idiom which implies that the initiative is not all on the part of the fisherman. Cf. Mini's death in Ch. 2 VI; it too is in part voluntary.

8   *ākhi-ḍāhā* N – it is just possible that this could refer to the jealousy of the informer rather than to the greed of the crone.

in your house.' 'In my house? Who can you mean? I don't see anyone. There's nothing in my house.' 'I mean the stone who came up in your net that day, Wayelung. She is in your house.' 'I've never seen her.' 'Look, take your net as if for fishing, go to a corner of the verandah, cover yourself with a winnowing fan and wait there in hiding. The person who cooks for you is in the storage basket and will come to earth with a tinkle. First she will take a brush and go around sweeping the floor. This will bring her down to the corner where you are hiding. Then you should say as follows: "Heavens! Who are you? Don't you recognise me? I am the miserable orphan on whom you took pity, for whom you have been cooking, as I now realise. Don't you know me? Don't you recognise me?" So saying, hold her tight.'

That is what they did. But at first she was not pacified. 'When I decided to look after your meals, to care for your hunger and misery, I came up in your net. You swore at me, picked me out and threw me back in the water, breaking my back. Next I tried again upstream, and you broke my skull. The next time it was my arm.' So she poured forth her complaints. That is the *ḍiumla* for bride and groom arguing with each other.[9] At long last the two of them settled down together and formed a household.

Since the main lines of the story are now clear, the remaining versions will be given in the form of excerpts or summaries.

Kam The years passed... their brother lived entirely off the fish that he caught... all he had to live in was a cave... one day he brought up a little stone swinging gently in his net... he moved upstream... 'Drat it, what is this stone? That's three or four times I've cast... I'd better take it and keep it at home.' He put it in his bag... he put it in his storage basket... The next day... on his return... the meal was cooked, the floor swept, all beautifully ready for him. He wondered who had done it but ate the meal in any case. On the morrow he was off at dawn, and again on his return found the fire blazing and the meal cooked. He ate it and did what was necessary, shouting in a loud voice: 'Who is it, who is it that has been cooking for me?' But he was all alone. The next day it was just the same, and for the following four or five days. He decided to search out whoever it was. 'If the meal is cooked today also, I'll

---

9   Or possibly, 'for a husband and wife arguing with each other'.

follow the tracks and find this person and bring him back.' A fine meal was waiting, and he shouted all over the place... but nobody came. Having shouted uphill and downhill, he noticed a winnowing fan in the corner of the house propped against the wall. When he moved it aside, underneath there was a woman wearing a necklace, in fact covered with necklaces, bangles and ornaments. 'So it's you who came and cooked for me,' he said. 'I don't know who you can be meaning, good Sir,' said she. She wouldn't speak frankly. When one takes a bride, she never speaks frankly. You know the flirtatious or pseudo-modest manner of women, when people take the bride to her new house – that's the meaning of it. Arguing and explaining, eventually he won her over. 'The other day you cast your net, and as I wanted to do your cooking I came up in it. You picked me out and threw me back in the water damaging my ribs. Further upstream you cast again. 'Let's try again,' I said to myself, 'Let's try to get married.' So again I came up, but again you threw me back and I was bruised all over. The third time you decided to take me, and carried me home in your lap.[10] That's who I am, and that's how you've been treating me.' Gradually he soothed her feelings, and they had a meal and settled down together. Their household was established and the years passed.

Mj IVa   In fact Khakcilik survived and later he cast his net and brought up Wayelung. From there all beings were born.

IVb   Long ago Khakcilik fished up Wayelung in his net. They lived in tranquillity as husband and wife, and so everything originated, all the kings, all the high Hindu castes, everything emerged from that beginning, as is still recognised, only the languages do not coincide and have not for a long time (?). In the Brahmans' language she is Sitara;[11] we call her Miyapma, but it is the same being. The languages have not... ? for a very long time.

IVc   (in response to question) The *tukciluŋ* was the one from the river. Wayelung, Khakcilik's wife, whom he fished up. He took her up to heaven and she became his wife. The two of them created all things.

---

10   Presumably in a fold of clothing, in spite of earlier mention of the bag.
11   I do not know of any such goddess – cf. Sita, Tara or Shitala?

PB b He brought her up in the net, put her in the storage basket and went off to work. Meanwhile she came out of the basket and did the housework. She wondered whether to fly away, but he grabbed her fast and made her his wife.

CP Taking his knife he cut a bamboo fishing rod and fixed it to a line made from a creeper. He went down to the Lake (*diridin*) and cast. He brought up a *gaḍera* N fish and put it in his basket, and as night fell returned home. He prepared his meal and ate it, made ready his bedding and slept the night through. At dawn the sun rose, he ate and made his way down to the lake again. Casting his hook, he brought up the deep-water stone, the ancestor stone... She descended from the storage basket and prepared the meal. Grab tight hold of her in your arms, he had been told. 'Who is this grabbing me? My beads are scattered, my ribs are broken, I am black and blue all over. I won't have it.' 'This is the one I shall take for my wife,' he thought. 'I shall get you more beads, and ornaments of gold and silver, and fine clothes.' They talked it over and reached agreement with each other.

This last is the only version to mention that Khakcilik's fishing tackle included a hook. All other versions mention a net, though the word may cover, or have once covered, some sort of basketry fish trap. Nowadays, a stone used for crushing condiments is smooth-surfaced and three or four inches in diameter. It is possible that in addition to her fish-like and stone-like qualities, Wayelungma is something of a bird. In describing her descent from the storage basket two authors use the verb *juks-* 'jump down,' which in the Jaw-Khliw cycle often refers to birds alighting. This is not very cogent, but PB definitely mentions her contemplating 'flying away' (*hut-*), rather than for instance 'fleeing'.

Among the longer versions, Kam again stands apart from the rest. One difference is that he omits the motif of the old woman and the informer. The informer is in any case a shadowy figure. For CB and Ph (on another occasion) it was a woman who unmasked the old crone. TR just says it was a certain person (*kunai mānis* N), while the expression in Karb is unclear to me. The inclusion of the old crone and the informer allows room for a lot of repetition, which appears to be enjoyed by narrators and audience alike. The crone can repeat parts of Khakcilik's questions (themselves repetitious) in the process of answering them, and the informer can give a foretaste of the scene of the capture. The informer also has the effect of relieving Khakcilik of any initiative in the matter.

The longer versions generally have Khakcilik hiding under the winnowing fan by the grindstone (TR) or elsewhere, in order to leap out and catch his bride. Only Kam reverses the picture, and has the bride hiding in her finery behind the fan (although she was originally deposited in the storage basket). By omitting the motif of capture at this point, Kam diminishes the symmetry of the story, which depends on there being two captures. The first capture, down at the river, is grudging, and essentially due only to the woman's persistence. As a stone she is not edible, and even though she might perform the minor domestic function of crushing condiments, the main reason for taking her is to keep the net free for fish. The second capture is deliberate and planned in advance, now that she has proved her domestic worth. There is no mention of love in any romantic sense. She enters his net because she has decided to do his cooking (Kam), and Khakcilik eventually comes to love her because she prepares his meals and lays out his bedding (Ph).[12]

We return later to the general meaning of the story, and to the sense in which it serves as precedent for recent Thulung custom. But we can note here the insistence of one version (Mj) that the marriage of Khakcilik and Wayelungma was the origin of all beings; this apparently amounts to a claim that the episode is a duplicate version of creation. He even refers to Khakcilik as taking his wife, who comes from the bottom of the primal waters, up to heaven.

V. The building of the house

Ph One day Wayelungma suggested they should build a house to live in. 'How does one do that?' asked Khakcilik. 'This is how. Off you go and cut some poles and stakes.' Off he went to cut them, but when he returned they were all without forks. 'These are no good. We need the other sort.' 'I don't understand. What sort do you mean?' 'You see that *neomli* bird down there, look at its tail. You see how it is forked. Well, that's the sort of pole to bring.' Now that he understood, he went and

---

12　A similar attitude has been remarked on among the Lepchas (Gorer 1967: 83f): 'Love... is considered to be the result of mutual benefits, and foremost among these mutual benefits is the gathering and preparation of food... 'When I go out to work and come back tired, my wife has food ready for me and looks after me; then I love her!'

fetched some poles with proper forks. Wayelungma had a child, and as they were planting one of the poles, Khakcilik did not know how to do it. Wayelungma had the child in her arms and went to explain. She put the child down on the ground, and while the two of them were forcing the pole down into the hole, they killed the child. Nowadays when we are building a house we sprinkle the ground with the blood of a fowl. That's the origin of the custom. When we have finished a house we have to sacrifice a fowl.

Karb In order to build a house Wayelung showed Khakcilik some stakes, and got him to bring a whole range of wood for building. After building the house they looked for Jaw and Khliw.[13] But first they decided to build the house and she showed him the type of wood. Khakcilik went off to fetch the main struts and came back with nothing but straight poles, lots of them. When there were enough straight poles, Wayelung said: 'For the main pillars, you see that *cakcagrɔ̄* bird [a Black Drongo] – the bird had come and alighted on a branch just beneath them – from now on just bring pillars. 'Look at the tail of that bird down there, that's the sort of pillar we need.' So he brought pillar after pillar, until at last they decided there were enough and he could stop. Now they flattened the building site and dug a hole in it. They had at the time one little child. When we Thulung build a house we do not allow children onto the site; it is said to be bad luck (*kholo*). Well they had dug a hole for the pillar and now it was time to plant it. The mother had been carrying the child in a cloth slung on her back. But the pillar was too much for a single person to manage, it needed both husband and wife. Together they summoned up their strength to get the pillar into place. Meanwhile the cloth suddenly came undone, and the child fell into the hole just as they were letting go of the pillar. He was flattened, dead, killed by the two of them. They sprinkled the site with his blood, and so they built the house and lived there, year following year, Wayelung and Khakcilik.

Kam Then Nagimo said: 'You must celebrate your brother's wedding[14] – we must build a house.' They dug the site, scooping out a terrace,

---

13   This sentence belongs in the introduction to VII. Karb almost omits the main part of the present episode, but remembers himself in time.

14   Kam is probably just thinking aloud: it appears unlikely that Wayelungma (the name Nagimo is discussed later) should in fact address the sisters, and the

and Khakcilik went to cut poles; but he brought back nothing but straight ones. A *cakcagrə̄* bird came down on a branch just in front of him. 'You must bring pillars with tops like that bird's tail,' Nagimo instructed him, pointing to the bird's tail. 'That's the sort we must put up.' Now at last Khakcilik felled them and brought them back. So they prepared the site and got ready to plant them. They had dug a hole and both of them came to plant the pillar in it. As they picked it up and summoned their strength to plant it, their child, who was crawling about, went down the hole they had dug, and they brought the pillar down on top of him. They looked around for him, but could not find him anywhere. It was no good. 'He must have crawled into the hole,' they said. They took out the pillar and there was the child, dead, crushed flat by the pillar. That's the reason why, when we are building a house, children are not allowed onto the site. So they built the house and lived there. Two generations lived there, including the grandmother, or three generations with Khakcilik's child.

CP Khakcilik impregnated Wayelungma, and in her womb Cindiringma was conceived. He sharpened his implement on a whetstone and went to the forest to cut down a trunk. He trimmed it, carried it home and put it down in the courtyard; but it was without a fork. 'Khakcilik, look up there in the tree, at the tail of that bird,' said Wayelungma. So he went again to the jungle and felled a Shorea tree and brought it back to the yard. 'Good, Khakcilik, that's a fine one.' Cindiringma was born onto the earth, was washed, and grew stronger. When husband and wife began to put up the timbers for the house, Cindiringma was in a cloth slung on Wayelungma's back. They discussed how to do it, and dug a hole. Khakcilik thrust the pillar into it, but it was still unsteady. He asked Wayelungma to come over and help. Just as they were sinking the pillar for a second time, Cindiringma fell into the hole. Now the pillar was perfectly firm.

They both wept, but then Wayelungma told Khakcilik to cheer up, as she was still of an age to expect further children. They made the timber framework for the house, tying the joints with strips of bamboo and bark. They set in place the hearth stones, the edging stones, the threshing stone, the threshold stone. Then they made the courtyard and the house was finished.

---

grammar is unclear.

TR. Wayelungma told him to go and cut stakes so as to build a house, but instead of stakes with forks he just brought straight poles. 'Those won't do,' said his wife. 'Bring ones like the tail of a *jhyāpyu* bird.'

The name of Wayelungma's child is given only in CP, who commented that *cindiriŋ* was the noise of Wayelungma jumping from the storage basket; compare Karb IV, which gives a similar sound, *ciŋliŋ*, in the same context. It is possible that the name is related to Nepali *cingringnga* 'with a noise as of a thin metal object falling on the ground,' and *cingring-cingring* 'with a tinkle, as of small thin metal objects knocking against each other'.[15] However it is still not clear why the child is named after a sound.

The final syllable of the name raises the question of the child's sex. Although the translations refer to it as male (this being the unmarked gender in English), the original texts leave the matter open: most Thulung words are neutral as to gender. Where gender is indicated, suffixes opening with *m* are feminine (e.g. *ma, mo, me),* while suffixes opening with *p* and *b* are masculine (Allen 1975a: 95). However, the suffix system is probably not sufficiently clear and regular to make a present-day Thulung assume that Cindiringma was a girl; the situation is as in Tibetan, where *ma* and *mo*, though often feminine suffixes standing in opposition to zero or to *pa* and *po*, are not always so. In any case the final -ma in Thulung names is often optional. The Nepali version of the episode (TR) might have answered the question, but unfortunately it omits the motif.

All versions present the death of the child as an accident: the parents may have been negligent, but they did not intend to kill the child. However, the episode is surely a charter for a foundation sacrifice. From a purely technical viewpoint, a hole containing a crushed body would be less effective in supporting a pillar than the empty hole before the child crawled in. But according to the myth (especially CP), it is only after the death, and no doubt because of it, that the pillar is safely planted and the building can proceed.

The different versions agree that the bird with the forked tail was the black King Crow.[16] Probably, the bird has some significance other than simply serving as a teaching aid that happens to be available at the right

---

15   The inserted additional syllable is not an objection since Nepali *gunri* 'mat' is regularly pronounced *gundiri* in Thulung.

16   Ph refers to a *neomli*, which was said to be an older word for *cancagrə̄* (= *cibe* N). TR gave *jhyāpyu*; cf. the dictionary form *jhyāpi* N, given as synonymous with *cibe*.

moment, when Wayelungma is attempting to instruct her husband; one might recall the essential role of a bird's tail in some versions of episode II of the Creation. From a technological viewpoint, a forked pillar would be more efficient than a straight one in supporting a central ridge-pole; but there may be more to it than that. The post used for human sacrifice among some of the Gonds of central India was generally forked. In citing this fact (originally reported by Verrier Elwin), Macdonald (1952: 332) argues that such posts are symbolically female, basing his case on a report by Hutton: the Angami Nagas state that for them forked stakes represent female sexual organs and straight ones represent male ones. Probably, a similar contrast can be seen in the Thulung myth: of his own accord the man at first brings nothing but straight poles, and it is only on his wife's instructions that he then brings forked ones. The last chapter offered two instances of female trees, and we can probably recognise a third one here.

Though it is not stated, we can doubtless assume that Cindiringma was the first child of the marriage from which (according to Mj IV) 'everything originated'. If so, one recalls that in the Creation it was Tiger, the first-born of the four brothers, who was killed. Cindiringma died at the bottom of the felled tree that was in the process of being 'replanted,' whereas Tiger died at the bottom of an undisturbed tree. However, two of the versions mention Cindiringma as being 'crushed' or 'flattened', and there is no evidence that the bottom of the central pillar was pointed like the arrow that killed Tiger.

VI. Agriculture and Brewing

TR Some days later his wife asked him who his relatives were; they ought to hold a family ceremony (*kul garnu* N). Going into the forest they felled trees and sowed eleusine seeds before coming home. When the eleusine was ripe, they began to cook ritual beer. When the mixture was cooked, they sprinkled on ritual yeast. They put it in an earthenware pot covered with a stopper, and stored it.

CP After discussing what to do, they cleared a patch of jungle by cutting down the trees and plants with their implements. They let the sun dry out the clearing, and then he prepared tinder from the plantain tree and kindled a fire. Another day they went and hoed the clearing and sowed lentils, eleusine and rice. The rains came. Returning home, they prepared a meal, ate it, got ready their bedding and slept. When they got up at dawn, Wayelungma told Khakcilik to go uphill and see whether the *hirimi* tree had flowered; then he was to report home. Next he had to go downhill and see whether the *roḍingo* N tree had flowered, and come back and tell her. They spent the night, and in the morning he went to the clearing to see whether the shoots had come up yet. The crops were flourishing and he held a sacrifice. On his return they spent the night. Khakcilik was sent uphill to see whether the *hirimi* was now ripe. Finding that it was, they weeded the clearing. Next he was sent downhill again to look at the *roḍingo*. They decided that their crops were ready. From split bamboo he made a close-woven carrying basket, and from split cane he wove a tump-line. Taking the basket and sickle he went to the clearing and harvested the crops. At dusk he carried the basket of grain down to his barn and stored it there.

He transferred some of the grain to a flat basket and put it to dry on the frame over the fire that he lit. They threshed the grain on a threshing stone and winnowed it. He poured the grain into a square basket and washed (it?). He ground the grain, made a preparation of *gahate jhār* N, and kneaded it with some water. He sprinkled on some yeast and incubated the mixture in a basket, which he placed uphill of the fire. One morning he was told to smell it. Then he spread it on a winnowing fan, dried it in the sun, and hung it up in the storage basket.

He carried some more grain from the barn and put it on the flat basket over the fire to dry. He threshed and winnowed the grain and transferred it to a square basket. He washed an earthenware pot, then poured in rain water and heated it. He added the grain and blew up the fire. They took down the flat basket and put it outside in the open air. He cooled the mixture on it, then mixed in yeast by hand. Transferring it to a close-woven basket, he added fern and incubated. He sprinkled on more yeast, and put the basket uphill of the fire. He was told to smell it. In the morning he washed an earthenware jar, dried it in the sun, and made a banana leaf filter. He put the jar uphill of the fire, and transferred the beer mixture by hand into it. He covered the jar with *buletre* N leaves and smeared the edge of the seal with a mixture of ash and water to make it airtight.

The details of the sequence of events in this narrative episode are not always clear, partly because it is told in the curt and formulaic style of ritual language, partly because no comparable lengthy versions are available. No doubt the first part of the brewing sequence describes the preparation of the yeast tablets. The problem of gender arises again, in a slightly different form from the last episode. Although I have translated 'he' where there was any doubt, the Thulung verb does not express gender and possibly one should understand that Wayelungma herself carried out many of the activities, as well as instructing Khakcilik in some of them. For instance, brewing is nowadays typically women's work (though not exclusively so).

The only other version of this episode is very brief.

PB Then what he did was to set a trap for a dove, and taking the grain out of its crop he introduced agriculture.[17]

In numbering the episodes we have followed the Tingla versions in placing the origin of agriculture after the building of the house; PB has the reverse order. Both episodes need to be seen both in their own rights, as precedents for the activities they describe, and also in the context of the whole myth, as leading up to its culmination.

VII. The Family Reunion

Ph So they settled down. One day Wayelungma asked him how many sisters he had and where they had all gone off to. 'I had two sisters, Jaw and Khliw, but after trying to kill me, they went away. As to where they went, one went to Luwale, one to Wayecaptiu.' 'We must send for them,' said his wife. 'But how?' 'We'll send a flea.' (The sisters were now at Jawaji.) Off it went, jumping along. Finding the sisters busy at their loom, it gave them a sharp bite. 'Ouch! Whose is this insect? What's this about? Our brother died long ago. What's the meaning of it?' So they bit the flea and killed it also.[18] So then they sent a fowl – a cock – and off it went, crowing on its journey, to the sisters' loom

---

17 Cf. Bushell (1880: 531) on a method of divination current among the Chiang on the Chinese borders of Tibet. They 'pray until a bird like a hen pheasant comes and settles on the sorcerer's hand, who cuts open the crop, and if he finds inside grains of corn it will be a fruitful year, if only sand and stones, there will be famine and pestilence.'

18 The 'also' probably refers to the fate of a previous emissary, a louse, accepted by Ph on another occasion as being properly part of the story.

at Jawaji. 'Kəkəriiika khakciliiipo, bangpa,' it crowed.[19] That's the origin of one of the marriage intermediaries. Hearing the word *baŋpa* they exclaimed: 'Whose is this cursed bird?[20] Our brother is dead.'

They threw the shuttle at him, then picked it up and threw it again. As they went on trying to hit him, the cock led them to Khakcilik's house, but they were overcome by shame and flew away again. Now they were both pregnant, and while Khakcilik was wondering what to do his wife told him, 'Those two will have the cravings of a pregnant woman. We must make a preparation from *kheli* and *rici* plants, and that will make them come.' So they soaked the two herbs, and the sisters, having the cravings of early pregnancy, came down to eat it, and this time they stayed. When they were thinking of going they said to each other: 'This brother of ours – we once tried to kill him. Now that he is alive and well, what are we going give him? We must give him bride-price.' That is where the bride-price comes from in today's weddings. The one who went to Luwale gave one, two ... (narrator counts aloud) six bride-price vessels, while the one who went to Wayecaptiu gave seven. They collected the contributions and presented the vessels, then flew off again and went their ways. Wayelungma and Khakcilik built their house and supported themselves, and the years passed.

Karb 'You say you have sisters called Jaw and Khliw. We must send for them.' Khakcilik agreed and the idea was settled. First of all they sent a scalp louse. Off it went and found the sisters busy weaving down at Jawaji. The louse went as *baŋpa* and gave them a sharp bite. With that louse as *ɖiumla*, when women are at their looms, you know how lice crawl up and bite them. When they felt the bites, they looked for the louse and squashed it. So back it went with its head cracked open. 'I'm sorry, Khakcilik, I couldn't manage with your sisters. Look what they have done to my head.' Next a flea volunteered to go. They gave him a good send-off as *baŋpa*, with a fine meal and lots to drink. Now it was the flea's turn to bite them, and it went on its errand jumping. But it too had its head crunched, and hopped homewards, dragging itself along (?). 'I'm sorry, Khakcilik, I could not bring your sisters. Look how they have crunched and broken my skull.' They wondered what on

---

19   On another occasion Ph said that in order to crow the cock jumped onto the part of the loom called the *carisəŋ* (*cari* N = 'bird,' *səŋ* = 'piece of wood').

20   Literally 'Whose are these lumps of meat (*cokʈā* N)?'.

earth to do next, talking it over and going through all the possibilities. Eventually they decided to send a cock. 'For this undertaking, give me a fowl's wing. I'll go and look for Jaw and Khliw. I'll get them.' The cock went off and beside their loom he crowed *al-al-al-a*, meanwhile letting fall one of his head feathers. 'Kǝkǝ-ǝǝǝ-ǝ Khakciliiipo,' he crowed. 'Who does this cock belong to, coming here and crowing out the name of Khakcilik? The cursed creature.' They threw the loom rod at him, and now he let fall one of his wings. 'Whose can this be, this creature that drops cock's wings?' With some difficulty they extracted themselves from the loom. Then the cock went a little further off and crowed again as before, letting fall another wing. Still wondering whom he belonged to, one of the sisters again threw her loom rod at him. It missed, and the cock jumped on a little further. 'I must fetch that rod' she said, 'and also pick up that wing and have a look at it' – she was curious. The cock moved on and crowed as before. 'Whose is this cursed bird?' Again she threw the rod and missed. In this way the cock lured her on and on until they reached Khakcilik's house. She looked around and realised it was the home of the brother they had killed... (?) Again she flew off, or rather the two of them did.

Afterwards Wayelungma saw them at Wamajuji.[21] She thought about it, and looked carefully. Seeing that they were pregnant, she discussed what to do with Khakcilik. Realising that the sisters were not going to come down, she told him to fetch some *rici*. Khakcilik went and picked some, and they spread it out to dry. When they saw it, Jaw and Khliw, who had flown away, now wanted to eat it, and so at last they came down and there was a real meeting of brothers and sisters, with much exchanging of questions about children and marriages and weddings. 'Where do you live, what journeys are you making, how are you keeping?' For days on end there were greetings and renewals of acquaintance. Before going home, the sisters handed over all the bride-price and wedding presentations. Even nowadays, the one called Jaw is down in the Lowlands (somehow associated with?) a Ficus tree, while Khliw is up in the high hills living in poverty. Jaw is rich, living in the lowlands, where creepers flourish, and trees and their fruits, where she eats well. She is really quite rich, and flies around with a powerful whoosh, while to the north Khliw flies around

---

21   Not otherwise known.

just eking out her existence. When she is seen, you can scarcely recognise her (?).

TR Some days later they prepared to celebrate the *sekro* rite, and Wayelungma asked her husband whether he had any relatives. He explained that he had two sisters, but did not know where they were. They discussed the matter and sent a louse with an invitation to them. The louse went off and bit one of the sisters on the stomach, but she found it and killed it. Next they sent a flea which went off jumping on its errand. It too bit one of the sisters on the stomach. They tried to kill it also, but it jumped out of harm's way and they lost it. Having had no success so far, they now sent a cock. When it reached the place where the sisters were, it cried out 'Kəkəriiika Khakciliiipo ha'. 'It is saying the name of our dead brother,' said Jawa and Khliw. 'Let's catch it.' They pursued the cock and in this way reached the house of their brother, where the *sekro* was in full progress. On seeing this, the two sisters were flabbergasted and decided to depart at once for heaven. However as they were pregnant, the others used a sort of magic substance called *khosku* to bring them down again. But one problem remained. 'We thought we had killed our brother and here he is alive. We must honour him properly.' One sister flew off to the south and another to the north. When they returned, the one who had been south brought four copper pots, and the one who had been north brought seven. Presenting the copper pots, they honoured their brother duly and accepted the invitation. Ever since that day, the elders say, the custom of giving four or seven pots has been current. Since the one who went north brought seven pots, the Khaling Rai give seven, and since the one who went south brought only four, four is the custom around here.

PB After they had settled down, Jaw and Khlew were flying around. They spread out some *rici* and the sisters flew down to it. The two of them hammered the Jaw and Khlew vessels;[22] Khakcilik at their natal home somehow propitiated them (?). In this way the creation was formed. They set up a household and made everything.

---

22 The term *jawsam khliwsam* applied here to the vessels is not otherwise known.

Ant   Later the two of them became pregnant, and they looked for their brother, Khakcilik. They wandered about flying without coming down to earth. Khakcilik knew that they were pregnant, and dried some *rici*, and down they came. That's how getting married was instituted, by Jawma and Khlewma, and it has led to a lot of trouble and confusion for us. After the two sisters had gone off with their husbands they presented a great deal of wealth to their brother. Yes, it is from there that our troubles have come. It's a long story.

Kam   His wife asked whether he had any brothers or sisters. 'There were no brothers but I had two sisters, Jaw and Khliw. But I don't know where they have got to now. One went north, one south.' 'We must send for them,' said Nagimo. 'But how?' he asked. The sisters had gone off to get married, and were now pregnant, as was Nagimo herself. 'We must fetch some *rici* and put it to dry on a winnowing fan, on top of that wall. They will see it drying there, and will fly down to it.' So they put out the *rici* nicely on the winnowing fan, and when the sisters saw it, down they came. Suddenly Khakcilik appeared. On seeing him they were overcome with shame at having tried to kill him, and flew off in confusion. Nagimo was clairvoyante, and knew everything. 'What's all this?' she asked him. What did you do to your sisters? They don't seem to like you. What did you say to them, what's the meaning of their flying away?' 'It wasn't anything I said to them, it's just that they take offence very quickly.' 'Your sisters are pregnant. We have to summon them.' 'But how?' 'We must send a cock.' They made the arrangements, and sent him off. 'Kəkə-əəə-ə Khakciliiipo,' he crowed. and they heard him. 'Listen, younger sister. What's that thing saying our brother's name? We must kill it.' Again it crowed as before. 'What's this our brother has sent to fetch us? We must kill it.' Again they dried the *rici* and tried to lure them down. 'Our brother has put out a snack for us. Let's go and eat it.' So they flew down to it, and this time they recognised each other and exchanged greetings before the sisters flew off. The elder one came north, and her family are the Dumi and Nachiring; the younger went to the Chamling, to Jeoplidel. The elder sister in the north became wealthy, while the younger accumulated practically nothing. Then they originated the custom of giving bride-price vessels. As for the *baŋpas* that we send, it was the cock who originated that.

As has happened before, Kam's version deviates considerably from the others. The motif of spreading out the *rici* appears twice, both before and after the unsuccessful mission of the cock. I see no particular point in the former appearance of the motif and am tempted to dismiss it. The whole episode is located before the Building of the House, which explains why Nagimo, as well as the sisters, is pregnant.

The other versions show only minor differences. Karb's story about the cock's wings is not entirely clear, but apparently the cock took with him the wings of some other fowl as an additional means of attracting the attention of the sisters. It is interesting that the birds despatched by Miyapma in the Creation were also held to be mythical precedents for the present-day marriage intermediary, and that in both cases there are descriptions of the emissaries' gait or mode of progress: Kekuwa hovered, (the Thulung word also means 'danced'), Jigiyom progressed with bursts of rapid movement, the flea jumped, the cock went along crowing. These may be just incidental details, but if the myths were once acted out in rituals, as is possible, they would have rather the status of stage directions. It appears typical of the cultural area that the women should use part of the loom to attack the cock. In Tibet the arrow and spindle are symbols of the male and female respectively (Nebesky-Wojkowitz 1956: Index VIII), and among the Lepchas 'in stories the heavy bar of the loom is the woman's chief weapon' (Gorer 1967: 68).

After the emissaries' failure to effect the reconciliation, the aim is finally achieved by means of the herbal preparation. The *rici* (*bhakiamilo* N) has a bitter taste, and *khele* (*ciraito* N) is used in Nepal in the form of an infusion for malaria. I know nothing relevant about any particular use of them by Thulung, nor about Thulung pregnancy customs. Possibly the word *rici* appears in the story because of its phonetic similarity to *rīci*, the dual form of *ri*, meaning 'sibling of opposite sex to ego'; *rīci* appears frequently in the story, referring to the two sisters, but the similarity was not pointed out to me by Thulung. Most informants understood the fluid as attracting the sisters because of its taste and because they are pregnant. In referring to it as *khosku*, the gluey preparation used by mediums to entrap spirits, TR offers an alternative interpretation which might be no less valid: in 'luring' them (*chem-*), the cock is doing to the sisters just what mediums do to spirits (Allen 1976b).

On the question of which sister went north and which south, and which became richer, the versions differ (some of the data are in II); no single version fully agrees with any other. Three of them claim that Jaw went north, but Karb, who gives the most detailed account of this motif, dissents. TR and Kam present the one who goes north as the richer, though TR does not say which sister it is; for Ph and Karb the one who goes north is the poorer, though they disagree as to which it is. It may or may not be relevant that Khliw is the variety of hornbill called *dhanes*, which is apparently related to Sk Dhanesha, god of wealth; cf. also *dhan*, the ordinary Nepali word for 'wealth'. In the Creation it was the elder brother, the bear, who went north, and the younger, the monkey, who went south, and there was a suggestion that the monkey was associated with wealth. However, one cannot use one story to emend the other. Perhaps too, the relationship between north/south and wealth/poverty could have been different at different times or in different contexts. For instance the natural richness of the jungle is no doubt greater to the south, but with the appearance of the Sherpas, the Thulung might have seen cultural wealth as lying to the north.

The Myth as a Precedent

At various points the narrators make comments relating the myth to the contemporary world. For the most part they relate it to the cultural world rather than the natural, but according to Mj II, the myth explains the thin skin of one of the hornbills. It seems too (though the passage is obscure) that in Karb IV the myth is used to account for the distribution to north and south of the two species of hornbill. As for cultural comments, one focus was the foundation sacrifice. Kam and Karb use the incident to explain the ban on allowing children onto building sites, while Ph relates it to the sacrifice of a fowl on completion of a house. With reference to Khakcilik's capture of Wayelungma, both Kam and Karb remark on the conventional protestations of contemporary brides when taken to their new homes. Presumably they had in mind also the traditional 'marriage by capture', the removal of a bride from her home by real or simulated physical violence, with or without her connivance; the custom certainly used to be practised by the Rai and is still current among the Limbu (Sagant 1969a). Karb also relates the Jaw-Khliw myth to a taboo on using long faggots for a fire (I), and to two facts: that the Kiranti are essentially hunters (IV), and that lice bite women seated at their looms (VII). Apart from the question of the marriage gifts, which we come to shortly, one presumes that the narrators took for granted that many of the other incidents of the myth were precedents for customs or activities that are either still current or only relatively recently obsolete. For instance, the myth contains potential precedents for fishing, swidden farming, brewing, house building, agricultural sacrifices and for the use of the *hadibom* in giving life to bare bones. In a sense a precedent is given for the use of an effigy for aggressive magic, though the undertaking is unsuccessful. It is interesting that none of the comments are moralistic. Episode II might be thought to inculcate obedience to an elder sister and the avoidance of excessive teasing of a brother-in-law, while episode III implies that daughters should obey their mothers; but no such interpretations were offered.

The final episode provided the main single focus for the narrators' comments. Ph, Karb and Kam all in one way or another explicitly treat the emissaries as *baŋpas*. This word definitely means an 'intermediary or go-between who conducts the negotiations leading up to and culminating in a wedding.' Nowadays, two of them are appointed by the bride's side and two by the groom's side. There is no evidence that the word ever had any other meaning, for instance that it might have meant the bearer of an invitation to a ceremony in honour of the ancestors. It is true that TR interprets in this way the ceremony at which the reunion takes place, stating that it was a *sekro*, which is the largest ritual of the type. But he, as well as Ph and Kam, explain the vessels given by Jaw and Khliw as bride-price vessels, the precedents for the four vessels that are still customary at a Mukli or Tingla wedding. Ant actually states that at this ceremony Jaw and Khliw founded the institution of matrimony, and laments the size of the gifts they gave their brother. Probably he is thereby reflecting the government's attitude that excessive marriage payments are a cause of peasant indebtedness and should be discouraged. In any case, he confirms that in general the Thulung understand episode VII as a wedding ceremony; and it can only be the wedding ceremony of Wayelungma and Khakcilik.

Although there is no doubt that the episode is interpreted as a marriage ceremony, the details of the interpretation are problematic. Thulung bride-price pots are nowadays given by the groom's parents and/or kinsmen to the party who come from the bride's side, who take them to the bride's parents; the largest pot may ultimately be kept as dowry by the bride. It is not clear why in this case the pots are given by the groom's sisters. Moreover, the significance of the *baŋpas* is no less puzzling. In the Creation two of them (or just possibly three) go from the bride's side to the groom's, and although there are none from the groom's side, the fact is not particularly problematic in that context. Here however, they go from the groom's side to his *sisters*.

As the narrative stands these puzzles seem to be insoluble. Either the myth must be dismissed as in certain respects unintelligible, or one must fall back on diachronic considerations. The simplest hypothesis is that, at an earlier period in the history of the myth, the central wedding was not between Khakcilik and Wayelungma, but between Khakcilik and one or both of his sisters. We noted when discussing episode IV that one narrator seemed to regard Khakcilik's marriage as cosmogonic, and brother-sister marriages are exceedingly common in cosmogonic myths. Moreover, as we shall see in the next section, such a marriage occurs in Limbu mythology. Supposing that Khakcilik's marriage was once incestuous, it is not particularly surprising that an episode shocking to later sensibilities should have been modified. We have already met a comparable situation. Deliberate foundation sacrifices make perfectly good sense in certain world views, but contemporary Thulung would certainly find shocking the idea of parents deliberately sacrificing their first-born. It may be significant that, out of the five versions of episode V, the only one to omit altogether the motif of the sacrifice was that given by the youngest and most educated informant. But if it is significant, it would only represent a further step in a change of sensibility that must have been in progress for some time. The other four versions without exception present the sacrifice as an accident, and the uniformity suggests that the development had already taken place at a time when Thulung culture was more unified than it has been in recent generations.

The theory of a brother-sister incest underlying the present story explains why Khakcilik should have sent *baŋpas* to his sisters, but not why the sisters should have brought him the pots. In the myth as we have it, the gifts are motivated by the guilt the sisters feel at having tried to kill their brother in episode I. This is itself a curious little story. What is odd is not that the sisters should have practised aggressive magic, but that there should be no explanation given of their failure. It is almost as if the story were mocking some outdated piece of superstition, and one might wonder if the incident was only inserted in the myth at a relatively late period when the incestuous theme was being disguised. But there is much here about which one can at present only speculate, but which might fall into place if versions were available from other subtribes.

Comparisons

Many examples could be cited of the use of effigies in aggressive magic, but they would add little to the understanding of episode I. In episode II the motif of the flowers that reflect the fortunes of the person in whose name they are planted recalls Tibetan beliefs about the 'seat of the soul' (*bla-gnas*, cf. Stein 1972: 227 ff., Nebesky-Wojkowitz 1956: 481 ff.). A single individual or community may have a number of different 'outer souls,' which may take as 'seats' a whole range of objects or beings, e.g. particular trees, animals, birds or fishes, a piece of stone, an animal carved in stone, a mountain, a grove or a lake. Damage to the seat of the soul is associated with (or causes) harm to the individual or group. Typically, outer souls appear at birth rather than, as here, being deliberately established by the individuals concerned. However this difference is not enough to render the rapprochement pointless.

In the context of Tibetan outer souls, neither of the above authorities mentions flowers.[23] However, among the Tamang (Höfer 1974: 177), one of the principal tasks of an officiant at a seance is to search for the soul and the 'life-tree' of the patient; if the patient is a woman he has also to search for her 'flower'. The passage thus associates not only flowers and outer souls, but also flowers and women. Similarly, Limbu priestesses (Chemjong 1966: 26) recite the story of the creation of flowers, and bring into relation a particular man and a particular flower; the withering and subsequent revival of the flower are reflected in the health and spirits of the man. Thulung vocabulary also makes comparable links between flowers, women and the flourishing or withering of a human (Allen 1972: 92f).

I have not been able to go far in studying Tibetan birds and the associated beliefs, but it is interesting that the owl is referred to in Tibet as a 'demon-eater' (Stein 1939: 355). It is traditionally the enemy of the crow (Stein 1957c: 228f). In the folklore of western Tibet the *gnyan* spirits of the sun and moon were imagined in the form of birds (Tucci 1949: 739 n.27, citing Francke). The name Khliw might just possibly be related to *khleomu*, the Thulung for 'moon,' but there is no similar link between Jawma and *nepsuŋ* 'sun'.

---

23   It is interesting that a yellow (male) and blue (female) flower occur in certain Tibetan accounts of the creation (e.g. Haarh 1969: 213). Compare the yellow and blue toads that are born at the same time as the epic hero Gesar, as his protector gods (Stein 1959: 305); there is a close association between protector gods and outer souls.

Episode IV offers considerable scope for comparisons. We start with Tibetan material since it was the first to be written down. The relevant Tun-Huang manuscripts were published in text and translation by Thomas (1957: 31, 42). I give first the second of his two versions, abbreviating and paraphrasing. Thomas's translations do not always make sense, and according to Stein (1971) they are often erroneous. Nevertheless they seem to be adequate to establish that there is a relationship between the Thulung and Tibetan myths concerning capture of a wife.

(i)   rBeg-ga rbeg-shi is the youngest of seven sisters. A fiend eats six of them and the parents, then threatens her. She is helped by an ass. Six peacock brothers arrive, and she changes into a peacock. The scene shifts. A certain man has six sons by his first wife ('the right hand house'), and Gyim-po nyag-cig (rendered 'Gyim-po Notch-one' or 'Number-one') by his second wife. The former go fowling with silken snares, the latter with a goat-hair snare. In spite of being released a number of times, the peacock returns to the snare. Gyim-po tries repeatedly to hit the bird by throwing stones at it, but fails. Around the house the peacock is not to be seen. He dreams of a pretty young girl. His mother goes out to gather herbs, while Gyim-po goes out to pasture the goats, then returns and has a meal. He wonders if 'this thing' is real or supernatural and hides behind a dung heap. Something young and pretty appears. He seizes the peacock to take her as wife.

(ii)   Tseng-'gi rBag-zhing, the second of three sisters, is warned by an ass after her father and younger sister have been eaten by a fiend. She tells her mother, changes her name to Bya ma-bya'i rma-li or Bye'u rma-bye'u-gi thing-tshun, grasps the tail of a bird and flees. The six Gyim-po brothers are rich and go fowling with snares of silk, while Gyim-po nyag-cig is poor, and uses snares of horse-hair. It is not clear whether he catches anything. He puts his sling in the sleeve of his right arm, and going home, 'he set down and stayed in the reed pile.' The next day at dawn he goes to gather wood. When he returns, food and drink is laid out for him and he eats.[24] He wonders what is the explanation.

---

24   Thomas's translation actually reads: 'He coming (back) to house and home, the place where was set the portion of food for one meal was heaped with moisture; where for one full serving of drink a ladle was set in the ashes, overflowed with curds (?). The meal not touched (?) by Gyim-po Number-one was consumed, the drink not drunk was consumed.' Compare Stein (1971:

Pretending to be on his way to collect wood, he hides among the swine of the dung-hill. From within the reed pile Bye'u rma comes and lays out the meal. 'Among women there has been none fairer than this one.' So he makes her his wife and associate.

Both versions also deal with the funeral of Gyim-po's father, but this need not concern us. I shall not list all the motifs which the Tibetan versions share with the Thulung ones. A major contrast is that Gyim-po is a fowler and not a fisherman, so his wife has nothing to do with any river or lake; but we have already noted hints of a bird-like nature in Wayelungma, and also suggested that Khakcilik may in earlier versions have been married to his bird sister. It is at least curious that Bya'u rma would be pronounced Jawma in contemporary Tibetan; also that *jawwa* is the Thulung for 'peacock'.

Another point of contrast is that the Tibetan versions allow Gyim-po six brothers or half-brothers, as well as, in one case, a mother who is still alive. However the Tibetan versions agree with the Thulung in emphasising his poverty (in contrast to his brothers with their silken snares), and also perhaps his loneliness (his brothers are six while he is one, as his name announces).

Two other versions come from Tichurong in north-west Nepal (Jest 1971: 72-4).

(i) A prince wipes out all the Magar except for one pregnant woman who escapes. Her son grows up and looks after cows. Each day he goes to the Milk Lake, where seven birds alight and transform themselves into young women to wash. He is forgetful and puts a stone into his belt to remind himself of what he has seen. Even so he forgets, and the next day he takes a larger stone with the same purpose. In a dream he sees the seven birds, and on waking he finds the stone and remembers to tell his mother about the incident. She instructs him. The next day six of the birds fly away, but one remains behind. As he has been instructed, he drops into the lake some blood from a severed cow's tail. The bird turns into a fairy. He takes her home and she becomes his wife. She remains silent until one day, when the mother is preparing a meal, the fairy bursts out laughing. The boy thinks it is the weeping

---

528ff), who summarises and compares the two versions without actually translating this passage.

of the cow's tail, but his mother tells him it is his wife's laughter. The couple become clan founders.

(ii) Seven fairy sisters bathe in the Milk Lake. Enchanted by their beauty, the clan ancestor hides the clothes of one of them so as to capture her.[25]

The pattern of six siblings versus one appears again. In both Tibetan versions it applied to Gyim-po and his brothers, and in one of them it applied also to his bride and her sisters, as well as (obscurely) to the captured peacock plus the six peacock brothers. Note too the motif of the stone from the Primal Lake carried home about the person of the groom. By making the fairy-birds wash in the Lake, the Tichurong version combines the watery origin of the Thulung bride with the bird nature of the Tibetan one. The term 'fairy' reminds one of Kam's description of Nagimo in all her jewellery hiding behind the winnowing fan. For the bride's laughter compare perhaps the tinkling sound with which Wayelungma descends (Karb IV).

The Lepcha version (Gorer 1967: 459ff) is one of the two major Lepcha myths. The comparison is particularly interesting because it is not confined to episode IV of the Jaw-Khliw cycle, but also contains echoes of VI and VII:

Tarbong is the youngest son of the Creator Goddess Itpomu. She instructs him to get bamboo and thread, and set up snares in the trees. The first day he catches birds but the second day he finds in the traps only wooden penises. He throws them away. His mother tells him to go and hide so that even the birds cannot see him. A beautiful girl called Naripmu or Naripnom arrives and starts to make the penises. He tries unsuccessfully to rape her. His mother sends him to his eldest brother Komsithing.[26] The

---

25   This very sparse version could no doubt be parallelled from many areas; thus Thompson and Balys (1958: 408) have several entries under 'Man falls in love with woman he sees bathing'.

26   Actually Komsi-thing, Itpomu's eldest child, is the husband of her second child Narzong-nyou (Gorer 1967: 225ff). The latter 'is really the chief Lepcha goddess... responsible for a great number of institutions... Komsi-thing is also responsible for a number of habits and institutions but he is in a way a foreigner.' The marriage produced only one normal child, whom they buried after he had been killed. Thereafter they separated, the husband going to Tibet with all the riches that Tibetans still have, Narzong-nyou remaining in poverty. I cannot follow up all the points suggested by the Lepcha material, but the

latter advises him to journey to various places to get copper vessels, cloth, millet, and so on, but he does not dare to go in search of fire. A bird is sent without success, but an insect brings back a brand, together with flint and tinder up its backside. Another insect volunteers to get yeast from an old woman. It learns from her how to prepare beer. While it is delousing her, the woman falls asleep and the insect steals her yeast. The beer is brewed. The elder brother goes to Itpomu for butter. A large feast is held, with the giving of gifts. Only now does Tarbong possess Naripmu. This was the origin of marriage.

In the Tibetan versions the bride-capturer was a fowler, and here he starts out as one; even when the bride is captured at the water's edge in the Tichurong versions, the capturer is not presented as a fisherman. The comparison is therefore less with the Khakcilik of episode IV than with that of VII. We have already suggested, because of internal inconsistencies, that the Thulung myth at one time concerned the marriage of Khakcilik and his bird sisters, and we can now further suggest that at that time the two means he used to make contact with the sisters were two techniques from a fowler's repertoire. What are now conceived of as emissaries would correspond to the use of lures (though I encountered no knowledge of this technique among the Thulung), and the spicy or sticky preparation would correspond to the use of bird-lime (certainly a known technique). If this is correct, we can now recognise in the Thulung story four distinct types of capture, two appropriate to birds, one appropriate to fish, and the one in the house appropriate to human brides.

I mentioned earlier that the Limbu, immediate neighbours to the Rai and their fellow Kiranti, still practise marriage by capture, and one might expect them to have mythic precedents for the practice. In any case, they provide interesting comparative material for the themes of the Building of the House and the hypothetical brother-sister marriage. The following is from Jones (1974: 260).

> After the creation of the world, a boy and his sister decided to build a house. The boy went into the woods to cut a tree for the wood they needed. After repeated failures to fell it, his sister came to help him. She made offerings of food, liquor and beer at the base of the tree, and only then was the boy able to fell it. With the help of friends he brought it back to the village, and by accident it fell and killed his sister. (She becomes an evil spirit causing accidental and violent deaths).

---

main one here is that Tarbong's mentor is the dominant female partner in a brother-sister marriage.

The building of what is presumably a first house (i) cannot be carried out without the advice of the female partner to the marriage, and (ii) is attended by an 'accidental' death. The notion of a primal incest in Limbu tradition appears also in Chemjong (1966: 27): when mankind was at the stage of animal life, a brother and sister became consorts, and when the brother died the sister became the wife of her own son. The son also died, and both husbands became evil spirits. There is also another story of brother-sister union located 'at the start of human life' (ibid: 34ff).

Chemjong does not give a myth concerning foundation sacrifices, but he does give the following account of Limbu housebuilding (ibid: 79f). A hole should be dug in the centre of the site and in it should be placed a copper pice. The 'King pillar' is set up, and its base is sprinkled with the blood of a sacrificed pig. The priest then prays to the deity Okwanama, supporter of the earth, for the health of the future inmates of the house. Here the pig corresponds to the fowl in Ph V, and the coin to the dead child.

A Tibetan parallel is the building of the Jo-khang (the 'Cathedral') at Lhasa. When Srong-btsan sgam-po (died 649 AD) constructed this temple in the new capital of Tibet, he is said to have located it over a subterranean lake in the Plain of Milk. The lake 'represented the heart of a she-demon lying on her back'. Her outstretched limbs reached the boundaries of Tibetan settlement, and were nailed down by three tetrads of temples arranged concentrically at increasing distances from the Jo-khang (Stein 1972: 38). Thus the central Tibetan temple was envisaged as founded on top of a demon that had been killed and buried. There is a similar story too about the original palace of the Yarlung dynasty. Gri-gum's daughter, who married the usurper Lo-ngam, was pregnant at the time when her brother reconquered his father's territory, and she asked to be buried alive in the castle that was built after the victory (Macdonald 1971: 243).[27]

In both these cases the victim is female, as is the 'accidental' victim in the Limbu story reported by Jones. This might support the view that Thulung Cindiringma was female. Stein (1957c) discusses Tibetan Buddhist rituals in which the officiant stabs a model or drawing of a naked human figure lying chained up on its back, and compares the figure to the demon underneath the Jokhang. However the figure is not necessarily female (ibid: 202), and it is actually called a *linga*, a Sanskrit loan word whose meanings

---

27 Another Tibetan foundation sacrifice is discussed in Ch. 5 XI.

include 'penis'. The gender of foundation sacrifices in the area needs further study.

In discussing Cindiringma's name, we thought it might be onomatopoeic. It is striking how often the stories we have considered connect birth with sounds. Thus both versions of the birth of gShen-rab associate the event with bird song. Kam III mentioned Mini's birth cry, and the tree birth in the story reported by Hermanns was accompanied by an 'unpleasant noise'. In Ant III the birth of Mini was immediately followed by Miyapma's *roko-roko poak-poak*, which probably included the tapping of metal on stone. Further miscellaneous examples can be added from Tibet. When a much-desired son descended from heaven to found the dGa' clan, a spontaneous noise was heard (Stein 1961: 49). An important category of the protector deities of the Bonpo are the *dbal* goddesses who were born from eggs in three groups of nine. Two of the groups were born from eggs broken open by different sounds (Nebesky-Wojkowitz 1956: 312f). The exact relationship between birth and sound varies in the different instances, but the association is worth noting.

Civilising Heroes and Heroines

Wayelungma's career falls into two phases. During the second, she is clearly a civilising heroine, as we shall see, but during the first, the impression she gives is rather different, and even her humanity is not securely established. It is conceivable that in episodes III and IV she foresaw and planned the whole course of events, but she by no means had everything her own way. Her mother tells her to go away and drown herself. Several times she is repulsed by Khakcilik and thrown back in the water, sustaining bruises and broken bones. For a matter of days or months she has to put up with the old woman claiming credit for domestic services she herself has performed, and she owes to someone else's initiative her release from this galling situation. Although her ultimate capture was no doubt welcome and her protestations about it insincere, the incident appears to have been violent and something of a shock: she claims at least that she lost her beads and again sustained bruises and broken bones (CP IV). Her persona at this stage of her career is so different from that of a civilising heroine that one wonders whether Wayelungma, as we have her, may have conflated two originally distinct characters.

During her second phase, Wayelungma is entirely in charge of the situation, and her only failure is over the emissaries. She seems to retain no trace of her past existence as a stone, and her role is consistently that of mentor to Khakcilik. She converts him from a life of fishing to one of swidden farming, i.e. she introduces agriculture (if we ignore the mention of rice in some versions of I, and accept Kam's statement that there was no agriculture at the period when the sisters left home). Whereas previously Khakcilik had been living in a cave (Kam IV), she teaches him to build a properly founded house. She instructs him in the brewing of beer, and in how to hold a proper family ceremony. Roughly speaking, she is responsible for the Neolithic Revolution. Furthermore, she was clairvoyante and knew everything (Kam VII).

Wayelungma's character in her second phase is emphasised by the contrast with Khakcilik's. Except for fishing, whatever he does, Khakcilik needs to be told how to set about it. He is slow in understanding, and liable to bungle. His character shows no particular development, though he experiences a change of mentor: during the capture of his wife it is some unnamed individual, or his 'fate', who gives him instructions, while thenceforth it is Wayelungma herself. The lack of initiative on the part of the groom is also a striking feature of most of the wife-capture stories. It is less apparent in the rather fragmentary Tibetan versions, but even in one of them the dream that is mentioned may offer him guidance, as does the dream in the longer Tichurong version. Both in the Tichurong and Lepcha versions it is the groom's mother who instructs him how to capture his bride, and perhaps this was the function of the mother who is mentioned in one Tibetan version, without being any given any significant narrative role. The Lepcha myth resembles the Thulung one in giving the groom a change of mentor after the capture of his bride, in this case a change from mother to elder brother.

Khakcilik is almost the only male in the Thulung story. The owl makes a brief appearance after he has finally been provoked into punishing intolerable teasing. Khakcilik's father Pacoksi is no more than a name. We hear nothing of Wayelungma's father, nor (for reasons suggested already) of the husbands that Jaw and Khliw are supposed to have married. The lack of creative or innovatory activity by males stands in contrast not only to the character of Wayelungma, but also to that of the two sisters. Jaw and Khliw are less clearly civilising heroines than Wayelungma, but they have a number of innovations to their credit. They introduced the giving of bride-price vessels, and according to PB they actually made them themselves. Earlier on they had brought from north and south to some central place new vegetable species including cotton and lentils (Ph II). Perhaps one can understand them also as having introduced weaving, about whose origin I collected no other traditions.

All of this contrasts markedly with Tibetan traditions, in which the innovations that led to civilisation are almost invariably attributed to males. For instance it was said of the youngest son of Gri-gum's wife that he 'subjected cattle to the law... turned grassy plains into fields... before him there was no harvesting of grass or grain in Tibet'. For other technical and social innovations ascribed to him and to other ministers and kings of the Yarlung dynasty see Stein (1972: 50ff). It appears that females play a part only in the introduction of Buddhism, which supposedly owed its initial impulse to the Chinese and Nepalese wives of Srong-btsan sgam-po (see further Ch 5 II and X).

The closest parallel I have found to Wayelungma is a man called Mig-can, who was born from a cosmic egg as demiurge. He ordered the universe, regulated the course of time, invited gods for the protection of created beings, and overcame demons. 'Once he jumped into the sea and was caught in a net by a fisherman' (Tucci 1949: 711).

Thus we meet again the contrast stressed at the end of the last chapter: where Tibetan written tradition emphasises the male, Thulung oral tradition emphasises the female.

CHAPTER 4

Migrations of the Ancestors

Introduction

In the last two chapters many of the characters have been in some sense part of the natural world, whether as stars or animals, stones or birds. From now on the traditions will lack this 'fabulous' quality, and the characters will be unambiguously human. At the same time we move closer to the realities of geography and history. Whereas the last two chapters have each mentioned only two place names, henceforth every event will have some geographical location. If there was cultural history of a sort to be derived from the last two chapters, it was not because the events narrated actually took place. The question of historicity now begins to arise, even if the verdict must often be negative or doubtful.

The present chapter starts with the ancestors existing in some primeval dwelling place, and describes their emergence and subsequent wanderings up until the foundation of Mukli. It may be that this body of traditions is less well known than those dealt with in other chapters, or it may be that the relative scantiness of the material collected is due solely to the fact that I learned of its existence only towards the end of my stay and was therefore unable to make specific enquiries about it from other informants. There will seldom be more than two versions available for any one episode, which greatly limits the need and scope for analysis.

The backbone of the chapter is the narrative given by CP. On this occasion he undertook to tell me the *loa* ('word, matter, language, story') of the *seor-reor*. *Seor* is a difficult word, which we shall here render 'ancestors'. *Reor* has stylistic rather than semantic significance, converting the basic term into a ritual expression; as before, this nuance is expressed by writing Ancestors with a capital A. CP begins his account from the hearth stones, the present seat of the ancestors, and undertakes a brief verbal journey from there across country to the location of the Primal Lake, before beginning his narrative proper. Although his whole account was spoken, not chanted, the opening reads as if it were the transcript of part of a ritual. Whereas his version of the Jaw-Khliw cycle was dictated throughout in ritual language, in this case by the end of episode I the language had taken on the rhythms and grammatical characteristics of ordinary narrative; however, it continues to be noticeably rich in ritual expressions, which often replace ordinary nouns. This shows that for him the narrative belonged within the sphere of ritual, though I cannot say whether it was ever told at rituals in the spoken form present on the tape. The Lokhim versions were told in ordinary narrative style, and although ritual expressions occur occasionally, their frequency is too low to point to any special association with ritual.

For reasons already discussed, one episode of CP's version has been excerpted from its context and was included in Ch. 2 as episode VII. His final episode, the Foundation of Tingla, is deferred until Ch. 5 IX. As before, Kam is the only narrator who attempts to set the myths of the present chapter within a single continuous version of Thulung history. It is not clear how CP or Karb would have related them to other episodes, for instance to the Creation.

I. The Primal Lake

CP The ancestor stone (*seorluŋ*) here, the other hearth stones, all the spirits of the niche and seat, all the pillars and roof-ties,[1] the side door and threshing stone, the front door, verandah and courtyard, from the village shrine, from the sacred tree (?), down via Ləramdu Cəramdu and Beneseo Luringma, down via Bolongga, over the great river, via Nayongma Heyongma, down there (is) the Primal Lake, the home of the Ancestors. Down there they followed their Destinies entirely, all

---

1 At this point I briefly interrupt. The inventory of the house is not analysed here.

of them, living there. They acted according to the *ḍiumla*, down in the Primal Lake.

Verbal journeys between the hearth and the dwelling place of the spirits are a prominent feature of Thulung ritual (Allen 1974). No such rituals were tape-recorded in Tingla, but part of a rite resembling a Mukli *huṭpa* was dictated to me by CP. We shall excerpt only that part of the text that relates to the present episode. After listing the ritual paraphernalia that are being used and addressing two pairs of deities, the text begins an inventory of the house, which differs only insignificantly from that given above. After progressing to the shrine and sacred tree, the verbal journey on which it then embarks is slightly fuller than in CP I.

Tingla Ritual	Episode I	Gloss, if available
loramdu coramdu	ditto[2]	Place of the *ləhəḍam* tree and *coaram* creeper
moredu bandamdu		Place of the *more* tree
glokulangka kraṭpusənglam		the big river and the bridge
beneseo lurengmalam	ditto	Beneseobdel, or Panchen village
meordali siriksalam		Necha village
cocuku congmayalam		Kuybhir village
həiu bolonggalam	ditto	(associated with a bridge)
glokulam		bloku morsalangka the big river
nayongma heyongmalam	ditto	(associated with a hollowed tree trunk used as ferry)
huiu cataralam		Chatra, or Bara Chatra
bari yekhop thari yekhop		'the god's dwelling' (? analysis)
...maidanmalam		*maidān* N = plain
...agidin nagidin	nagidin agidin	Primal Lake (see below)

When it comes to details, the interpretation of ritual texts is very problematic, and the purpose of the comparison here is quite limited. Apart from suggesting the location of the Primal Lake, it confirms that the first part of episode I is indeed a fragmentary ritual journey of a type previously identified. I do not know why CP felt it necessary to begin his narrative in this roundabout fashion. However he was doing so deliberately, since when

---

2   I have not exaggerated the consistency of my note-taking by standardising the spellings. The postpositions *-lam* and *-laŋka* mean 'from' and 'via'. The omissions at the end of the text are of expressions having no geographical significance.

I interrupted his inventory of the house to ask whether he was really telling me the Story of the Ancestors, he replied that indeed he was. The simplest explanation is that he set out to tell the story as he had previously heard it told, and that this had been as part of a ritual. However, there may be more to it – perhaps some feeling that the past of the Ancestors could not or should not be reached except by starting from their presence. Whatever his motive, it is not disconcerting that the journey is so cursory, that it omits so many of the place-names appearing in the other text. We have met something similar before: in introducing the Death of Mini, DB made a cursory allusion to the main body of the Creation myth by using a few phrases from two episodes.

The description of conditions of life down in the Primal Lake is somewhat obscure, but it apparently suggests a sort of paradise or golden age, during which the Ancestors lived in a state of harmony and wholeness. The term for the Lake, *nagidin agidin*, is composed of *din* 'lake', *agi*, which may or may not be Nepali *aghi* 'first, previously', and *nagi*, which we have already met in Wayelungma's alternative name Nagimo. The expression 'Primal Lake' was used to render *diridin* in Ch. 2 Ph I, and various non-Thulung primal lakes were also alluded to earlier. Although the Ancestors begin their career in a lake, nothing else points to their having a fish-like or non-human character.

To a Rai, 'down' strongly implies 'south', and there is much evidence, both here and in later episodes, that the Ancestors are thought to have come from the south. More precisely, the route to the Primal Lake lies to the south-east, via Bara Chatra, a settlement on the Sapt Kosi some eight miles west of Dharan – nowadays a well-known Hindu pilgrimage centre. A Kangel informant volunteered the suggestion that the Primal Lake was situated at Bara Chatra. However, AS gives the equation *diridin* = *samudra* N, i.e. 'Ocean', and perhaps the reference is to the Bay of Bengal, into which the Sapt Kosi ultimately drains. Interestingly, the Lepcha tribal priest is said to take the soul of the deceased on a journey down the river Tista 'to the ocean', before finally disposing of it in the home of the dead (Nebesky-Wojkowitz 1951: 34). The Thulung journey seems to be on land, except where rivers are crossed, but it is worth noting that its watery destination lies in the direction taken by the rivers of the area.

II. The Exit

In this episode the ancestors of the Thulung, together with those of some other Rai subtribes, emerge from their original dwelling-place by means of a blood offering, sometimes of a bird, sometimes of a human.

CP Then Khimci came out from there. 'I did it by making a Blood Offering,' he said, (for) he had sprinkled the blood of a *le-pikpuri* bird (Red-vented Bulbul). After he had done so, the Door closed again. 'How did you get out, elder brother?' asked (another brother). 'It was by making a Blood Offering,' he replied. But the other misheard him, and thought he had said that it was by killing his younger brother. So he sprinkled the Door with the blood of his younger brother and came out. The priest (*dewa*) came up from the *dewa*-stone, the medium (*sele*) from the *tiri*-stone, the minister (*muliu*) from the *muliu*-stone. Then the Ancestors came out.

The mishearing arose because the ritual expression for Blood Offering is *loakbe bukbe*, while the Thulung for younger brother is *loak*. The *le-pikpuri* bird is the *kāli jureli* N. Khimci was a Sunwar, or better, the ancestor of the Sunwar, and probably we should imagine him representing and accompanied by younger brothers, women and children. The identity of his questioner is not stated, but evidently the question is posed on behalf of the Ancestors.

The triad of priest, medium and minister is particularly problematic. The stones from which they come are presumably the three hearth stones, imagined as present on the far side of the Door. It may be possible to understand the passage as including the triad among the Ancestors who come out through the Door. However the verb applied to them is not actually *luk-* 'come out, come through, emerge', but *ge(t)-* 'come up, come north', whereas both in this and in the other versions all the other characters are said to come *out*, before coming *up*. The contrast suggests that the reference to the triad may be a formula or fragment from some extraneous context that has been incorporated here without being clearly synthesised into the narrative.

Karb Of old, when the Earth opened, down at the Place of Origin – as to what happened, I do not know the full story; one or two things I do know and I shall tell you. When they opened the earth, according to what I heard, there were just four brothers. Chamling was the eldest, Ombu the second, Kulunge the third, and Phuliukuceo the youngest. When they opened the Place of Origin, this is how they came out. Chamling killed a *le-pikpuri* bird and sprinkled the Place of Origin with its blood, sprinkled the door and came out. 'How did you get out?' asked his younger brothers, 'We shall come too.' He had done it, he said, by killing his younger brother and sprinkling his blood. This was how he himself had come out, and the others did likewise, each of them down to the third killing some creature. But the youngest became stuck, and asked his elder brothers how they had managed. They said it had been by killing their younger brothers. But the youngest had no younger brother, so he cut off his little finger, sprinkled blood and came out.

This time the Thulung ancestor is named as Phuliukuceo, and the emergence is from earth, not water. As before, we must understand that each of the four named brothers is accompanied by fellow members of his subtribe, including unnamed younger brothers who could be sacrificed. The narrative line is confused, since first it is stated that Chamling emerged by killing the bird, then that he did so by killing his younger brother. The motif of mishearing is absent, and it is not clear why the eldest brother should mislead his younger brothers by saying that he had killed a younger brother, if he had not in fact done so; nor indeed why the three elder brothers should mislead the youngest in the same way. The confusions are not clarified by the other Lokhim version.

Kam Khakcilik had four sons: Kirantsor the eldest, Banasor the second, Geanasor the third, and then Ramli, our forefather, the ancestor of the Thulung. They were dwelling down there at the Place of Origin. After they had come into being, they emerged upwards, Kirantsor, Banasor, Geanasor and Ramli, from eldest to youngest, and at the same time Chamling and his women-folk also emerged. Kirantsor came out first, and in the process our ancestors gave rise to something of an evil force (*khlamya*). 'O mother's brothers and elder brothers, how did you get out?' asked the Nachiring, Dumi and Chamling. 'It was by killing my younger brother,' said Kirantsor: so they too killed their younger brothers. Actually, he had brought his people out by means of a *pikpuri* bird – you know the large *le-pikpuri*. He had cut the bird near its cloaca and squeezed the blood out and sprinkled it, so as to make the earth open. That is why we do not eat the *le-pikpuri* – you must have heard them spoken of as taboo (*kholom*) – the bird with the red colour round the cloaca. So Kirantsor came out, by killing the bird and sprinkling the Place of Origin, whereas Chamling emerged by killing his younger brother. All four brothers came up... 'But you did not kill your younger brother – all of them are here. And I killed mine in order to come out. You are a sinner (*pāpi* N).' Thus they quarrelled, as they came north from the Place of Origin.

The name of the eldest brother, Kirantsor, evidently derives from Kirant, the Nepali term for East Nepal; sometimes it appears to be used to stand for the whole quartet. I cannot identify the elements Bana-, Geana- or -sor [?cf. Sk. *asura* 'demon'], but they do not seem to have anything to do with Rai subtribes. In addition to the quartet of named brothers, four subtribes are mentioned by Kam, namely Thulung, Chamling, Nachiring and Dumi, but for a number of reasons, including the intonation of the passage on the tape, the total cannot here be regarded as significant. No other narrator mentioned that Khakcilik had four sons.

No version of the episode was tape-recorded in Mukli, but the story was recognised by Ph. He agreed with the Tingla version that the first brother to come out was a Sunwar, but with the Lokhim versions that the failure of the youngest to sacrifice a bird was due to deliberate deceit on the part of his elder brothers, rather than to a misunderstanding.

In order to grasp the relationships between the versions, it is useful to divide the characters into those who shed the blood of a bird and leave earlier, and those who shed human blood and leave later.[3] The second category contains CP's unnamed ancestor who kills his younger brother, Karb's Phuliukuceo who for want of a younger brother cuts off his own finger, and Kam's Chamling. One appreciates that Thulung today might find offensive the notion that their own subtribal ancestor committed human sacrifice using his own younger brother, while the ancestors of other subtribes did not. Many of them are apologetic about the tribal traditions of animal sacrifice, which some have abandoned as being old-fashioned and primitive (*jangali* N). So perhaps the explanation given for the sacrifice, namely misunderstanding or the trickery of others, is a way of excusing

---

3   Karb actually talks vaguely of the second and third brothers killing 'some creature'; perhaps in earlier versions they all four killed different creatures. The offerings are actually said to be 'cut' (*phəl-*), but the word is probably here used in its common meaning of 'sacrifice'.

something that once needed no excuse. The reinterpretation would be comparable to explaining away the sacrifice of the first-born of Wayelungma and Khakcilik as an accident. Following the same line of thought, the substitution of the finger for the younger brother in Karb could represent a further toning down. Finally, by attributing the fratricide to Chamling, Kam altogether exonerates Ramli, the ancestor of the Thulung, and attributes the blame to someone who in the next episode will turn out to be a villain.[4] It is thus entirely understandable that the episode should have changed in the direction CP to Kam, whereas I cannot think of a motivation for the converse shift.

CP cannot be convincingly construed as referring to any sort of quartet, but both the other narrators refer to a quartet of named brothers; and in both cases it is the youngest of them, Phuliukuceo or Ramli, who is the ancestor of the Thulung. The pattern is the same as that formed by Mini and his three elder brothers, and the similarity between the two origin stories can hardly be coincidence. However, the comparison cannot be pressed very far: the brothers in this chapter are not sufficiently characterised, either here or in the next two episodes, and cannot be confidently linked to four social functions. At the most, Phuliukuceo's lack of a younger brother to sacrifice recalls the emphasis on Mini's uniqueness, and the later villainy of Chamling, the eldest in Karb, might be compared with Tiger's matricide. One notes too that for Karb the quartet is homogeneous – consisting of representatives of four subtribes – and that it forms a totality – the four members standing for all the occupants of the Place of Origin, or at least for all who leave it. In contrast, the characters in Kam are heterogeneous. His named quartet consists of the Thulung subtribe ancestor plus three names ending in -sor which are probably Nepali and are not linked to subtribes; other subtribes appear in the story, but outside the quartet. Karb's version is not only more satisfying aesthetically, but shows less evidence of external influence. This is a second reason for regarding it as a better representative of older tribal tradition than Kam's version.

The cosmology of the episode raises several problems. CP accepted the idea that the Door was like the outlet of a womb, and this is evidently one possible interpretation, or level of interpretation. The vocabulary of opening (*hor-*, *hoas-*) recalls that used in the story of Mamaciuniu, and the

---

4   The triumph of Chamling in the next episode and the death of three members of the quartet in the following one may be due to the evil force originated by their deception of Chamling; but the narrative does not say so.

particular difficulties associated with the last-born recall Miyapma's intense labour pains at the birth of Mini. The notion of a Door is not clearly related to the notion that the primal home of the ancestors was a Lake, and for the Lokhim narrators at least, the door is explicitly an opening in the earth. Karb also talks of the opening of the Place of Origin, Khuliu. This is a difficult term, whose semantic ramifications I do not fully understood.

(i) Probably, though not certainly, it is related to the noun *khul*, which I recorded in the meaning 'shaded area at the foot of a tree', and which in turn is doubtless related to the verb *gul-* 'cloud over'. Speaking metaphorically, one may say of a story one does not know well, that one does not know it from its *khul* (*pheddekhi* N), 'from its base, foundation or beginning'. Assuming Khuliu is related to *khul* in this sense, the nature of its second syllable is unclear; there are reasons both for and against relating it to *yu* 'down to, down at'.

(ii) Another area of meaning appears in the ritual expression *khul ripsi* or *khuliu repsiu* (= *purkhā* N), 'ancestors, elders; those who are both aged and highly knowledgeable'. The expression occurs particularly in lists of, or salutations to, those present at ceremonies, and may be interspersed among kinship terms. Thus we can include here AS's entry *khuliu* = *sasurā* N, i.e 'father-in law', which was not accepted by my informants. The link between semantic areas (i) and (ii) is perhaps quite close (cf. Fox 1971), and in giving the meaning of the ritual expression Ph related *ripsi* to the verb *rip-* 'to shade'. Unfortunately the variability of ritual vocabulary is such that in doubtful cases the views of a single informant can only be accepted with reserve.

(iii) AS also gives *khuliu* = *kā̃shi* N. This can only mean the holy city of Benares. Standard Nepali is *kāshi*, but the nasalisation appears to be a dialectism since it is used consistently by older Thulung speakers, especially when talking of the opposition between Kasigotra and Lasagotra, which is to say roughly between subtribes claiming an origin respectively in India (Benares) or Tibet (Lhasa) (see Ch. 5 X). AS's association of Khuliu and Benares was rejected by those informants to whom I mentioned it, but we have seen that the general Thulung tradition is of an origin in the south, and presumably AS is alluding to a version current in either Dewsa or Darjeeling.

(iv) Ph had heard used in ritual contexts the expression *khuliu hamḍi* or *hamṣta* (plural or singular), which he thought referred to the time when the clouds parted and people emerged from primeval darkness.

But whatever is to be made of *khuliu* as a lexeme, the cosmology implied by the narratives needs further consideration. Since the Thulung material is relatively scanty it is not worth pursing the theme at length, and the following remarks are somewhat concise and dogmatic; for wider documentation see Stein (1957a and b), who draws on material not only from China but also from Siberia, Central Asia and Tibet. Within this area, there are numerous contexts in which the cosmos is conceived as consisting of two (or more) 'levels', separated by a constriction or difficult passage. For instance, Stein mentions in this connection the reverence of the Chinese for grottoes consisting of two superimposed cavities, with a pool of water in the bottom. In many instances the constrictions are located between the ordinary inhabited world and the heavens above, rather than, as in the present episode, between the ordinary world and the underworld; but the two sorts of opening can be regarded as equivalent. Points of passage or connection between different levels of the cosmos are normally located at its centre. The house (or tent) is regularly equated with the cosmos, and often has in its middle a central pillar or roof-hole which is climbed up or through in the course of rituals. Sometimes a tree-trunk or sapling is set up specially for the ritual to enable a shaman to climb through the roof-hole to 'another world'. Central pillars are often associated with human sacrifice, as we saw in connection with Cindiringma.

Ideas of such wide distribution in the Asiatic and Tibetan worlds might very well be represented among the Thulung also, which suggests that the passage through the door in the present episode might be an undertaking comparable to that of a shaman who climbs through a roof-hole. Admittedly, a Thulung would be unlikely to accept the idea without extensive explanations, if only because this particular operation is not carried out by the local shamans. Moreover, this interpretation still leaves unexplained why the first ancestor to leave opens the door with a bird, while the last has to shed human blood. On the other hand, up to a point at least, and unlike the womb interpretation, it does explain the necessity for some sort of sacrifice: even today, in what is probably the older type of Thulung shamanic séance, a blood sacrifice, often of a bird, remains essential (Allen 1976b). It also fits well with area (i) of the meaning of *khuliu*, assuming that this is relevant: the ancestors would be starting off at the base of a tree that served as a ladder for their ascent.[5]

III. Territorial Dispute

This episode is absent from CP's account.

Karb   After he came out, the four brothers were together over at Majhuwa Diktel. They were each looking for their own territory and it was necessary to make a partition. '*I* shall stay at Majhuwa Diktel,' said the eldest, but each of the others said just the same. 'No,' said Chamling, 'We are the eldest, so it must be us.' Each claimed it for himself and they fell to quarrelling. Eventually they agreed that they would have to make a partition somehow or other, and while they were discussing the question, the second brother, Ombule, proposed that they should have something to eat before deciding. While he was wondering what to have, Chamling, who was a cunning fellow, said, 'It does not matter. Why not ground meal?' – he himself had brought parched rice. With parched rice one can speak, with ground meal one can't. 'Where would you like your land?' asked Chamling, and as the other could not speak because of what he was eating, all he said was 'Om-om-om'. 'Aha! You want Ombu. Off you go.' And he gave him Ombu.

   That left three brothers, but none of them would give up his claim – Majhuwa Diktel was very good land. So they quarrelled in earnest. 'Well, younger brothers, let us call upon this earth and heaven of ours. The one for whom rain falls from heaven to earth, the one to whom the earth beneath replies, he shall be the ruler of Majhuwa Diktel.' Chamling then dug a hole, buried the young of a *cempra* bird and smoothed the earth flat again; the others were not there and did not bring birds. Each of the three set up a sapling. 'Right, let us invoke,' said Chamling. 'But we do not know how to,' said the others. 'This is how,' and he gave them instructions. 'What you must say is "Sola Panja, Majhuwa Diktel is mine", and thereupon you must strike down at the earth.' If there is a bird underneath, it will squeak (he thought to himself), but when the others made their claim to Majhuwa Diktel and clapped, there was not a sound. When the second and third

---

5   As has been emphasised previously, the analysis of ritual expressions is difficult and often speculative, but perhaps CP's term for the Door, *giculi ladikhre*, contains the same element as *khrekhrem* 'ladder'.

brothers repeated their claim, and shook the sapling, no water fell. 'Right' said the eldest, 'Now it is my turn to invoke. Listen carefully.' As he made his claim and clapped, the little bird chirped *chya chya chya chya*. 'Did you hear that?' he asked, and the others admitted it. 'Now I shall shake the sapling,' he said, and as he did so, he stated his claim a second time. Previously he had put some water in a length of bamboo;[6] and when he shook the sapling, the water came down and wet them – the three brothers were sitting together like this. 'Did you hear?' he asked. 'Yes.' 'Both of you?' 'Yes, both of us.' 'Well then, clearly Majhuwa Diktel has favoured me. The place is mine,' he said; and so he occupied it. 'Well, brothers, this earth, this land of ours has favoured me and selected me. You two must look for your own place.' The others accepted this. So the second brother followed the Arun river and reached Salewa Lungkhim, and the youngest, recognising that he too must find his own place, followed the Dudh Kosi and came up to Phuliuku, to Mukli. So they each found their own territory and lived there.

Majhuwa lies a mile or so south of Diktel. Both villages are probably still inhabited by Chamling. If Sola Panja is a geographical term, I did not locate it. The Ombule now live around Manebhanjyang and between the Dudh Kosi and Sun Kosi, as neighbours of the Chamling. The third brother, who is referred to after the departure of Ombu as the second, was given in Karb II as Kulunge. Although he is described as going up the Arun, nowadays the Kulung are usually thought of as living on the Hongu Khola, i.e. in the watershed of the Dudh Kosi rather than of the Arun.

When Chamling shakes the sapling and the water falls, one would expect him to ask the others whether they 'felt' it, rather than whether they 'heard' it. Either the verb *theos-* does have this second meaning, or the narrator repeats the earlier question inappropriately.

Kam And so they came to Sapsuwa Majhuwa, over in Chamling territory, Kirantsor and Ramli, in fact all the four brothers. There they stayed until Chamling became jealous. In one place (where Thulu was?) there was splendid rich forest, where game was plentiful – in those days they lived by hunting, there was nothing of all this agriculture,

---

6   It is possible, but unlikely, that if the 'sapling' was a bamboo, the water was placed in a segment of the pole itself.

none of these cereal crops. All they had to live on was what they could catch: deer, wild goat, wild sheep, fish.[7] There were none of these big rivers then, just marshy areas here and there. That is how they lived. Well, Chamling looked for an excuse for a quarrel: 'O elder brothers and mother's brothers, what are you doing living on land that I was the first to claim?' 'No, I occupied this area first,' said our forefather; he had claimed it much earlier. Chamling spent one night here, one night there, uphill and down. He cut the wild plantains when they were only so high, he cut the *moasa* when it was only just black (?). 'Let us go around and see who has laid claim to the land by marking trees with sickle and axe,' they said. Chamling had gone around doing this in order to chase away Thulu. Our forefather paid no attention to the matter... and as they went round it was the same everywhere. 'Let us put it to the trial. Whoever wins, let it be his,' they said. So they decided to put it to the trial. They hammered flat a good patch of earth and held a court of decision. Chamling said: 'Now we must plant saplings on this patch of earth which we have hammered.' On the top of his sapling Chamling put some water, in the earth beneath he buried the young of a *cempra* bird; our forefather buried nothing whatever. 'When we hold the trial and judgment, the one on whom the heavens send down rain, the one to whom the earth replies, he shall be owner of the land.' Chamling had caught and buried a *cempra* bird, and put water on the top of his sapling. 'Sapsuwa Majhuwa is mine, mine by first mark of sickle and axe, mine first and foremost, mine for good or ill, my property (?), my territory (*kipaṭ* N),' said our forefather, and clapped the earth below. Not a thing happened. Not a drop of water fell, the earth stayed silent. Then said Chamling, having made his preparations: 'There now, elder brother, you received no answer, not a thing; the sky sent not a drop, the earth did not reply. Now listen to me! Will I get an answer, or will I not? Sapsuwa Majhuwa is mine, by recent mark of sickle and axe, for living and spreading, it is mine.' So saying, he clapped, and the bird said *kya*. 'Do you hear that, brother?' he said; 'Now I will shake the sapling.' As he did so, down came the water in a stream. Our forefather stood up, he had lost the trial, Kirantsor had lost.

---

7   The intonation shows that the list is not intended as exhaustive.

Although the translation is doubtful in places, the general lines of the story are clear. Kam's version omits the incident of Ombu and the meal, and appears to reduce the actors to two, namely Chamling and 'our forefather', who is variously referred to as Thulu (= Thulung) or Kirantsor. The remarks on ecology are interesting, but I do not know whether there really was a time when the ancestors of the Rai subsisted in East Nepal solely by hunting and gathering. We shall meet other passages (Ch. 5 VIIIb) that couple the cutting of the *moasa* and the wild plantain, but the significance of these motifs is not totally clear.

A prominent feature of Kam's version is the amount of Nepali vocabulary relating to land ownership and legal procedures. Marking trees with a sickle is widely recognised as a means of staking a claim to ownership; the same procedure is current in the neighbourhood of the Central Valley. The lengthy formula used for the claim by Chamling's opponent is entirely in Nepali. Karb's version lacks this amount of Nepali vocabulary, so perhaps it is more traditional in other ways too.

The word 'sapling' inadequately translates *lingo* N (Karb) or *tharsəŋ* (Kam), which refer alike to tall bamboo poles, or small trees, from which the lower foliage or branches respectively have been removed. For one contemporary use of the *tharsəŋ* in Thulung ritual see Allen (1974: 10, where the term is misspelt). A *tharsəŋ* is also set up in the middle of the courtyard during a *sekro* ritual. In the ritual I observed, as in the present episode, the earth of the courtyard was hammered flat before the pole was erected, although the courtyard was already virtually flat. Karb refers to the hammered plot as a *khalo* N, which generally means 'threshing surface'.

After uttering one's claim the procedure was evidently to call first upon the earth, then the heavens, to ratify it. The method of calling on the earth is alluded to five times in the two versions, by means of three different expressions. Karb talks of 'striking down at the earth', which is not quite the same as 'striking the earth', and also of making a *boak* or *bhoak*, which is no doubt onomatopoeic. Kam uses the Nepali expression *beḍi toknu*, which is not adequately elucidated in the dictionaries. Sharma's *beḍi* 'iron anklet to be hammered round a convict's leg, fetter' is of little help. Turner comes closer to the present context with the following entry:

> (?) *bẽṛi* s. Trial by ordeal.– *b°* *ṭhoknu* or *hālnu* to be tried by ordeal, in which the two parties throw a rupee or wooden shoe each into a pool, and he, whose rupee or shoe sinks, is held to be guilty.– *b°* *pasnu* to be tried by ordeal of plunging the hand into boiling water.

My commentator understood the expression *b° toknu* as *simā lāunu*, 'fix boundaries', and associated it with the gesture of striking the open palm with the closed fist.[8] The repetition of *boak* or *bhoak* two and three times in Karb implies that the gesture was repeated. Perhaps, after 'clapping' in this way, the disputant had to touch the earth, to make it clear to whom he was addressing his request for endorsement.

This detail is of some interest because of the similarity between the Territorial Dispute and the well-known episode in the life of the Buddha.

> Mara, the Lord of Death, leads a personal assault upon the sage as he sits in meditation beneath the Tree of Enlightenment at Bodhgaya. Having failed to disturb his serenity by his taunts and attacks, Mara challenges him to produce a witness to his fitness for Buddhahood. The sage touches the Earth with the fingers of his right hand and calls upon it as his witness. The Earth quakes in testimony.[9]

Similarly, in stories of his previous lives, the earth by quaking bears witness to his heroic acts of self-sacrifice (Snellgrove 1957: 18). In Buddhist iconography the moment of enlightenment is regularly depicted by showing the Buddha in this 'earth-witness' posture, seated cross-legged, left hand in the lap, palm upwards, right hand in front with extended fingers touching the ground or extending towards it, palm inwards.

The two stories differ widely as regards the context of the earth-witness motif. The Buddha is engaged in a cosmic struggle against the forces of evil and illusion, while Chamling is simply outwitting his brothers in the course of a territorial dispute. The Buddha calls only on Earth, the Rai ancestors on Heaven as well. The Buddhist story has only the one *bodhi* tree, while Kam implies at least two saplings and Karb mentions three. Nevertheless, we are surely dealing with variants of a single story. Although the Thulung has more than one sapling, it has only one that is associated with the victor, and presumably the latter, like the *bodhi* tree, can be linked to the protean family of cosmic trees that join heaven and earth. Although the text does not say so, perhaps the victor's sapling was the middle of the three in Karb's account, in which case the point of the Ombu episode could be to reduce the four disputants to an odd number and so make a symmetrical

---

8   Perhaps the Thulung text should read *thoknu* 'knock' rather than *toknu* 'decide'.

9   [Or else (Thomas 1975: 74, from the *Mahāvastu*) 'with his right hand (he) smote the earth. Then the great earth roared and sounded forth a deep and terrible sound.')]

line-up possible. Since the disputants are seated when the water falls on them (Karb), presumably they are under a sapling and in this posture throughout the trial.

The various sounds are worth noting. In the Thulung, the 'clap' that elicits the chirp of the bird is rendered by the syllable *boak*, which recalls the *poak* associated with the movement of souls in Ch. 2 Ant III. Auditorily, this clap is more like the Buddha's earthquake than the chirp that corresponds to it functionally (i.e. as the earth's testimony). The marking of the Buddha's victory with a rumble or roar recalls the fact that a transition or break-through is very commonly associated with percussion (Needham 1967).

The 'heaven-witness' motif, absent from the Buddhist story, is also less salient than the earth-witness motif in the Thulung versions. In first describing Chamling's preparations, Karb forgets to mention the bamboo tube of water, and Chamling's initial instructions to his two brothers omit mention of shaking the sapling. After the water wets them all, Chamling asks, oddly, whether they have 'heard' it. Kam does not mention shaking the sapling when describing the claim made by Chamling's opponent, and when Chamling calls on heaven the account is briefer than when he calls on earth.

When cosmic trees link heaven and earth, an offering of some sort is often made at the base of the structure – cf. the pig's blood at the base of the central pillar of the Limbu house (Ch. 3 Comparisons). The *cempra* bird (*bhaisi carā* N, literally 'buffalo bird') can possibly be seen, not only as playing its obvious role in the trick, but also as an offering that converts a mundane sapling, such as the others set up, into an effective cosmic axis allowing Chamling to communicate with Heaven and Earth; nothing suggests that the bird is rescued from its hole. Another characteristic of cosmic trees is that they are sometimes inverted. Common in early Indian mythology, similar inversions can be found in East Asia (Stein 1957a: 178). Perhaps the Thulung story contains a hint of the same idea, since a bird is more naturally associated with the top of a cosmic tree than with its base (cf. e.g., the turquoise bird at the top of the willow or poplar at the birth of gShen-rab). Conversely, primal waters are typically located at the base of symbols of the centre, whereas here the water is at the top of Chamling's tree.

In one way this episode is reminiscent of Ch. 3 I, where Jaw and Khliw tried unsuccessfully to kill Khakcilik by destroying his effigy. The implication appeared to be that such symbolic behaviour was intrinsically futile, not that the failure was due to, for instance, some fault in the execution. In the present episode we are presented with the paraphernalia of cosmic symbolism, and the situation is set up as if an important decision is seriously to be left to the supernatural powers – such procedures must be commonplace in the historical and ethnographic literature on dispute resolution, and the Buddhist story provides a good example. Instead of this, however, Chamling perverts the course of justice by means of a trick which, in real life, would be absolutely transparent.[10] It is as if the narrative were making fun of the procedure, just as in Ch. 3 it made fun of destroying effigies. This sceptical tone is at odds with the atmosphere of most Thulung traditions, in which the efficacy of symbolic behaviour goes without question – for instance, the blood offerings in II do effectively open the door. I am not sure whether diachronic conclusions can be drawn from the unserious character of the episode, but its absence from CP's account does contribute to the latter's consistency.

IV. In the Central Valley

CP So they came out, cutting the *moso*, cutting the Wild Plantain, swimming and hunting. They came up via the Sun Kosi river, and then they arrived over in the Central Valley (*nepaldu newardu*), and became the rulers. There they stayed, making themselves ornamented headdresses from *omri* fibres, making themselves Plumes and Brass Cymbals.[11] There they ruled, and accumulated rich Stores of Grain (?), splendid Robes, women's garments, satchels, and everything else (appropriate). They were kings and rulers.

The first sentence presumably refers to means of subsisting off the jungle in the course of migration: the *moso* or *moasa* tree (*bohori* N) was formerly used for making bird-lime to trap birds, the plantain is of course closely related to the banana, and the 'swimming' might be a reference to fishing as well as to crossing rivers. One notes the material culture appropriate to kings and rulers. The satchel (*sidimo*) is nowadays worn by priests as part of their ritual attire, but Khakcilik apparently wore one for

---

10 [The Panchatantra tells a comparable tale of formal dispute resolution involving trickery. The villain (a thief) hides his father in a hole in a mimosa tree, and when the goddess of the tree is asked who is guilty, the father bears false witness. In this case, the malefactors are unmasked and punished (Ryder 1949: 144-49).]

11 Here, as in CP VI, the correct translation may be 'Brass Objects'.

everyday purposes when he went fishing (Kam); we shall meet it again worn by Ramli when he goes to court a princess in Ch. 5 II.

Kam The view to the east is short, but when we look towards Nepal there is a wide open plain before us.[12] So our forefathers went to Nepal – Kirantsor, Banasor, Geanasor, and Ramli the youngest, and ... soon took power and set up a small kingdom there. Then Prithvi Narayan appeared, the Newar Raja. They fought a battle against him, and the Newar Raja was defeated, and driven off towards Bhatgaun. He came to a place called Kasi, the other side of Dapche Danda, and slumped down in the corner of a terraced rice field. Beside his leg, a dung beetle (*bhundiuyu, gogar* N) was trying to climb a ridge of earth, but each time it neared the top it fell back to where it had started. At long last it succeeded. Taking heart from the example of the insect, Prithvi Narayan decided to return and renew the battle. This time he was victorious. Our forefathers were defeated and the three elder brothers were killed. Geanasor met his death at a place related to Dhobi Dhara, Dilli Bazar, Kalo Pul and the river that runs in front of the Sinha Darbar. Kirantsor's effigy (*sālik* N) is in Hanuman Dhoka, Banasor's is this side of Sinha Darbar, Geanasor's is at Paspatithan, close to Gaurighat. I have seen all of them myself.

Just as the battle was starting the three elder brothers had called Ramli and said to him: 'Whatever happens, the enemy is onto us, and whether we live or die, we three shall stay. Leave the city while we are fighting. You are just a child, you are too young for this. You must get well clear of the city.' So Ramli was escorted away, over Sange Pass, while the three brothers battled on, and met their fate at the hands of Prithvi Narayan.

As in CP's version, and as is still common in the language of older people, 'Nepal' is used in the old sense of 'Central Valley'. The historical Prithvi Narayan was of course not a Newar but a Nepali-speaking king from a small state west of the Central Valley, whose place in the history of Nepal was briefly mentioned in Ch. 1 II. For those more familiar than I am with the Central Valley, Kam's reference to the effigies might offer clues to the nature of the Kirantsor trio.

---

12 This remark about the view appears also in a passage from Kam not used here, and is possibly something of a proverb or cliché.

The two versions of this episode share the tradition that at some stage in their past the ancestors of the Thulung were rulers of the Central Valley. This is a 'Thulung-centred' version of the tradition, well established in the literature on Nepal, that some two millennia ago there was a dynasty of Kiranti Kings in the Central Valley. The tradition was widely known locally, and some informants had views on the number of kings in the dynasty (e.g. thirty-three). I was also shown a primary school text-book which gave the names of two of these Kiranti kings. In view of the uncertainties attaching to ethnic nomenclature over long time spans, the chances of the tradition having any solid historical foundation are slim, and in any case, so far as the Thulung are concerned, this episode is surely to be seen rather as a mythological claim to association with an ancient and prestigious cultural centre, comparable to references to Benares and Lhasa. However, as in other such cases, e.g. the purported origin of the Chetris from Rajasthan, or that of the Newars from the Nayars of Southern India, one need not dismiss the possibility that small numbers of migrants may have been absorbed into the Rai, or even the Thulung, population.

V. Journey Eastwards

CP   As to where they arrived next – they came across and settled at Rajagaun. There they lived and quarrelled, ate and drank, and then they came across to Kirantichap and struck coins. There they stayed, all the ancestors together, carrying on their various activities. Thence they came to the Tamba Kosi, and then via Namdu Kabre up through the Jungle, up to Salungma Thanglema, where there is the Mortar for pounding grain. After staying there they came and settled at Junbesi Salabesi, and intermarried (?).

This is a reasonably straightforward account of the more northerly of the two main routes leading eastwards from the Central Valley. Rajagaun has not been identified. Kirantichap lies four miles south of Dolakha. Nowadays no Rai live there, but some Newar shopkeepers there told me that the name originated from a royal charter (*chāp* N 'stamp, seal, print'), which had granted some land in the area to a Rai in recognition of military services. Whether or not this is true, CP's version evidently derives from a different understanding of *chāp*. The river just east of Kirantichap is given on my map as the Bhota Kosi but it is one of the two branches into which the Tamba Kosi divides. Namdu, now mainly inhabited by Tamang, lies half a day's journey east of Kirantichap on the main route. Salungma Thanglema may be the Salung two miles south-east of Junbesi, though this does not seem particularly plausible. The 'Mortar' is possibly a natural rock formation: Okhaldhunga (N = 'mortar-stone') is said to have been named after such a feature. The last words of CP's version are *sālā-bhenā* (N) *bacci e*, 'they (dual) were (or stayed there as) wife's younger brother and elder sister's husband'. The phrase is obscure, but relates to the etymology or folk-etymology of Salabesi, which lies two miles south of Junbesi. According to another Tingla informant, the Thulung ancestor Ramli lived at Salabesi and his elder married sister at Junbesi. Another view is that the name commemorates Mapa's wife's younger brother (v. Ch. 5 IV). There are now no Rai at all resident in the area of the two villages (Oppitz 1968: 107).

Kam   So our forefather fled away from the city and came gradually eastwards across to the Solu Khola.

A journey eastwards is of course essential if continuity is to be established between ancestors who reign in the Central Valley and those who found the present-day Thulung villages. The chief interest of the episode lies in CP's statement that the journey was not continuous, but was broken by more or less prolonged residence at particular places. One may interpret this as a recollection of a period when the Thulung were in fact migratory shifting agriculturalists, but it is probably more important to recognise the typical pattern of the ritual journey. For the Thulung at least, such journeys are typically interrupted by pauses (*ŋeluŋ*). Moreover in talking of the ancestors arriving at new localities, CP twice uses the expression *bloara deop-*, apparently literally 'to appear suddenly at', an expression never used in ordinary prose conversation, but very frequent in chanted ritual journeys.

CP moves on next to the episode of Mini and the Sandalwood Tree, which has already been treated.

VI. In the North

CP   After washing, the next place he arrived at was Sunta Paramata[13] and Khuciu cave. He went up there, and stayed for a certain period. The

---

13   Or Suntala Parmatala.

next place he went was straight up to Tarangga. There the ancestors set up a Loom, made Brass Cymbals, and performed all the *diumla* and the like. They stayed up there – I don't know how many years it was – and then they arrived at Ramanjo, and there they established an *oganem* and performed all the *diumla*, carrying on their various activities and establishing an *oganem*.

Sunta Paramata was said to be 'below Dudh Kund', but neither it nor Khuciu cave has been precisely located. Tarangga, said by CP to be above Namche Bazar, can be confidently identified with the Tarnga or Tarangan which lies on the Bhote Kosi a few miles north of Thami in Khumbu. After making the tape, CP stated that Ramanjo was the ritual name of a place a little beyond Rapcha, but the name was given by several informants as that of the founding ancestor of Tingla, and CP himself uses it to refer to a founding ancestor in Ch. 5 IX. So possibly in the present episode we should read Rapcha in place of Ramanjo.

The episode alternates curiously between singular and plural verbs. Previously CP has always referred to the Ancestors in the plural, and his hesitation here may well be due to the immediately preceding episode concerning Mini.

An *oganem* (*nem* = 'house') appears to have been some sort of communal building. They have long been obsolete, and I could not learn their precise function. In later episodes (as Ch. 5 II) the *oganem* at Mukli is evidently a palace, but 'palace' seems inappropriate for buildings constructed during a migration.

No other narrator closely parallelled CP's version of this episode, but I shall introduce here two extracts whose original context can be determined from Table I. The first concerns a Kulung called Lunam, while the second starts with Lunam's son Mapa, ancestor of the Khaling.[14]

Karb (a) Now that their enemies, the five brothers, were dead, they looked for a place to live. Buckwheat seeds, barley seeds, short-haired barley seeds (*uwā* N), what excellent grains and vegetables, up at...[15] They went up to the strangers' settlement, up to Pangmuje Phorosa and Teangmoje Sangmoje. There they went and stayed. We people

---

14   I have standardised the name. Many narrators prefer Moapa, while Ant gives Moape. No other sources relate Khaling and Kulung in this way.

15   The lacuna is of about one line.

nowadays, their distant descendants, we hardly know these things, but they say that in the old days the territory (*kipaṭ* N) of the Kiranti extended up to there. The looms are still up there to this day. There they sojourned.

An intervening episode concerns the dealings of Mapa and Sherpas (Ch. 5 III).

Karb (b) Thereafter Mapa came to Jubing, and they came south above Cocium.[16] Mapa's son was Kangpas. Kangpas crossed the river to Rapcha, the place of the *pheaklim* tree and the *soaksam*, a place of great virtue, and there he was king. There they stayed, and nowadays all of them are Lasagotra, though they say they are Kasigotra – Kharithok(?) Khal they are called. I suppose that all the Khaling are the descendants of Mapa.

The places named in Karb (a) can be confidently located. Pangmuje is the old Sherpa village of Pangboche; the Phorosa to which it is coupled is the neighbouring Phortse; Teangmoje is the monastery Tengboche familiar to Western readers from accounts of Everest expeditions; and Sangmoje is probably Shyangboche near Namche. Rapcha appears in Ch. 5 DB IV as the place where Mapa became a god, and the village once enjoyed a certain religious pre-eminence. Its *pheaklim* tree (= *phipiri* N) was in some way also associated with the Creation. I do not know whether the *soaksam* was a separate species, nor in what sense the place possessed 'virtue'.[17] The notion of Kasigotra is discussed in Ch. 5 X.

CP's story is about the Thulung ancestors, while Karb's concerns the ancestors of other Rai subtribes. However they have in common that the ancestors in question travelled north and lived for a period in Khumbu, that while there they set up looms, and that thereafter they settled at or near Rapcha. Similar themes occur in Khaling tradition (Joiner):

The starting point for the Khaling migration was Chatra (= Barachatra). Maphe and his wife quarrelled with his brothers who were ancestral to

---

16 The place name, difficult to hear on the tape, is perhaps the Chochmi or Chochimi that lies just east of Wanku.

17 The word translated 'virtue' is *lacchin* N, = 'sign, mark'; but in Thulung usage I suspect contamination by *lacchimi* 'goddess of fortune, prosperity', i.e. Lakshmi.

other Rai groups, and he and his wife were chased up to Khumbu. They sojourned for a time at Dingboche where they cultivated Sherpa barley (? *uwā*). Thereafter they came down the Dudh Kosi to Jubing.[18]

We thus have three related migration stories. CP's and the Khaling story agree in starting at or in the direction of Chatra, and in leading up to the foundation of the narrator's village. Karb, a Thulung whose home village adjoins Khaling territory, makes the story apply to the father and son of the Khaling ancestor, and forms a sort of bridge between the other two. This will be relevant in Ch. 6 when we consider the diffusionist hypothesis that some Thulung narratives have spread from the north relatively recently.

Altogether, the tradition of a period of residence in Khumbu is curious. One sees why the Rai should claim a period of residence in the Central Valley, but it is less clear why they should claim to have lived in such a cold and nowadays alien region as Khumbu. Present-day Rai in my experience never live above 8,000 feet, whereas the villages in Khumbu are above 12,000 feet. Let us consider two possible ways of explaining the tradition.

Firstly, might the tradition contain a grain of historical truth? It is inconceivable that large numbers of Rai ever spent long periods in Khumbu, but it is possible that small groups lived there at certain periods, or that temporary visits were made, e.g. in the course of hunting expeditions. We need to mention here the Sherpas' claim that when they arrived in Khumbu from Tibet they found the area uninhabited by human beings (Oppitz 1968: 50); but this need not be taken at face value. For one thing, it might have been in the interest of Sherpas to claim that the land was uninhabited when they occupied it. Moreover, what the tradition actually says is that there were no humans, but that the forests of Khumbu were the home of a large variety of wild animals and birds. The list of species includes the *miti* and *dremar*, more familiar to non-Sherpas as species of yeti. Even if these terms

---

18   A link between Khumbu and weaving is made in the following report about the Khaling funeral rite, though the precise relationship between the rite and the migration of the ancestors is problematic.

'The priest (who specialises in this rite) as I understand it sends the dead man's spirit SE to Chatra and then brings him back to Jubing, and thence north up the Dudh Kosi past Namche to a place on the path between Tangboche and Pangboche called Dwonglamza. We got a Sherpa living there to point out the precise spot to us. It is a small clearing with a small stream. There are two trees which are said to be used for weaving, and at night one can hear the sounds of chickens and people' (Joiner).

are nowadays understood as referring to types of bear (and the point is debatable), it is not impossible that they were once understood as referring to indigenous peoples such as the Rai who, from the point of view of the Sherpas of that time, were so primitive and alien as to stand outside the category of the completely human. The folklore concerning yetis, including that reported by Oppitz, often ascribes to them remarkably human attributes, such as stealing Sherpa cattle and women, being afraid of malaria, and trying to imitate Sherpa agricultural practices.

Historical types of explanation are difficult to dismiss altogether, but hardly suffice to account for the Thulung and Khaling traditions. A second approach – a functionalist one – is to interpret the traditions as claiming that, historically speaking, the Rai owned all the territory up to the Himalayan watershed. Karb was not the only Thulung to believe that the Rai once had a nominal title to the whole tract, though his mention of 'strangers' (if the translation is correct), settled in Khumbu at the time of the visit, contributes little either for or against this explanation. Alternatively, or in addition, perhaps a claim was being made to connection with a place of high cultural standing. Nowadays the Thulung are well aware that, from a Hindu point of view, the Bhotes are beef-eaters and stand low in the caste hierarchy: intermarriage is strongly disapproved of for this reason. However in earlier times, the cultural achievements of the Sherpas might have inspired the respect of the Rai, and the references to looms and the working of brass may be seen in this light.

The functionalist type of explanation seems to me more plausible than the historical type, but still inadequate. A different approach will be presented after the final episode when we look at the migration as a whole.

VII. Foundation of Mukli

CP Then a Wild Boar appeared. Seeing that it had rich fertile Soil on its Body, our ancestor followed it. 'I wonder where it is, this rich Soil that the Boar has on its Body. I must follow the animal,' he said to himself. He wrapped some Ash in a Plantain leaf, tied it on the Boar's tail, and pierced a hole (in the packet), so as to follow the animal and find the fertile Soil. The boar set off and he followed behind ... and the line of ash from the hole led him down to Phuliuku. Thus our Ancestor came down to Phuliuku, and there too they established an *oganem*, and lived and quarrelled, following their Destinies in all things.

Whereas CP has the founder of Mukli arriving presumably from Rapcha, i.e. from the north, Kam has him arriving from the west.

Kam Thus our forefather lived all by himself with his two dogs up at Tumse. After he had been there for a long time, his two dogs chased a wild boar and killed it, over at Mukli, at Phuliuku. What they could carry (of the meat) they brought back themselves, and what they could not manage they left lying there ... and came back to look for their master. They would run up to their master and jump around him, nuzzling him (?), so that he would know that they had killed an animal but could not carry it all back. When he looked at the dogs he noticed great thick clusters of burrs, all over them. 'This must be a Place where Grain and Vegetables would flourish,' he said. Taking a *pĩḍālu* leaf, and making a packet of ash with it, he tied it onto their tails, and made a hole in it with a sharp stick. Off ran the dogs, leaving a trail of ash, and our forefather followed along behind. It was down at Mukli, at the place called Phuliuku, that they had killed it, a vast great boar. He broke it up into pieces and left half of it down there hanging up in a tree, and the rest he carried back with the dogs; half of it he made the dogs carry, half he carried himself, and what they could not manage he left in the tree. So they went away and ate it.

Kam does not state in so many words that this episode led to the foundation of Mukli, but his following episode has Ramli returning to an *oganem* at Mukli, and not to Tumse. Comparison with CP also strongly suggests that this must be the point of the story, and I cannot see what other point it could have.

The division of the meat by the dogs into what they can and cannot carry foreshadows the similar division made by their master later. The point of the first division is not clear, since the fact of the killing is apparently conveyed to the master not by any meat that the dogs carried, but by the way they jumped round him. In other respects too, the logic of Kam's version is obscure. If the dogs were as intelligent as is implied, why should they not have guided their master directly to the carcase, without the necessity of leaving a trail of ash? The master apparently understood from the way the dogs danced round him that they had killed some animal, and would presumably have followed them to it even if he had not noticed the burrs (which, as was agreed in Mukli, were good evidence of suitable land for agriculture). There is much greater economy and internal plausibility in

CP's version, where it is the boar himself who gives evidence of the good agricultural soil and who leaves the trail of ash. Even here, the idea of tying to a wild boar's tail a packet of ash in such a way that it would leave the required trail can hardly be regarded as practical. Whatever one is to make of the packet of ash, the tail of a pig is associated with guidance on a Thulung ritual journey in at least two other contexts (Allen 1974: 10).

Only two versions of the episode were tape-recorded, but others were briefly encountered. In Dewsa I heard that Ramli's forebears fled from Kathmandu and settled at Junbesi; the story that followed concerned a dog which ran from there to Mukli in one night, and mentioned his tail. In Mukli one informant stated that Ramli had arrived there from Paphlu, following his pigs.

Although the details of the episode are fanciful, for the first time we meet an account of an event which is almost certainly historical. All Thulung that I talked to were unanimous that Mukli was the first permanent Thulung settlement, and there is no reason to doubt the tradition. The emphasis on the agricultural potential of Mukli is also realistic. The hillside at the site of the original settlement faces south to south-east, which gives it at least as many hours of sunlight as any other Thulung village; it is well watered; and its relatively easy gradient in the altitude range 5000-6000 feet gives it further advantages.[19]

The Migration as a Whole

CP's continuous and stylistically consistent narrative proves that in at least one Thulung village an attempt has been made to conceptualise as a whole the events leading from the emergence of human beings on the surface of the earth up to the foundation of the first permanent settlements. These events take the form of a journey which starts from the plains (or possibly the Bay of Bengal) and ends in the hills. CP does not mention the period of residence at Majhuwa, but if the ancestors followed the Sun Kosi they had to pass close to it, and through traditional Rai territory. The same river leads them virtually to the periphery of the Central Valley. Thereafter they follow a more northerly route back eastwards into the Rai heartland, then divert northwards to Khumbu, before finally settling down.

If one can include CP's outward journey to the Primal Lake, the whole journey consists of three subordinate journeys, successively to the south-

---

19   [For fuller discussion see Allen 1997c.]

east, west and north, each starting from and returning to a centre. At first sight, one might try to relate the three journeys to the three hearth stones, one downhill and two up; but there is nothing to substantiate the idea. The journeys follow each other in a clockwise sequence, which is the normal manner of enumerating cardinal points in Buddhist Tibet; but again I doubt whether this is significant. Khaling tradition apparently knows only the first and third of the three journeys and Karb too says nothing of the visit to the Central Valley. This suggests that the westward journey is a separable motif: was it added to the others so as to incorporate the story of a Kiranti dynasty in the Central Valley, at the period when the political and cultural importance of Kathmandu began to make itself felt? If so, the Thulung myth at one time consisted of two journeys. We noted that the Place of Origin was located in the direction towards which rivers flow, and if there were only two journeys, the second would be in the direction *from* which they flow – Khumbu is the source of the Dudh Kosi.

More information is needed, but it is not clear that linking the journeys with rivers will explain all the questions that arise about the migration of the Thulung ancestors. One difficulty is the relationship to the death ritual. The journey of the dead soul might be expected to reverse the route taken by the ancestors, but in fact the Thulung dead are conducted to the south-west, in a more or less straight line which ignores the direction of flow of rivers. For the Khaling, the two journeys are more similar to each other, but the destination of the dead is five miles short of where the ancestors resided in the north, which in any case is not at the very source of the river.

Another difficulty is that if the rivers are the key to the question, it is odd that this was never pointed out. This might simply have reflected the lack of good informants or my inadequate enquiries, but one Thulung told me that after living in the Central Valley, some of the Rai settled for a time at Tingri Maidan (= Tingri Plain, well across the watershed into Tibet), 'but they did not like it there'. Moreover the pattern of two chanted journeys, one to the east or south-east, and one to the north, appears also in the Thulung *hutpa* rite described by Allen (1974: 8ff); it too sometimes terminates at Tingri. The origin of rivers in Khumbu was not only ignored by informants, but in these instances it would not even be relevant.

Although the 'river theory' cannot fully explain why at least two Rai subtribes claim once to have lived in Khumbu, it points, I think, to the right type of explanation. The northern journey must not be considered in isolation from the southern one. In Ch. 5 X we shall meet another Thulung story in which northern and southern journeys are coupled, and we shall find that the pattern is widely distributed in the Bodic area in connection with myths about founders and origins.

The Balance of Sexes

The move from chapters 2 and 3 to chapter 4 is marked by the abrupt and almost complete disappearance of females. Given that the Thulung language so seldom renders sex, one needs to see whether this is an artifact of translation. The word *seor* does not necessarily imply masculinity, since Wayelungma was once referred to (Ch. 3 IV CP) as the *blokuluŋ seorluŋ*, 'the deep-water stone, the ancestor stone'. The words *wa* and *loak*, translated respectively 'elder' and 'younger brother', can also mean 'elder' and 'younger sister'. Women's garments are specifically mentioned in CP IV, and the references in VI to looms and weaving certainly imply female activity: weaving is now a female prerogative among the Thulung and their neighbours, and the only weavers mentioned in the myths are Jaw and Khliw.

None of these points can be given much weight. Both Karb and Kam talk of the four 'brothers' using the unambiguous Nepali *bhāi*, and the sex of Ramli (and Mapa) will be confirmed in the next chapter. In Kam II the term for mother's brother cannot refer to females, and when Chamling exits with his 'Women-folk' it is certainly implied that he is male. Kam uses throughout, not *seor* 'ancestor', but *iki bep* or *iki bāje* N, which without context would be understood as 'our grandfather' (but is here rendered 'our forefather'). CP moves from *seor* to Mini and back again. In the face of all this, in spite of the looms, this is clearly a chapter in which all the emphasis is on males.

CHAPTER 5

Later Legends

Introduction

As its title implies, this chapter lacks any obvious unifying theme. It consists of what remained after subtracting from my total corpus of Thulung narratives those used in previous chapters, those analysed in other publications, and a few that were omitted for the reasons given in Appendix 1. However, the material is more consistent than the method of compilation might suggest. The first seven episodes and the ninth all refer to the characters Ramli or Mapa, whom we met briefly in the last chapter, and the actors in the eighth episode are of the same general type. Only the last two episodes stand apart from the rest and apart from each other; they form a sort of annex – interesting, but too short for an independent chapter, and even less appropriate in any other chapter than here. As for the first nine, apart from their personnel and their location in the north-west corner of the Rai tract, they have in common a certain uniformity of tone. Violence, or the threat of violence, is prominent in about half of them. Often the upshot is some kind of social change: the composition of an endogamous group is altered, innovations are made in economic or ritual life, or one population is replaced by another. In general the tone and language are secular, and with the exception of CP's episode IX, nothing suggests that the stories were ever recited at Thulung rituals.

Since the various Thulung episodes do not form a continuous whole, it has been more convenient to look for external parallels episode by episode, rather than waiting until all the Thulung material has been presented. Similarly, there is little scope for discussion of the chapter as a whole, and such general points as arise are treated in Ch. 6.

As table 1 shows, two narrators between them covered episodes I-VIII, and I have adjusted their order only in one respect. In Mukli (Ph and DB) the ordering of the first two episodes reverses that in Jubu and Lokhim. Both episodes tell of the wives of Ramli, and the reasons for preferring the Jubu-Lokhim order will be given after both episodes have been considered. Meanwhile, one should note that in episode I Ph refers to a wife whose acquisition he describes in Ph II. Ph had been present when DB told his version of I, and their accounts are so similar that DB's need not be given in full, especially since it has already appeared in Allen (1975a).

I. The Slug-eating Wife

Ph   After the bride's parents returned home, the couple lived together here for some time – I don't know how many years. Then she began to waste away. Day by day she declined, getting thinner and thinner for no apparent reason. 'I must go south to your parents and brothers, and ask them what has gone wrong with your ancestral spirits,' said Ramli. When he arrived, they asked him why he had come. 'Since your daughter came north, she has gone into a decline. I have come to ask whether there is something wrong with her ancestral spirits, or whether something else is the matter.' The people down there were slug-eaters, and when he raised the question of ancestral spirits they knew what was wrong. 'Stay here for the day, don't go till tomorrow. Your brothers-in-law are going hunting.' The next day, off they went carrying their bows and arrows, and came back bringing a bamboo tube full of slugs. Some of them they prepared and cooked, others they left raw; and they presented them to him with the following instructions: 'Take this north to our daughter without looking at it on the way, and give it to her. It is her medicine.' When he arrived, she took it off somewhere and ate it. The next day she was already better, and thereafter she grew steadily stronger. In a couple of days she had put on so much weight that she got stuck going out of a door. 'Good gracious! What kind of people can they be if they eat this sort of thing?

It's horrifying! I shall have to get rid of her.' He set out to take her back to her parents.

They had just crossed Cirku bridge when he proposed a pause. While they were resting, he offered to look for his wife's lice, and as he was doing so she fell asleep. He laid her down gently on the ground, and going back across the river, destroyed the bridge. Having planted a stone, he came north, and ever since then between male or female Bahing and us Thulung there has been no intermarriage. Since Ramli planted the stone and uttered his vow there has been no intermarriage (*seor*).

The Thulung cult of the 'ancestral spirits' (*səsi-roksi*) cannot be fully discussed here. In some villages at least, they are particularly associated with in-coming wives. They are recognised as occasionally causing illness, but it is not clear why Ramli immediately assumes that this is his wife's diagnosis. Apparently, the woman ails because her spirits ail, and her spirits ail for want of her accustomed diet. However, other relationships might link the spirits and the slugs; perhaps, for instance, her vital spirits *are* slugs. The word *dawāi* N, translated 'medicine', can certainly refer to substances whose mode of action is less purely physical than the English word suggests. The slugs (*ciple kirā* N) were said to be about three inches long, and are still regarded by Thulung as disgusting. No doubt the hunters' bows are intended to mislead Ramli.

DB's version diverges in the following respects. No mention is made of Ramli's diagnosis, and it is his wife who sends him south; he is to bring back her 'eating-stuff'. Ramli brings back two tubes, the first containing seasoned slugs, the second raw ones. On the final journey south the couple stop at a stone resting-place (*cautārā* N) at Kharbari (not located), where Ramli's wife falls asleep with her head on his thigh. The woman is simply abandoned, no mention being made of destroying or blocking the bridge.

As to the origin of the woman, II DB refers to her, not specifically as a Bahing, but as belonging to the family or region of Waye-Luna or Wayecapciu-Luna. In contrast, PH II takes the name Wayecaptiu as relating to a group living to the south of Ramli's parents-in-law, who are themselves clearly Bahing. As a free-standing word the element *waye* in the name means 'low-lying land'.[1] Luna however seems definitely to be associated

---

1 *Wayebuŋ capcebuŋ* is the ritual name for a species of flower (or possibly for a category of flowers) used in garlands.

with the village of Necha, which is sometimes regarded as Thulung, sometimes as Bahing, sometimes as not quite either. Cirku (or Cirpu, according to another informant) is close to the junction of the Dudh Kosi and Solu Khola, and the bridge would therefore in fact have led to Necha.

Ant Ramli the Kiranti was king over at Depku, and married a woman from down at Benoseobdel. As she seemed to be in fatal decline, she sent her husband Ramli down to her parents' home. All night long his mother-in-law cooked slugs, which she then gave to him. On his way north he wondered what they were, and looked and saw they were cooked slugs. After his wife had spent the night eating them she became stronger, so much so that she could not get out though the door and became stuck. Ramli pretended to his wife that her mother had told him to bring her down to her whatever happened. So he took her off, together with their one son, and abandoned them. After returning north he vowed that his family should never again marry women from Benoseobdel.

Depku is a hamlet in the east of Mukli, not otherwise particularly noteworthy or associated with Ramli. Ant was the only narrator to locate the woman's home at Benoseobdel, which is now one hamlet within the village of Panchen. I have no other evidence of prejudice against marrying women from Panchen, who appear to be as pure Thulung as anyone else. The motif of sticking in a doorway recalls Khomda in Ch. 2 II Mj.

Kam Our forefather Ramli, the youngest, came east to Solu Morku, and while he was living there he married a Bahing woman. They lived for a while below Tumse ridge where the Kangel path goes down, the path for Mukli and Nele Pasal[2] comes across, and the path from Solu goes steeply downhill – that's where our forefather's house was at that time. I once showed it to your grandmother[3] – on a platform just so high, like the one...(?) The ruins of Ramli's own house are still there, with some of the stones just as he left them, but not very high. That is where he lived with the Bahing woman and his two dogs. The dogs killed game of all sorts, deer, wild goat, wild boar – in those days

---

2   *Pasal* N = 'shop'. The weekly bazar at Nele was founded in the early 1960's, but Kam's name for the place probably goes back to an earlier period.

3   Kam is addressing my host in Lokhim, who had accompanied me on the visit.

game was plentiful. They lived in the midst of jungle surrounded by wild animals of all sorts, which their dogs hunted and brought to them as food.

Then the Bahing woman went into a decline, getting worse day by day. In those days around here they used to sow just a very little *sakyo*, like *malindo* – that made up their agriculture, together with some amaranthus and *nemsi*:[4] otherwise they ate nothing but meat, day after day. When the woman had wasted down to almost nothing, she sent him down to her natal family. 'I must be dying, I am sure. I have barely any strength left. Go quickly and take the news to my brothers.' Off he went to his in-laws in the Bahing settlement – actually his wedding had not been formally completed. On his arrival they asked with some surprise where he was journeying and why. 'Nothing special. I just came to see you and bring greetings.' 'How is our child?' 'She is still alive, but I don't know, something is wrong. She has become so wasted she can do little more than breathe. It is only her skin that keeps her together. She sent me down to you because she thinks she is dying.' They gave him a meal, recognising the trouble as soon as they heard that she was wasting. The Bahing are slug-eaters, as you know – that is the name we call them. Up they went to their cattle shelter to look for slugs, which the Bahing and Rumdali call *nelepo*. They brought them down, cooked them, and told him to take them to their girl. Some of them cooked a meal, others cut a bamboo tube with a cover, others busied themselves in other ways, while Ramli just sat there, saying nothing to anyone and no one saying anything to him. They fried the slugs and put them in stoppered containers – for their own good reasons, and after they had given him a decent meal, they gave him them in the bottom of a sack together with various gifts – gifts of meat, I suppose. 'Mind you don't look in this tube!' said his mother-in-law. 'Take it and give it to my daughter, but don't open it or look inside.' However Ramli was curious and somewhat anxious. On the road he decided to open the container, and inside he saw the slugs. He closed it up again carefully, deeply upset. 'Do they really eat this sort of thing? What is it for if not for eating? I'll take it and see what happens. My wife will know what to do with it.' When he arrived,

---

4   *Malindo* and *sakyo* or *sawyo* were equated with *sāmā* N, a weed that grows among rice and is nowadays thrown away. *Nemsi* = *silām* N, which I have not been able to identify botanically.

he opened the sack. 'Look and see what your family have sent you in this tube. They told me not to look in it and I didn't. But what can it be?' When he gave her the sack, she took the whole thing into the house. Ramli stayed around outside, extremely uneasy. Wondering to himself whether she would eat the stuff or throw it away, he peeped in. Immediately she had the sack indoors, she gobbled down the slugs.

This was too much, and Ramli decided to take her back to her own home. 'How can I possibly settle down with this woman? I am not going to keep a person with such disgusting eating habits.' Some time later he wondered how she was getting on. Day by day she was getting stronger, and in six or seven days she had become quite big and round, walking with a waddle, with cheeks as red as a rhododendron flower. So that was what they were like, he thought. 'Right,' he said to her, 'Now you are better, let us go down to your natal family. Your relatives have all been worried about you. Now you can walk, let's go and see them.' The Bahing woman was delighted. They got together gifts of meat – tiger, bear, wild boar, all kinds, which their dogs brought back to them every day. Some they cooked, some they took raw. Ramli gave them to his wife to carry, putting them all in a cloth on her shoulder. And so they set off.

Down at Solu Morku river, between Tingla on the one side and Tumse on the other, where the path goes along to Seobdel,[5] there was a bridge known as Murku bridge. When they came to the mouth of the bridge, Ramli pretended to go aside for a call of nature. He took the bundle he had placed on her shoulder, and put it down on a ridge between the fields. Meanwhile his wife had crossed to the other side of the bridge. Ramli now picked up a vast boulder, big and long. Digging a hole at the entry to the bridge, he planted the boulder firmly in it. It is still there. 'Let my descendants and family never take Bahing wives,' he vowed. His wife saw that he had set up the boulder, and Ramli gestured to her with his hand signalling her to be off. Then he picked up the bundle and came straight home again. That is how he got rid of his Bahing wife.

Kam locates this episode before the Foundation of Mukli, and the dogs mentioned here are the ones which, in his account, led Ramli to the

---

5   Seobdel is for Benoseobdel. Tumse is the ridge five minutes' walk west of Nele.

slain boar. Nowadays too, it would be unusual for a man to make a solo visit to his wife's natal home. Ramli's misleading remark on his arrival there is a matter of politeness: it would be discourteous to broach too abruptly the reason for his coming. It would nowadays also be unusual to take cooked meat as a present, so perhaps the raw-cooked duality has been transferred from the slugs to which it applies in the Mukli versions.

Although in Kam's version the stone could be interpreted as actually or symbolically blocking access to the bridge, in the Mukli versions it seems to be associated with the making of the vow, perhaps symbolising its durability. The custom of setting up a stone when taking an oath has been reported in modern times from Kham and Sikkim, and is mentioned on a Tibetan stele of 730 AD and in the Tun-Huang Chronicle (Stein 1972: 200).[6]

If we follow the two versions that definitely present the woman as a Bahing, we can envisage an historical interpretation close to that of Ph himself. With reference to the story, Ph pointed out that in Mukli at least it was still thought unwise to marry Bahing women. He gave two examples of such marriages that had come to grief, one owing to the premature death of both partners, one owing to quarrels between co-wives, which resulted in the non-Bahing wife leaving for Darjeeling with her two school-age children. However, according to Shafer's taxonomy, Bahing is among the languages most closely related to Thulung, so it is not implausible that they were once spoken by a single intermarrying population. One might imagine that recognised symbolic actions once existed to mark the severance of marital relations between segments of a single subtribe. A difference in dietary habits between the two subtribes, whether real or imaginary, is also not implausible, especially in the light of Kam's reference to Slug-eaters; and although a sense of superiority based on such dietary differences is of course typical of the Hindu world, one need not here ascribe the idea to Hindu influence. Thus the episode could contain elements of historical truth, as well as serving as a charter for a contemporary attitude.

However, before going further with the Thulung story, we should take account of parallels from the area. The motif of putting a woman to sleep by delousing her appears rather curiously in the Lepcha story of the origin of marriage, where the delouser is himself an insect (Gorer 1967: 461). More interesting for our purposes is a parallel from Tibet, whose fullest

---

6   All four Thulung versions use Nepali *kiriyā* for 'oath' or 'vow'. I do not know a Thulung equivalent.

available version comes from a text of 1376 translated by Ariane Macdonald (1971: 230-2). I abbreviate the end of the story, which is not relevant. The main characters are king 'Bro-mnyen (or 'Brong-gnyan) lde-ru, twenty-ninth in the mythological dynasty; his queen Klu-rgyal ngan-bu mtsho, a woman from the mChims people of Dvags-po; and their son, who was to be the grandfather of Srong-btsan sgam-po.

> At first the queen is like the daughter of a god rather than a human, but later she begins to grow ugly. The king asks her what is wrong: 'Is it a matter of the food or the clothes you are getting?' She attributes her transformation to the lack of an article of diet that exists in her natal country but not in her present home. The King tells her to make arrangements for the food to be brought, and she sends a reliable serving maid. The servant fries in butter a large number of frogs and returns with loads of them on horses and half-breed cattle. The two woman hide the frogs in the treasure house, and on eating them recover their former strength and beauty. The king thinks that he too should eat a substance that has such desirable effects. He ignores the warnings of his minister, and sends his wife on a journey to other parts of the kingdom. While she is away, he opens the door with an imitation key. When he sees the mass of dead frogs, he experiences a profound sense of disgust and apprehension. 'This is no human being that I have married, but a demon,' he thinks to himself. (As a result of his state of mind) the king falls ill from leprosy, and when the queen his wife gives birth, their son is blind. The king, the queen and one of his ministers are buried alive. Just as he is entering the tomb, the king leaves his blind son instructions to worship the protector spirits of his ancestors and to summon a healer who will cure his blindness. The instructions are followed and the blindness is cured.

A few additional or variant details can be found in the two versions given by Hoffmann (1950: 299f, 317). The wife is at first healthy and exceedingly beautiful, but then she develops a greenish complexion and grows thin. The queen eats the fried frogs in secret, without people being able to see. There is no mention of the minister or of a deliberate plan to get the queen out of the way. In the briefest version, it is *because* the queen belonged to the race of serpents that she hid the frogs (apparently described as low or vile) in a store-room.

The point of the Tibetan story is not very clear, and Tibetologists approach it in different ways. Hoffmann (1950: 158) discusses it in relation to the Tibetan concept of serpents (*klu*), arguing that an indigenous concept was in fairly early times glossed over with the Indian notion of the *nāga*.

He regards the king's leprosy as punishment for his discovery of the secret and for his reaction to the frogs, and cites another story about a Buddhist sage who punishes a later Tibetan queen with leprosy. The Tibetan for leprosy, *klu-nad*,[7] is a translation of Sk *nāgarog*, and the association of serpents and leprosy indicates Indian influence.

Haarh (1969: 334-9) uses the story in a chapter on the death and burial of the Tibetan king, claiming that ritual regicide was an established institution. He argues that 'the essential importance of these accounts is to be found in the facts *that the king resigned and took his own life because of the physical defect caused by the leprosy*, and *that the recovery of the heir's eyes was the condition for his accession to the throne*' (ibid: 338).

Macdonald uses the story when discussing the completeness of the Tun-Huang Chronicle, one of the most important Tun-Huang manuscripts. When the Chronicle omits stories such as this, which are well known from later literature, it is not because the stories are of later origin, but simply because the Chronicle is not a complete compilation of the narratives current at the time when it was composed. It would be astonishing, she considers, if the story of the frog-eating queen had not in some form or other inspired the bards of the early period from which the Tun-Huang documents date. On the other hand, she maintains, the king's instructions to his son about the worship belong to the period beginning in the tenth century when the old traditions were being recast in Buddhist moulds.

The Tibetan story differs from the Thulung in points of detail. Frogs replace slugs; it is a servant, not the king, who goes for them; they are carried in large quantities on pack animals (which Thulung do not use), rather than in a tube in the bottom of a sack; the king's son succeeds him, unlike the son who is abandoned in Ant's version, and so on. Moreover the parallel breaks down after the king's 'mind is broken' (to translate Kam literally). Up to this point, however, the two traditions are clearly related. Their common core is a male king/ancestor who marries a woman from a different region, who is not a human being of the same kind as himself. Without a supply of frogs/slugs from her home region she wastes away, and only recovers when her supply is restored. She and (where relevant) her relatives try to keep secret the nature of the food-stuff on which she is dependent, presumably because they anticipate the husband's adverse

---

7   Leprosy is also called *mdze-nad*. There are two types, 'red' and 'grey' (Nebesky-Wojkowitz 1956: 291).

reaction. However the latter is curious and finds out surreptitiously. When he does so, he is both disgusted and shocked.

The Tibetan parallel prompts a deeper look at precisely what it is that makes the woman unfit to be Ramli's wife. In the Tibetan version not only does the wife's name contain the components Klu-rgyal 'Serpent-queen' and *mtsho* 'lake', but some sources state explicitly that she belongs to the race of serpents; presumably (Hoffmann), that is why she needs food of such a watery character. It may be significant that Dvags-po lies to the east of Yarlung, i.e. downstream from it, and also that it has a reputation for 'barbarism' (Stein 1972: 41). In being a serpent, the queen is a sort of throw-back to her predecessors in the mythical royal dynasty; the first twenty-two or -three queens left no bodies at their deaths since they were not mortal women but 'the daughters of gods and/or serpents' (Hoffmann 1950: 158). In the Thulung episode the wife and her people are presented as alien insofar as their dietary habits are disgusting, but at first sight nothing relates them to serpents. Whereas frogs, having a tadpole stage, are necessarily associated with water, slugs are not. Nevertheless, if one looks for them, certain clues relate the slug-eater to the world of serpents rather than to that of fellow tribesmen.

Only two versions state unambiguously that the wife belonged to the Bahing subtribe. We do not know for sure that the river (or Kharbari) formed the boundary between Thulung and Bahing territory – my impression is that in this area it is ridges, rather than rivers, that typically form territorial boundaries between ethnic groups. All that is really clear is that she comes from the south, from 'low-lying' land, which connotes either land close to the rivers that form the lowest point of valleys, or more remotely, land towards which rivers flow. Benoseobdel lies low down in Panchen, while Cirku bridge lies close to the very lowest point in the village; moreover to cross the bridge is to go yet further south. Kam's bridge is apparently located closer to Tingla, but the woman is still abandoned by the riverside. Again, if one follows DB, part of her parents' name is Wayecapciu, and one cannot help being reminded of Wayelungma, whose other name was Nagimo.

The comparison with Tibet does not mean that the historical interpretation of the Thulung episode should be rejected outright. The latter may indeed reflect the local history of marital relations between nascent subtribes, as well as later opinions about these relations; but there is probably an older or deeper level of meaning to the story. The last chapter showed clearly that Thulung mythology makes an association between the south, the Place of Origin and a primal lake, and in episode XI when we return to the connotations of frogs and serpents, we shall find that they too are often related to primal lakes. The implication may be that, in rejecting their wives, Ramli and 'Bro-mnyen are in some sense dissociating themselves from the watery beginnings of society.

However, the relationship between the present episode and the Creation does not depend solely on lakes and their inhabitants, as the following table shows. It mainly uses the Tibetan version of the present episode, but some details from the Thulung are included in brackets.

Thulung Creation	Frog-eater (Slug-eater)
1. The star appears beautiful: Miyapma summons him.	1. The queen is very beautiful: The king marries her.
2. Seen at close quarters the star is disgusting. The star is rejected.	7. In her private behaviour the queen is disgusting. (The slug-eater is rejected).
3. Star causes drought.	2. The King's country lacks frogs.
4. Star leaves abnormal water in hollow tree.	5. (Ramli brings cooked slugs in bamboo tube.)
5. Star leaves instuctions ensuring M will drink water.	4. King gives queen instructions ensuring she will obtain frogs.
6. For lack of water Miyapma becomes comatose.	3. For lack of frogs the queen languishes.
7. Miyapma drinks abnormal water.	6. Queen eats frogs.
8. Miyapma gives birth to Mini	8. Queen gives birth to blind son.
9. The star was leprous (Kam).	9. The king contracts leprosy.
10. Miyapma is buried.	10. King and queen enter tomb.

In both crises it is the female who needs the water/frogs, and nearly dies for lack of it/them. Apart from the difference in the order of the elements, there is one major contrast between the two stories. In the Thulung Creation, the male star is the outsider and Miyapma is the focal character, her home being the main location. The other story presents the reverse situation: the female is the outsider, the king is the focus, and the action takes place at the home of the patrilineal Yarlung dynasty to which he belongs. If the second story were solely Tibetan, this would just be another example of the differing emphasis given to the two sexes in the two bodies of mythology. But the second story has a Thulung version as well as a Tibetan one, and the Thulung version is no less male-centred than the Tibetan; if anything, it is even more androcentric, in that Ramli suffers no enduring effects from his dealings with the slug-eater. What then is to be made of the relationship between the three stories? We shall return to the question in Ch. 6.

II. Contest for Rathongma

Ph Long ago at Phuliuku there was a king called Ramli, who went to the Bahing settlement to look for a consort. Some people called Wayecaptiu came up to the same house from the south, and encountered Ramli. The parents of the maiden wondered whether to give her to the people from the south or to Phuliuku in the north. Ramli had gone there dressed in clothes that were far from beautiful, and was covered in oil-dregs, while Wayecaptiu and the people from the south were clad in splendid garments and their persons too were altogether prepossessing, in marked contrast to Ramli. 'If we give her to Phuliukuceo in the north, Wayecaptiu will be angry, if we give her to Wayecaptiu, Ramli of Phuliuku will be vexed. What shall we do about it?'

'Right' said the father, 'We must set these people a contest and give her to the victor; then they will be satisfied.' After thinking about it he decided to make them fell trees. To the Wayecaptiu party he gave axes with a sharp edge – he took them up to the blacksmith's and had them dealt with, while to Ramli he gave a blunt old axe – without any sort of proper cutting edge. But Ramli noticed that the others had been given sharp axes while his was blunt and useless, so he took it and rubbed it vigorously on a rough stone, and only when he had given it a decent edge did they set off for the forest. When they asked for instructions the father indicated the hillside above. The Wayecaptiu party surrounded the trunk of a huge old tree and started cutting at it from all sides. Ramli gave a quick glance at the situation and set about just notching tree after tree on the upper side until eventually he came out on top of the ridge. Then he gave a whistle and along came the wind with a mighty gust, and with its help he cut down the whole lot all at one go. Meanwhile the Wayecaptiu party had at long last succeeded in cutting down just the one big tree. When they returned, people asked what they had done and where they had cut, and they had to tell how Phuliukuceo had been victorious by his own methods while they had only felled a single tree.

When the time came for the meal, the father again split them up. To Phuliukuceo they gave maize, to Wayecaptiu they gave a delicious meal of rice and meat, lentils and ghee. After the meal they got ready to sleep, and the maiden's mother told the girl's younger brother to go and keep an eye on this strange Phuliukuceo. He went to Ramli and proposed they should sleep next to each other, but Ramli was not to be persuaded. 'I have got diarrhoea, I warn you; you go over there and don't sleep near me.' And so he slept by himself.

'Here too this Phuliukuceo has got the better of us, just as in the tree cutting. What is to be done?' said the parents. 'Let us make them split wood for torches, and then give her to the victor.' They gave the party from Wayecaptiu perfect straight-grained wood, but what they gave Ramli was all twisted and full of knots. Ramli noticed at once that the others' wood was easy to split and his was all knots, but he heated his in the fire, and when he took it out, it was as easy to split as bamboo, while the fine wood they had given to the Wayecaptiu lot became like twigs and impossible to split. So here again Ramli was the victor. 'What shall we do? This Phuliukuceo has won. Let's just pretend to give him the girl. We'll take her up there, then when we return we'll bring her back down again and give her to Wayecaptiu.' So they told Ramli he was the victor and promised him the girl. As the party was bringing her up here, just as they were about to arrive at the houses, Ramli began taking off his clothes and hanging them on tree-trunks, first the shirt, then the other garments, one by one. And so they came up to look. But when they arrived at his house or *oga* – Heavens above! It was quite magnificent, all lit up, shining like candles. When one passed inside, it was enough to make one giddy. When they arrived, they were quite overwhelmed. 'If we don't give her to someone like this, who on earth *should* we give her to? We had no idea he was this sort of person.' So they left their daughter there, stayed for a while and then returned.

The general outline of the episode is clear. In contrast to the other suitors Ramli presents himself as dirty and unprepossessing, but by means of quick wits and magical prowess he eventually triumphs. Smaller points are best left until all the other versions have been presented. In this case the divergences from DB are sufficient to make it worth giving the latter in full.

DB Long ago, Ramli Raja went to Wayecapciu-Luna to look for a wife. Wayacapciu had a daughter and a whole crowd of young men had come as suitors. Ramli arrived all smeared with oil dregs, while the others were in their finest clothes; but in the end his magical power brought him success.

Ramli was given just cooked maize and vegetable juice to eat, while the others all had rice and meat. Ramli picked up the meat bones that were left over and put them in his bag. Then the girl's parents announced: 'Let us see then who can cut down the most forest. It shall be to him that we give our daughter.' Having made this promise, they distributed axes – sharp ones to the other suitors, a blunt one to Ramli; but as they went towards the forest Ramli sharpened his axe on a rough stone. Then he set to work, cutting all the largest trees just half way through, until eventually he reached the ridge. Then he gave a whistle, and the storm wind came and blew down all the half-cut trees in one tremendous pile. Meanwhile, the well-dressed suitors had not cut down a single tree all day long.

So Ramli was the victor, and the girl's parents wondered what on earth to do. In the end they made a second promise: 'Let us see who can capture the male and female seeds of the *le*. He shall be the one that gets our daughter.' At the place where the *le* couple dwelt, a dog was tied up. Taking the bones that he had collected in his bag after the others' meal, Ramli poured them out in a pile, and while the dog was busy with them, he undid its chain and captured the *le* couple.

Thus Ramli was acknowledged victor at last, and took the girl from Waycapciu-Luna, and brought her north. So far he had looked repulsive, smeared with oil dregs; but when they came up here to his palace, the path to the washing place at the spring was paved with coins, and when he washed he was like a ball of wool.

There are two versions from Ant, since the first was so evidently compressed that on a second visit I asked him to amplify it.

Ant (a) After that he married Rathongma, daughter of the Raja over at Capleti. Eight suitors had come for the hand of the princess.

Measuring out the number of trees, he made them all cut down the jungle. Meanwhile, Ramli put the meat they gave him into his two satchels. Taking axes, they went to cut the jungle. Ramli went along cutting trees just half way though, and then from the top collected the whole lot at once, forming one great pile. By the time he came down, none of the others was yet half way through a single tree. And so it was Ramli who took Rathongma.

Ant (b) As to how Ramli married Rathongma over at Capleti, there were eight suitors who had come for the girl, and the Raja made them cut down jungle, measuring it out by the number of trees. In the evening he gave them a good meal of rice and meat. Ramli ate only the rice and put all the meat into his two satchels, one on his left side, one on his right. When they went to cut the jungle, the others started felling the trees completely one by one. Ramli went along just cutting them half way through, then from the top of his stretch of jungle brought down four trees in one go and picked up the whole bundle.

After this he came down to the palace of the Capleti Raja, in which there was some *le*. *Le* meant the special mark of the *bhĩguma* N bird; the *le* was in the palace together with the *bhĩguma* bird – no, they call it the *saŋwa* bird. Two dogs were tethered there, preventing access. Ramli took the meat from his two satchels and gave it to the dogs. The dogs forgot their duty over the meat, and Ramli was able to take out the *le* together with the *saŋwa* bird, and hide them in a fold of his clothing. After he had taken everything out, the others returned from above. Thereafter Rathongma garlanded Ramli, and they got married and produced eight sons.

The name Rathongma (or Rathungma), while not attached to this particular story in Mukli, was recognised there, and was sometimes used proverbially to mean 'princess'. 'You are not a Rathongma, you know,' a man might exclaim in irritation to an over-demanding wife. Capleti is situated a few hours' walk to the south-east of Jubu. In a cursory reference Mj VII locates Rathongma's home at Sungdel, a few miles further on up the Rawa Khola. The number eight attached to the suitors probably comes from the eight sons born of the eventual marriage (for whom see Ant VII).

Kam So things continued, until one day he said to himself: 'What's going to become of me? Some time ago I brought in this woman, but then I got rid of her. What now, how am I going to manage?' In those days trees used to speak – and stones, everything in the jungle, all the boulders, even the house used to speak, and he addressed his question to them. 'There is a wife just suited to you, Thulu, away over in the Chamling settlement.' So they answered him, and off he set. The name of the Chamling woman was Rathongma, and as he went he kept asking the trees and stones the way to her village.

When he arrived he found that Rathongma's father was exceedingly wealthy and thousands of suitors had come, thousands of them for this one girl. So Rathongma's father set them competitions. At that time they were clearing jungle and he showed them the trees they were to cut down to win his daughter. Every day there was feasting in his house. So they set off, some of them with good axes, some with bad ones – there were lots of them, fifteen or twenty, but all of them Kiranti, from one subtribe or another – fifteen or sixteen arrived every day to sue for Rathongma. Most of them wore expensive white cotton turbans and clothes of all kinds of good material, while Ramli just had on his *thulumakte* and was not an attractive sight. Every day they killed buffaloes or sometimes goats – the whole thing lasted for days. The others were given proper rice meals, while Ramli just got ground maize served with a stew of bones. He collected all the bones and put them in his satchel. In those days the type of satchel called a *sidimo* belonged only to us Thulung, the sort that is worn by officiants, like the present day *jholā*[8]... anyway Ramli ate only the juice, and took away the bones in his satchel. The Chamlings looked on our forefather with disfavour, trying to avoid giving him the girl. That is why for the woodcutting they gave him a blunt axe and for the meal they gave him only maize and bones. However, he possessed magic powers. The task set was to cut down and pile up a quantity of sixteen trees on one occasion. Ramli could see what to do. Going up the side he cut the trees just half way through, and when he came to the top he cut the largest tree. And so he felled all sixteen at once into a pile, thus gaining the victory.

Even so, the Chamlings had no trust or liking for Ramli. The others had their fine white turbans, trousers and tunics, while our forefather was wearing a *ramlimakte*, such as is still worn by the Bahing when

8   Kam refers to the ethnographer's satchel.

they perform *nagi* or *sekro* rituals.[9] The price of a *thulumakte* is unbelievable, two hundred rupees, or twelve score rupees, and it is ornamented with *omri* fibre. Anyway, over the ridge, up at Mayung there was a *le* plant used for making large necklaces – you know the large amulets people put around their necks – at its base there was this necklace, such as is now beyond price. It belonged to Bhagavan – indeed it was like Bhagavan, himself, like the Goddess of fortune, Laksmi (?). So they set another contest, promising their daughter to whichever of the suitors pulled up the *le* plant. They sent a whole crowd of them to get it, but Ramli took a quick look at the lie of the land and went straightaway up along the ridge to the foot of Tentelekh, where the plant was situated.[10] Bhagavan's dogs (were waiting there). From his satchels he poured out one pile of bones downhill for the lower dogs, and one pile uphill for the upper dogs, ran in between them, whipped away the *le* plant and came down with it in his satchel. 'My journey is done,' he cried to the others – he used the old Thulung turn of phrase. 'Let me bid you good day'. While he was hastening south, the others were collecting sackfuls of *le* excrement.

Back at Rathongma's home he at first hid his success. The girl's father said: 'If they have pulled it out there will be no light, if they have not there will be.' The night was dark. Towards evening,[11] when the evening star (normally) shines, (that day) it did not shine. But as night drew on, Ramli's body began to glow like a firefly. All that the others brought was a great heap of *le* excrement. Rathongma's father was unhappy, because Ramli had been so unprepossessing. 'This Thulu was victorious in collecting the wood, and now he has brought the *le* plant. But how can I give my daughter to someone so unattractive? On the other hand, he has won'... (Ramli taunts them, and they try to ingratiate themselves with him). 'I must be a knave, dressed in these rags, not good enough even for nettles and ground maize.'[12] Suddenly

---

9   Kam uses *ramlimakte* and *thulumakte* interchangeably; *makte* simply means 'upper garment'. To judge from the Tingla *narimakte*, worn at similar ceremonies, Ramli was wearing an unlined cotton jacket with sleeves, probably dyed with local dyes and ornamented with *omri* fibre.

10   No doubt the 'Temke Range' ten miles east of Majhuwa Diktel, in which case the Mayung mentioned above may be the 'Mayam Danda' that continues Temke ridge to the north and east.

11   Literally: 'At the time when one shuts up the chickens'.

12   Both types of food, especially nettles, are proverbially humble fare.

he drew the *le* out and cast it down in front of them, shining bright, large and branching. Everyone was amazed and bowed down before it. The Chamlings, who had been given the meat and rice, slunk off without so much as a by-your-leave.

Meanwhile, Ramli was given the seat of honour and dressed up as bridegroom, now that he was clearly the victor in the contest. The next day they fed him with the finest food, and Rathongma's clansmen made him a tunic and trousers of the best white cloth, in place of his *thulumakte*. They also bound a white turban on Ramli's head as groom and a head-cloth on his bride, and prepared to send them off. 'Have a good journey to the *oganem*' – the *oganem* is still there, or at least its site is still visible, over in Mulki by the Phuliuku river. It is very long, like a compartment in a train. Anyway, they arranged to bring their daughter over after a certain number of days, in a wedding procession. 'You must have friends and neighbours, and fellow clansmen. You will want to assemble them and get ready everything needed for a wedding. Then we shall bring over our daughter and hold the proper ceremony.' They sent him off with these words, and Ramli took his leave. They had given him back his *thulumakte*, and (on his way) he took off his new clothes, and left the tunic wrapped round a tree trunk. He hammered a stake into the ground, dressed it in the trousers, and wound the turban round the trunk which he had dressed in his tunic. In their stead he put on his old *ramlimakte*.[13] He also brought with him the *le* plant they had given him…

On the agreed day Rathongma's parents set out to bring her over. Ramli had been saying: 'Shortly there will be people coming, and asking for me, people who gave me offence in such and such ways. When they ask to be directed to my house, tell them that it is way up there.' When they went a little further, he arranged for them to be misdirected again, and so on, playing a little trick or them. When at long last they arrived, he pretended to be apologetic: 'My dear parents-in-law, you seem to have had a terrible journey, up hill and down dale. I have been telling people that my parents-in-law were coming, and now you have had a really difficult journey.' Commiserating with them in this way, he took them to his house.

---

13   He would have retained some undergarment, probably a small loin-cloth.

There is no point in noting all the divergencies of detail between the versions, especially since some of the motifs are not explicable without further material. It is not clear, for instance, whether Ramli's avoidance of sleeping next to his future brother-in-law is simply a further example of his quick-wittedness in extricating himself from unwanted company, or whether there is more to it. Nor is it clear why he discards the rich clothes he has been given, and in such an odd manner. On the basis of Ph, one might sense an echo of the emissary cock dropping his feathers in order to lure Jaw and Khliw to their brother's marriage ceremony; but the resemblance is remote.[14]

A point of more general interest is the character of Ramli. In two versions he explicitly possesses magic powers, which certainly include the ability to whistle up the wind (Mukli versions); and it seems to be magic that brings him victory in the torch-making. His collecting of bones may suggest clairvoyance, though it could be simply a shrewd guess at the likely course of events. Clearly, he is particularly quick to notice things and to size up a situation: he notices the relative bluntness of his axes, he sees how to set about felling the trees and what to do with the knotted wood (all in Ph), and there are two similar observations in Kam.

His motive for appearing in humble clothes and smeared with oil dregs is not explained. Obviously, it puts him at an initial disadvantage and thereby magnifies his eventual triumph. It would not be alien to his character if this was in fact his motive, for he certainly enjoys his success. He takes real pleasure in the physical discomfort he inflicts on his parents-in-law, and is quite without magnanimity towards his defeated rivals. The narrator chuckled to himself when describing Ramli's mock humility after he brings back the *le*, and no doubt an audience would have taken equal pleasure in the passage. In Kam's version, the episode could be taken as a delayed vengeance by the Thulung following the Chamling's trickery in the Dispute over Territory; but the episodes are separated by several intervening ones, and the text contains no hint of such a link.

The exact nature of the *le* (also *li* or *liu*) is an unsolved problem. Clearly it is a substance of magical potency, but I do not know whether it should be conceived as animal, vegetable or mineral as several of these or none of them. In Mukli at least, *le* was thought of as a red mineral, from

---

14   Another remote comparison is with a Bon-po version of the descent of the first
      Tibetan king. After descending the ladder to earth and giving battle to demons,
      the king goes to the *smu-le-gong* tree and abandons his divine clothes in
      favour of human ones (Macdonald 1971: 209, cf. also 199).

which beads were made for necklaces. Until quite recently such beads were still being turned up occasionally by ploughmen who sold them to itinerant Limbu merchants for a few pice each; according to some, they would be resold in Assam. But the substance acquired by Ramli can hardly be anything so mundane. The material mentioned in Kam as collected in large quantities by Ramli's rivals, here rendered '*le* excrement', is also unidentified; presumably the expression refers to some inferior substance with a vague resemblance to the real thing.

The light or phosphorescence inherent in the *le* appears in Kam's version to be linked with the light of the evening star. The name Rolasila is not mentioned here, but since, as we saw, this is the star that Miyapma originally wooed, it may perhaps have enjoyed some supremacy among heavenly bodies. In similar vein, the dogs which guard the *le* belong to the supreme deity Bhagavan. Ant associates the substance with the *bhĩguma* bird (*saŋwa* or *-ma* in Thulung), and in another context, talking of the greatness of the Kiranti relative to other races, Kam compares them to the *bhĩguma* bird, 'who is king among birds, as the sandalwood tree is king among trees.' In view of these associations, *le* must be a symbol of royalty or supremacy, and it is natural that Ramli should take it back with him to his *oganem*. Conceivably, the resplendence of the palace, emphasised by Ph, is somehow linked with the resplendence of the *le*, which he does not mention.

No precise parallels from Tibet have so far been found, but there is a well-known story of the same general character. A harvest festival drama edited by Duncan (1955: 100ff) relates how Srong-btsan sgam-po's minister mGar was sent to bring the king a Nepalese and then a Chinese princess. At the court of the Chinese Emperor, ministers have arrived from the kings of the four quarters to sue for the girl on behalf of their kings. Several of them have supporters at court, but no one is favourable to the Tibetan envoy. The emperor sets a competition, promising the girl to the victor: a silk ribbon has to be steered through the eye of a turquoise. After the others fail mGar succeeds, by tying a silk thread to an ant or a body-louse. However, another half-dozen competitions follow before mGar is allowed to take the princess. In one, he and his escort have to finish tanning the skins of five hundred sheep and eat their meat, in another the competitors have to find the top and base of tree trunks that are of constant diameter, in a third they must find lodgings to sleep in overnight – the framework can accommodate an infinite variety of trials. Such competitions for the hand of a princess are a common theme in folklore generally, and there are numerous samples from India listed under 'Suitor Contests' in Thompson and Balys (1958: 220-1). In the absence of any precise parallels between Tibetan and Thulung traditions no definite conclusions can be drawn.[15]

Much the same is true if one compares Ramli with the hero of the Tibetan epic. Gesar's career falls into two parts, for which separate origins have sometimes been proposed. In his first phase he is called Joru, and is an obscure outcast, mean in clothing and appearance, scurvy (or bald), snotty and diarrhoeic, but roguish and wily. In the second, he is Gesar, the *cakravartin* or universal sovereign, sometimes worshipped as god of war (Stein 1959: 543ff). The two phases are separated by a contest (a horse race) in which the victor's prize is a princess and the throne. Insofar as Ramli in this episode and Joru share the more or less world-wide characteristics of a trickster, they have something in common, and if the *le* is really a symbol of supreme sovereignty, then perhaps the second phases of their careers are comparable also. However, even when we have further material, in particular from episode V, the resemblance between Ramli and Gesar will remain at best rather general and hence difficult to interpret.

We are now in a position to justify giving the Jubu-Lokhim versions priority over the Mukli ones in the ordering and labelling of the episodes. By placing the contest for the bride before the separation from the slug-eater, the Mukli versions can treat both stories as referring to the same woman; indeed, nothing in the Mukli texts even suggests that the narrators conceived of the two episodes as distinct. The Jubu-Lokhim order, in which a divorce precedes a marriage, implies distinct wives, and conversely, distinctness of the wives makes it more likely that separation from the one should precede acquisition of the other. In Kam the episodes are so distinct that they are not even juxtaposed – the separation from the slug-eater precedes the Foundation of Mukli. The comparison with Tibetan material not only supports the recognition of two quite distinct episodes, but also favours the order given here, in that the tradition situates the frog-eater story earlier than the visit by mGar to the emperor of China. Moreover, the Mukli versions came from close neighbours, one of whom had heard the other narrate, whereas it is most unlikely that Kam and Ant in their separate villages would have had any such occasion. Thus several reasons combine

---

15 I have not been able to consult the Tibetan suitor competition stories translated by Bacot and by Francke and alluded to by Stein (1959: 57). [Nor have I connected the stories with the Sanskritic (and Indo-European) notion of *svayaṃvara* marriage, which may be reflected in Ant's mention of the princess garlanding the successful suitor.]

to suggest that the Mukli versions represent the fusion of episodes whose earlier distinctness has survived east of the Dudh Kosi.

III. Introduction of Salt

DB Then Ramli came north. Up until this time, people had used no salt. Then one day Mapa Raja from up at Luwale went hunting at Mandre cliff. He left his ground meal in a bag at the cliff where he had spent the night, and went off hunting. Meanwhile some Sherpas came down, poured out his meal, and put lumps of salt into his bag instead. When Mapa returned, he looked at the lumps without understanding, and was very annoyed. Next time he came with his bag of meal and left it at the cliff, he thought to himself: 'Today I'll see who it is, this wretch who goes off with my food and leaves me stones instead.' He climbed into a tree and waited there with his bow drawn. Again the Sherpas came down, poured out the meal, and put the lumps into the bag. But just as he was about to shoot, they saw his shadow, and called out to him: 'Come down, good sir, come down, let us become ritual friends. Would you like to marry our girls?' Wondering what they were saying, he climbed down. The Sherpas put the lumps of salt in their mouths and bit them, and offered some to him. Dissolving it in warm water they drank some themselves and made Mapa do the same. Next they gave him their unmarried girls – the name of the Sherpa girl was Khamema. Each winter the trio of them came south, and each summer they went up to the Sherpa settlements.

TR's version, typed in Nepali, need not be given in full as it diverges only slightly and is generally less full. Mapa comes from Khalinggaun, which is merely a Nepali gloss for Luwale. He hunts every day from his base at Tare cliff. When the Sherpas see they are about to be shot at, they join their hands together to beg for mercy.

Karb Lunam's son was Mapa. At that time Mapa lived purely and simply by hunting. There was no Nepali spoken at the time and people did not know the Sherpa language, nor anyone else's. Nor did they know about using salt. Although the Sherpas knew about salt, (the people here) ate their meat just by itself. Mapa went hunting wearing his peacock-feather headdress. Each time he went, they stole his meat and in its place left him a bag of salt, looking like sand. In those days they used a bow and arrow, such as is now obsolete. 'Today I'll see who it is that takes my meat and I'll kill him.' So saying, he climbed into a tree to wait for them. When they came, bringing their bag of salt, just as he was on the point of shooting, his feathered headdress shook a little. Looking up they saw that it was a man. In those times there was no Nepali, and they were Lasagotra Sherpas, while Mapa was a Khaling. They did not understand Nepali, and their Sherpa language was no help. They beckoned him down with a gesture of the hand, inviting him to form a ritual brotherhood with them. 'Let us become relatives to each other. We shall give you our daughters. Come down. The thing to do is crush a little bit of this salt, cut up the meat and put the salt on it. Then it will taste really good. Try it.' He tasted it and found that they were right. 'Ymm!' he said. So some of them became ritual brothers, some of them became just good friends, and some of them inter-married.

Ant This comes later on. Someone called Mapa went hunting and the Sherpa stole his grain and ate it. 'Today I'll wait and shoot him with my bow. If I catch that Sherpa I'll kill him,' he said. The Sherpa told him to come down; rather (than shooting him), he should eat (what the Sherpa had brought). So Mapa tasted the salt. It was in the north, with Mapa, that the Sharpas taught people how to eat salt – we did not know how to. Mapa was the ancestor of the Khaling Rai.

Kam The person who taught us to eat salt was a Khaling. The people who brought it were the Sherpas from the other side of the range, they used to eat it up there in the north. The one who learned about eating salt and brought in the custom was Mapa, the forefather of the Khaling. One day he went hunting – up there they did not use dogs for hunting, nothing but bow and arrow. We too were a hunting people, but we used dogs which were self-born (?) – I never heard it said that the Khaling had dogs. They used to put feathers on the shafts of the arrows. Well, Mapa lived below Pakhe Pani. The Khaling are Lasagotra. They came out of the country of the Khambas from beyond the range, and then moved south. According to their original birth-place the Khaling are Lasagotra, whereas our Place of Origin is Kasi. We emerged from the Place of Origin, and our *ḍiumla* is not the same as theirs. Each people had a single founding ancestor, and the founding ancestor of the Khaling was called Mapa. He understood the language of the Khambas from beyond the range, and he spoke our own Thulung language, and that of the Chamling in the south. His clothing was (?) like that of Kirantsor. He had a garment like the Sherpa *bakkhu*, made from the skin of a wild sheep. He had scraped down the skin and wore it (?) inside out as a tunic. And on top of this he wore a feathered headdress.

Kam does not finish the story of Mapa, but goes on to talk about the image he has seen of Kirantsor with his plumed headdress, then about the ancestors' clothing, which consisted solely of animal skins, then about the absence of cash at that period. Mandrebhir is located some two or three hours to the north of Jubing on the east bank of the Dudh Kosi. Another Jubu informant located the event at Khuciu cave. The story seems to be among the best known in this chapter, though both Kam and Ant told it in response to a direct question. It was also known to Ph and in Tingla. It is current too in much the same form among the Khaling themselves, where the name of the Sherpa with the salt is Gelbu (Joiner).[16]

It is very likely that at one time the Rai did indeed subsist without imported mineral salt, and that when they began to import it, it was as a result of Sherpa initiatives. Although Karb says that it was Mapa's meat that the Sherpas took, the majority version – that it was his cereal – is much more likely, since the salt-grain trade has long been a fundamental feature of economic exchanges across the Himalayas (Fürer-Haimendorf 1975). Although the story claims that the Rai did not know what to do with the salt until formal social contacts were established with the Sherpas, there may well have been a period when exchange satisfactory to both parties took place without any face-to-face contact: relationships of this sort, called 'silent trade', have been reported from other parts of the world, e.g. Malaya. However, in recent times at any rate, trading partnerships between Rai and Sherpa have been a well-established institution.[17] Such relationships are regularly referred to, as here, by the Nepali term *mit*, which also covers relationships entered into for sentimental reasons as well as for mutual advantage. In principle, a small ritual is held when the relationship is contracted. With the spread of weekly markets the institution has lost its economic relevance, and seems to be on the decline for that reason. In two

16   [Gelbu is from Tib. *rgyal-po* = 'king'.]

17   Ph has as ritual brother the Sherpa Pasang Khambache, known to the wider world as the assistant of both Snellgrove and Fürer-Haimendorf, and in recent years a prominent figure in Kathmandu circles.

villages I was given a less prosaic explanation: it is a sin to harbour even a fleeting moment of resentment against a ritual friend, and since one can never be sure of being able to control one's feelings completely, it is safer simply to cooperate with people (*hit* N). It is probably relationships like this, lacking any ritual element, that Karb refers to as *iṣṭu* N, translated 'just good friends'.

Although the story relates to a real historical innovation, one can reasonably doubt the historicity of the narrative details. We have already met in Ch. 2 IV the schema of a bowman, there Mini, waiting in a tree for his enemy below. In both cases the Mukli versions refer to the bowman, while the non-Mukli versions (there CP) refer to movements of his plumed headdress.

As for Tibet, it is worth citing the story of how the father of Srong-btsan sgam-po discovered an extensive salt bank in the northern desert plain, before which time the supply of salt in the country was very meagre. The king hunts down a fierce wild yak, whose carcase falls off the king's horse onto the ground. When the king alights, he finds the salt (Das 1881: 217). Remotely too, one might recall again the story of the descent of the first king. A bow is among the accoutrements that he brings to earth. He descends by himself, to be greeted by a group of subjects who honour him. Some versions note the mutual incomprehensibility of the languages of king and subjects, who communicate by gestures (Macdonald 1959: 422).

IV. Ramli versus Mapa

DB It became the custom for Mapa to get salt from the Sherpas and bring it south, and its use spread. Ramli knew about this through his magic powers but did not have any salt himself, so he made ready a large basket and sent a porter. Mapa simply cut off the porter's hand and sent him back. Ramli was furious and decided to become Mapa's enemy. He addressed his sword, which was called Khapcium, bidding it go to Mapa and kill him. The sword went flying through the air and Mapa was cowed. 'O Ramli, good Sir, I shall give you your salt,' he cried. Knowing of this by his magic power, Ramli changed his mind, and the sword Khapcium turned round and came back south. Ramli sent a second porter and this time Mapa gave him salt. Since that time the substance has come into general use.

Cutting off hands is a proverbial mutilation in the area. It appears for instance in the ceremonial dialogues at marriages when the bride's side wonder if this fate has befallen their daughter. The Thulung claim that during the Rana period, a person who showed too much interest in writing or studying was in danger of having his hand cut off. The sword's name Khapcium is to be related to certain ritual expressions: *dewayum khapceyum* refers to the magic power (*yum*) of the priests (*dewa*), including no doubt their powers of aggressive sorcery. The root also relates to metal: *khapciu buliu* is given in AS as = *kãsa tābā* N, i.e. 'bronze-copper', and in Tingla *khapce bole* is the ritual name for cymbals (cf. Ch. 4 n.10). Another informant also mentioned that Ramli could summon his sword to fly through the air to his hand.

Beneath its fabulous surface, this episode too may contain an element of genuine history. There could well have been a period of hostility or violence between Thulung and Khaling over access to Tibetan salt. Since the route from Thulung territory northwards inevitably passed through Khaling territory, the latter were potentially in a very strong position.

V. Foundation of the *Bhume* Rites[18]

DB   Afterwards Mapa fell ill with leprosy. His wife and her younger brother carried him on a journey. They stopped for a rest up on Ratnangi ridge. I forget the name of the place, and at this point Mapa turned to stone. His wife tried to resurrect him but failed. Then her brother tried and he also failed. Mapa had three sons; to the youngest he had given the powers of a seer and the knowledge of invocations. News was sent and the eldest brother went, but failed to resurrect his father. With the second brother it was the same. The youngest, however, had the visionary powers and knowledge of ritual, so he got his mother to brew some beer, and took seven gourds of it together with seven leaf-plates of wheat and parched grain. As he travelled, he chanted invocations, making ritual use of an old cock, of *cimphin* and ginger, and of the gourds of ritual beer. He splashed some beer over his father, and cut the cock's mouth and sprinkled him with its blood. At that, his father suddenly came alive.

    They picked the father up again and carried him down to Salabesi. There he abandoned his wife and brother-in-law, and asked his

---

18   [A fuller discussion is given in Allen 1981; cf. also Allen 1986: 87-8.]

youngest son to carry him further. They went down to Yaliu but the wind made it impossible to stay long, and they went on down to Sase. The gnats would not let them stay there either, and they continued down to around the Sakhle. At this point, a stone suddenly turned round and allowed them to leave. While they were still there, one of Mapa's thumbs fell off. This was not good, and he asked his son to carry him on again. Next they came to Rindapu hamlet, in Dewsa, where they rested, and here too a *bhume* site was founded – the Sakhle *bhume* site had been founded where the thumb fell off, and another site was founded where they rested at Dewsa Rindapu. Then they rested up at Amras and another site founded. From there they went to Luwale, where another was founded. Then they went to Rapcha, where Mapa said to his youngest son: 'Right, you have a meal, I'm not eating. Go and look for firewood.' So the son put him down, turning him to face across the hillside, and went to look for wood. When he returned his father had become a stone, a god. Thus Rapcha ought to have been the first to splash him from a gourd, that is to worship him, but the people of Phuleli came down, and since they were the first to do it, they now have the right. None of us others has the right to perform the Sakhle *bhume* at Rapcha without the permission of Phuleli.

The porters would have carried Mapa in a basket on the back like any other load, this being the normal method of transporting an invalid. The ritual paraphernalia mentioned in the story are still used by Thulung priests, and do not need comment here.

The geography is relatively clear. Presumably Mapa set out from Luwale, mentioned as his home in DB III. Its location is not known precisely but was stated to be near Khali (= Khaldel), and may be identical to it. Ratnangi ridge runs north from Mukli, forming the watershed between the Solu Khola and Dudh Kosi, and Mapa had to cross it to reach Salabesi from the Khaling area. Yaliu is above old Mukli, at its 'head' (*sir* N) and on or by Thunki Ridge[19] – hence could well be windy; it was Mukli's original *bhume* site. Sase is much lower and just to the west of Phuliuku, a few hundred yards above and west of the present *bhume* site at Sakhle. I could obtain no explanation of the event involving the stone at Sase. Amras, the stop after Dewsa, is already in Khaling territory. If Luwale was really near Khali, the next stop can hardly be identified with the Bhumethan marked on the maps

---

19   Cf. *thumki* N 'hillside, hilltop, ridge'.

at the east end of Kanku. Rapcha is very close to Khali, if the two are not different names for one place.

It is unnecessary to present in full a typed version by TR since it probably derives wholly from DB. The only notable differences are that the first turning to stone is omitted, and that when the son finds the stone at Rapcha he goes off to get his ritual apparatus. When he returns, he finds that the Rapchalis have been the first to asperse his father.

The only other version collected was from SSJ, who had heard it from his father-in-law, a Khaling priest from Kanku.

SSJ An old man from Phuleli in the north went down to the plains and on his way back fell ill with leprosy at Halesi. Being unable to return he sent for his relatives from Phuleli to carry him in a basket. When they reached Sakhle, his little toe fell off, and he instructed the people there how to perform a *bhume* ceremony. At Kanku his right little finger fell off. At Khali the bearer looked over his shoulder and found there was no man in the basket, and that his aged relative had turned into stone.

The Khaling of Jubing assert that when their ancestors arrived from the south they found Phuleli already inhabited by Khaling of another sort who had come from the earth (Joiner); so there is a certain tradition about the antiquity of the place. Halesi is well known as the site of a large fair held thrice yearly and centring on a shrine which, nowadays at least, is regarded as Hindu.

Both versions appear incomplete in that no motive is given for Mapa leaving home, though one can understand that he wishes to return there once his illness becomes manifest. In DB's version the journey constitutes roughly a full circle travelled in an anti-clockwise direction starting from the north or north-east. The circle does contain the location of the Sandalwood tree of Ch. 2 VII, but nothing else indicates that the journey should be interpreted as a ritual circumambulation, such as Tibetan pilgrims so commonly make around sacred mountains. Other types of symmetry can be noted in the journey as described by DB. The party apparently stopped at four places before reaching their southernmost and lowest point at Sakhle, where the stone suddenly turned round and the first digit was lost; and the return journey also involved four named stops, if we include Rapcha, the terminus. Both the first halt and the last are marked by Mapa's petrification. But I do not know whether such points are significant, especially since we only have the two versions. It is only the second part of the journey, from Mukli onwards, that is duplicated by SSJ, and it is probably better to look at the two parts separately.

It is clear enough that the return journey serves as a myth of origin of the *bhume* sites. Presumably, even when it is not specifically mentioned, each site is associated with the loss of a digit or some other part of Mapa's body. Though the losses are rationalised as resulting from his leprosy, one is tempted to recall the deliberate offering of the little finger in the Exit (4 II Karb). It seems natural that Rapcha, which retains the bulk of Mapa's body, enjoys precedence over those sites whose origin is linked only with one of his extremities, and it is no less fitting, since Mapa is a Khaling, that Rapcha lies in Khaling territory. I do not know whether nowadays people from outside Rapcha might still sometimes wish to perform a *bhume* there, but Kam VI (ii) apparently reflects a period when the Thulung did go to Rapcha for ritual purposes – Ramli goes there to give his children ritual names. The exact relationship between Rapcha and Phuleli might be ascertained by field research among the Khaling.

The interpretation of the outward journey is problematic. The wife who sets out with Mapa would most simply be the Sherpa Khamema of DB III, but Mapa could have had more than one wife; the mother who prepares the ritual beer for the youngest son may or may not be the one who set out with Mapa. This youngest son (surely the most likely of the three) may or may not be the Kangpas given as Mapa's son in Ch. 4 VIb Karb. It may or may not be significant that Salabesi is very close to Junbesi and is coupled with it in Ch. 4 V CP; Junbesi also houses a particularly important Sherpa village temple associated with pre-Buddhist agricultural fertility rites (Funke 1969: 88ff). I cannot here attempt to relate this Sherpa cult to the Thulung *bhume* rites, but if they are related, this may be relevant to Mapa's first petrification.

An interesting feature of the outward journey is that during it Mapa 'abandons' his wife. The word *parjeot-* is a compound of *par-* 'throw, throw away', and could not, I think, be used to mean 'temporarily absent oneself from' someone. The same word is used by Ant when Ramli separates from his slug-eating wife and her son, and although DB's version is here so fragmentary, there are other reasons for comparing the two episodes. Salabesi lies well to the west of the natural route that would be taken by anyone crossing the Traksindo pass and heading south towards Mukli, and this suggests that Mapa went there for a specific purpose. Perhaps, as already suggested, his journey had something to do with the ritual centre there, but this is not at all certain. The first part of the name Salabesi means 'brother-in-law'; so could it be that Khamema, the non-Khaling, is being returned to the village of Mapa's affines, and being replaced as carrier of a basket (cf. Kam I) by a true Khaling male? This may be tendentious, but the second element in the name Salabesi (= *bisi* or -*besi* N) refers to a 'flat piece of land beside a river' (Turner) – compare the discussion of *waye* under episode I. Moreover, relative to Khaling territory, Salabesi lies just on the far side of the Solu Khola (or more precisely, of the two branches of which it there consists): Ramli's wife too was in most versions left just on the far side of the same river.

If this were all, the comparison would be rather weak. But as we saw, the Ramli story resembled in many details the Tibetan story of 'Bro-myen lde-ru, the only Tibetan king reported to suffer from leprosy. This affliction provides a link between the Tibetan and Khaling characters, independent of the features they both share with Ramli; and there are further points of contact. Both men die in unusual ways, the Tibetan going live into his tomb, Mapa turning to stone.[20] Both give their sons instructions bearing on ritual. Finally, both sons have unusual vision, the Tibetan being born blind, the Khaling receiving the gift of seeing visions (*ŋima-sema*); Thulung mythology contains several characters who 'know things by magic' (*yum*), but I met with no others who were supposed to see visions.

These rapprochements suggest that the first part of the present episode is a Khaling parallel version to episode I. This idea can be supported by material from the Khaling themselves. After their parallel version of the Introduction of Salt, Mapa briefly married the daughter of the Sherpa Gelbu. 'On the trip down the Dudh Kosi from Khumbu, the pregnant Bhoteni got stuck in a narrow place and died (?), from which time it was ordained that Bhotes and Rais shall not marry' (Joiner). The motif of the pregnant Bhoteni getting stuck in a narrow place echoes the fat Slug-eater getting stuck in the doorway. It is interesting that Gelbu became one of the three major household gods of the Khaling, but it is not clear whether or how the fact relates to the divinisation of Mapa in the second part of the present episode.

---

20   In view of this parallel, might one relate the stone into which Mapa turns to the stone which Ramli sets up when he takes his vow? There is another Tibetan parallel for Mapa's petrification: Srong-btsan sgam-po was an incarnation of the god Avalokiteshvara, and at his death he dissolved into that deity's statue, 'becoming a kind of sacred talisman of the kingdom, standing at its centre' (Stein 1972: 52). For Mapa's first and temporary petrification, compare also that of Wayelungma, the future civilising heroine.

If the first part of Mapa's journey relates to the story of 'Bro-mnyen lde-ru, might the second part relate to the journeys of Padmasambhava and gShen-rab mi-bo, the largely or wholly mythological Founders revered respectively by the rNying-ma-pa Buddhists and the Bon-po? The former travels through Tibet subjecting to his will the gods of the soil and the mountains; his progress, what the Indians would call a *digvijaya*, a 'conquest of the directions', culminates in the construction of the famous temple of bSam-yas (Tucci 1955-6b: 279f). The biography of the Bon Founder contains a number of similar fantastic episodes occurring in the course of a journey ostensibly in pursuit of some horses stolen from him by a devil (Hoffmann 1950: 340ff). However, neither of these journeys closely resembles that of Mapa. Mapa's progress can hardly be described as triumphant or victorious, even if it ends in the appearance of an important ritual stone at Rapcha, and his progressive mutilation has no parallel in the journeys of the Tibetan founders. This rapprochement must be rejected.

In assessing the historicity of the episode, one must remember that the main narrator was Mukli's most active and respected priest, and that the *bhume* sites he mentions include the one where he himself frequently officiates, as did his father before him. He says unambiguously that the site was founded as a result of a visit by a Khaling culture hero. Before fully endorsing this view, it would be prudent to review in detail all available evidence about the *bhume* cult both as practised by the Thulung and as reported from other areas. However, for the moment, I accept as probable that the Thulung *bhume* cult owes its origin in whole or part to influence from the north.

It is interesting that the story of the main village shrine is known to so few Mukli villagers. In part this must be due to the general decline in tribal ritual activity, but it may also be due to the lack of interest in or reverence for the relics of individual holy men. Whereas in Tibet one might expect Mapa's thumb to have been preserved in a commemorative chorten, the tribal religion is concerned rather with the ancestors in an anonymous and collective manner. Individual tombs of members of a household are located next to each other in a field a minute or two's walk from the house, but once the death ritual is complete, they are fairly soon forgotten.

VI. Salewaceo

Since in its fullest version (Kam) this episode is a quite long, a preliminary outline may be helpful. (a) Salewaceo is an outsider who seduces a Mukli girl and resides there. (b) The wedding ceremony is delayed because of a quarrel with the Sherpas. (c) Subsequently, further hostilities with the Sherpas lead to a quarrel over the distribution of plunder. (d) The Mukli party kill Salewaceo's child. (e) Their crime leads to a drought in which many perish.

Of the three versions recorded, all agree approximately on (a) and even more closely on (d) and (e); but Karb omits (b), and Ph omits (b) and (c). It might be possible to treat (b) as a separate episode, but Kam certainly regarded it as an integral part of the story.

Kam (a) Our founding forefather Ramli had one child, Ekli...[21] For his children's wedding he gave them ritual names, set up the hearth stones and established all our ceremonial. At the place for marital exchanges he gave away his sisters and daughters to his affines, took from them their women and arranged the weddings. I'll tell you the *ḍiumla* concerning this, though it is a long story, as long as what has gone before.

Ramli had this one daughter, and five sons. He decided to hold a ceremony and give them their ritual names. For this it was necessary to prepare sixteen measures (*muri* N) of unhusked rice, not using a pestle and mortar, but doing it all by hand, producing eight measures of husked rice. In addition, they needed eight measures each of *silām* N and eleusine, and not only ritual grain but also ritual beer. Next they needed sixteen haunches of wild boar, and sixteen haunches of deer, and on the day of the ceremony they had to sacrifice a sixteen-year-old pig, using the blood in the ritual.[22] In addition, they needed sixteen pheasants, sixteen quail, sixteen *bǝypu* birds and sixteen mountain pheasants (*munāl ḍāmphe* N). His sons and sons-in-law were to go hunting for the sixteen haunches of wild boar. You remember how Ramli went to the Chamling village – well, following that he had the one daughter Ekli. Salawaceo had heard about her and had come here to woo her. She was out looking after the goats, and the two made love. After much consideration, the girl brought him to her parents' house. 'Who is this man?' asked the mother, 'and what is he doing wandering round here?' 'I don't know where he was going to, but I met him while

---

21 A feminine from *ekle* N 'only child'.

22 The grain, beer and blood are stated to be *kholom*, which means approximately 'consecrated, taboo'.

I was pasturing the goats, and he stayed with me.' The mother feared that now the man had seduced her daughter he might make off with her, and she talked it over with her husband. They questioned the man at some length and eventually consented to the union.

After a while Ekli became pregnant. They built a little shed or outhouse for the couple, where they slept and spent most of their time, but they came into the main house for meals. However, the parents were still afraid that this man who had seduced her would take her off to his own village – wherever that was, so they performed a *ṭikā* N ceremony that formally recognised him as son-in-law. But they wanted to hold a proper wedding ceremony for their children, with all their kinsmen and full ceremonial. So they decided to send Salewaceo and four of their sons over to Solu, up above Okhaldhunga, to hunt for the wild boar. They did not send the youngest son, who was too young to be of any help.

(b) Meanwhile two Sherpas appeared, a woman and a man. Some *silām* grain was spread out to dry in the sun for the *miksinəŋ* ceremony, so it had to be kept pure. The Sherpas sat down on it and scooped up a couple of mouthfuls. Thereupon Ramli's people took them both and cut off their thumbs. The two of them went off mutilated and weeping, and returned to their village. The defiled grain was disposed of and a new supply was put out to dry. Meanwhile the hunting party had stopped for the night in the village of that very same couple, and were given an evening meal. The Sherpas and ourselves were great enemies, it was like in the old days when these people [i.e. the anthropologist's compatriots] and the Germans were at war. Well, after the meal, the Sherpas led the members of the hunting party each to his own sleeping place. As sleeping mats they gave them great wide animal hides and sewed them up inside – this of course was in revenge for cutting off the thumbs.[23] They were careful not to disturb them, and each of the five just went on sleeping inside his own great bag. They could not tell whether it was day or night. Meanwhile, down below, day after day went by, four or five days, and nothing happened, no news came. In Ramli's house everything was ready for the *miksinəŋ*, and every day the hunters were expected back with the wild boar. And there they

---

23 The narrator particularly enjoyed this part of his story, laughing and repeating it several times.

were, all sewn up in their leather bags, unable to tell whether it was day or night, unable to communicate with each other. Soon they began to suffer from hunger and thirst. 'Surely the Sherpas will come and let us out,' they thought; but they did not. At last Salewaceo cut his way out with a dagger that he had about his person, found his brothers-in-law all bundled up similarly, and released them too, while the Sherpas were out of the way. They came down, related their adventure, took new supplies of grain, and set off hunting again, taking good care to keep clear of that particular village. Salewaceo had magic powers and this time they killed what they needed, deer, three types of pheasant, and the wild boar. When they had brought them back, Ramli performed the *miksinəng*. 'Now that I have performed the ceremony with all the invocations, we must next go up to the *bhume* site to give the ritual names. Carrying the requisite grain they went up to the Khaling village of Rapcha, to what they called the Bhumethan. He took all his children up there and gave them their ritual names.

The ritual names he gave were like this.[24] Congkom were called Congdise comokha... Hadise were Nagise nagipa – that is the Captiuriu-Liumma people; the Laploace people were called Lindise capuka, and our own people Congdise comokha, that is, our whole branch (*suktium*) – nowadays each of us have our own ritual names, but those are the ones our forefather gave.

(c) After their return south, when all the ceremonial was over, Ramli's children and Salewaceo went on an expedition to collect bamboos. They were still angry over the affair of the leather bags, and they went over to the Sherpa settlement and made war with them. Having killed large numbers, they plundered the place. The one weapon the Sherpas used was an eight-inch dagger, with scabbards of silver and gold and the like. Salewaceo found an ornamented gold scabbard (*kothimorā* N). The four brothers tried to get it away from him, but whatever they did they failed, and they became thoroughly angry. They came south again, carrying their loads of bamboo, and arrived before him.

(d) They went into their sister's lodging and in their anger they burned their nephew.[25] The child was just of an age to be taken in the lap,

---

24   In response to a question by my host.
25   The sex of the child is never in fact stated.

and they blew up a really fierce blaze – all of this was to get rid of Salewaceo and his wife. The oldest brother, Jiugba, told his sister to fetch the baby – two sat on one side of the fire and two on the other. Each in turn asked to hold the child, and they passed it back and forth through the flames until it was dead.

Salewaceo knew that they had killed his child, but realised that he could not take on all his in-laws and would have to proceed carefully. The child's mother wondered when Salewaceo would appear and what had been the cause of her brothers' anger. When the child expired and the brothers got up, she went and cut some banana leaves and put one underneath the corpse, and one on top as covering. She had cooked her husband's meal and sat there waiting.

Salewaceo arrived and threw down his load...He entered the house and sat down. His wife gave him water – the brothers had meanwhile rapidly departed. Salewaceo was clairvoyant, you realise, and demanded to see the child before eating. She pretended he was asleep, but when he insisted she told him what had been done. 'The child is over there. But what happened with your brothers-in-law?' As he saw the child he cried out. The grandparents did not know what had happened, and the couple spent the night as usual, taking their meal in the main house.

(e) The next day somehow or other they planned to depart. They had a servant who had been given to Salewaceo's wife as dowry. Nepali speakers call them *gharti*, or else *kamārā* or *kamāri* according to sex, but in Thulung *ḍiumla* they are called *tayu* – servants who fetch water, go out looking for nettles and *ṭhoṭne* N vegetables, who do the washing up and other domestic tasks. Salewaceo's wife went with the servant to a nearby patch of forest to collect conifer wood for torches, urging her husband not to say anything to her parents... When they had brought them back, the two women were to set off for that vast fallen broken boulder at the head of Payo, the one that is visible from Wanku when one is on the route up to Khuciu cave, where there is that sacrifice to some god or other in Phagun or Magh – you know the one?[26] Anyway, they were to make a fire there, and when he saw the smoke rising he would follow them. Jiugba and his brothers were now

---

26 Kam will be referring to some Hindu deity who receives a sacrifice in February or thereabouts.

looking for an opportunity to kill him – those were wild times, murder and killing were commonplace, no one knew what went on. The couple were bound to depart for his village, and the brothers planned to follow him and strike him down from behind with their kukris; but again his clairvoyant powers told him what they were plotting. If they all travelled together the brothers would pursue and kill them. So all day he intended to sit indoors, heating the pinewood torches; then, when the signal was given, he would fly and join the others. The grandparents still knew nothing of their grandchild's death, nor of how their son-in-law was going to make off with their precious daughter.

Immediately Salewaceo saw the smoke coming from beneath the boulder at Payo, he slipped out of the side door, and was off, flying through the air. In no time at all he was up with the two whom he had sent on in advance. As he went, he snapped up all the mothers of the waters of Phuliuku river, and a complete drought fell upon the whole of Mukli and Dewsa. People searched high and low, but unless they went down to the Dudh Kosi there was simply not a drop of water anywhere, there was a curse on the place. Fearful for their future, they sent each of the brothers in turn, starting with the eldest, to implore Salewaceo to return their river. Each time he refused. Finally, they sent the youngest, Ramli, who was just a child, just so high; and at last the other agreed to come. They were to get ready sixteen vessels of beer, counting them out one by one,[27] sixteen measures (*pāthi* N) of grain, and two pigs, and assemble their friends and neighbours so that he could come and exorcise the curse… They should also watch the spout of the spring. When he set out, there would be a little moisture there instead of the dust. When he reached the ridge – Bukrum or Laure Ridge – just a little water would flow. But on no account were they to drink it until he had arrived and exorcised the curse.

However, when he reached the ridge and the water began to flow, they cried out in joy. 'Where did you go, what happened to you, Waters of the Earth? We were dying of thirst without you.' As soon as the water came, they drank their fill, without waiting for the curse to be lifted and before Salewaceo had held his séance. As a result the people of Phuliuku died out, and the only survivors were one or two people here and there who had not drunk.

---

27 Using the birth-order terms, *jeṭhā, mahilā*….

A few comments need to be made on incidental details which do not arise in other versions. Other informants also stated that personal ritual names should be given in the course of *miksinəŋ* ceremonies. This ceremony is the largest in the series performed by the priest in honour of the ancestors, and is nowadays regarded as quite distinct from the wedding ritual. However in the Jaw-Khliw cycle too, the ceremony at the end which apparently celebrated the wedding was described in some versions as a *sekro*, which is the Tingla equivalent of the Mukli and Lokhim *miksinəŋ*. It seems to be implied here that Ramli is establishing the ceremony, i.e. holding the first one of its kind; this may explain the necessity for the visit to Rapcha, which is not a regular feature of the rite. It is not clear why the rice had to be husked by hand (literally 'with the nails', implying that it was done grain by grain). Both the visit to Rapcha and Salewaceo's séance at the end require fixed quantities of grain as offerings. The Thulung term for such offerings is *sorium*, which is said to be derived for *sorah* N meaning 'sixteen', the number of measures (*pāthi*) originally used for the purpose. As an etymology this is unlikely, but the total accords with the emphasis on the figure sixteen in Kam's account of the requisites for the wedding ritual.

The first paragraph of the episode is interesting in that it appears to state that the women were exchanged directly between communities at a given public place (*kuṭumbu* N *goākhop*). Any such custom has long died out, but inconclusive conversations with other informants suggest that it may once have been current, i.e. a group of women from one community used to be publicly handed over to members of another.

It is common enough for young couples to inhabit a shed close to the family home where they eat. This ensures them some degree of privacy before they feel ready to move away and build their own house. By heating lengths of conifer wood, Salewaceo was no doubt drying them out so that they would burn better when used at night as torches.

Karb (a) There they lived for a long time, for generations. I don't know which generation it was, but Salewaceo the Kulung married the daughter of Phuliukuceo … The second brother's family[28] lived at some distance, while his in-laws were at war with Solu Khumbu; and they came to him to ask for help. 'O brother-in-law, the Sherpas have

---

28 Salewaceo was referred to as the second brother at the end of 4 III Karb, the episode which immediately precedes on his tape.

attacked us. Come to our aid.' He accepted and came over to join them.

(c) Kinsmen and affines together went north to attack the Sherpas. They put them to flight and pursued them all over their territory. Then on the way back south after the victorious expedition, they began to quarrel over a particular sword which had been found in a Sherpa house. The Kulung had magic powers, while the Phuliuku people were just ordinary laymen, without special abilities. 'Please give me the thing,' said Salewaceo. The Phuliuku people refused. 'Why won't you give it to me? You ought to because I'm a magician, an officiant, and when I'm performing a séance or ceremony for some purpose or other I shall need it.' 'Anyway you are not having it.' 'Why not?' 'Since it is now in our village, it is ours. If we had set out from your village (?), it would have been a different matter.'

(d) So they quarrelled, and resentment built up. 'This brother-in-law of ours is not going to give in. What shall we do about it? Let's set upon him and kill him.' With this in mind, the Phuliuku people conceived a wicked plan. 'We'll set off into the jungle with him to collect bamboos, and up in the bamboo thicket we'll kill him. Moreover – he had one child – we'll tell our sisters to kill the little child.' When the sisters asked how, they told them: 'Blow up the fire until there is a good blaze. Some of you sit at the uphill edge of the fire – or rather, one up there, one at the side, and one at the downhill edge.[29] Then one of you should say: 'Oh, what a pretty little boy our nephew is! Hand him over to me.' Then another one should say the same. Make sure the fire is really blazing well. Later you should roast him actually in the flames.' This wicked plan they then carried out according to the instructions, scorching him to death in the fire.

After killing the child in this way in the house, the brothers had planned to take the father up into the jungle and kill him too, whenever the opportunity arose. But the Kulung was a magician, and moving this way and that he eluded them. By now they had their bundles of bamboos all tied up and ready to carry, but they went on plotting. 'Some of us must get in front of him, others behind, and we'll catch

---

29 The narrator in fact does not mention the downhill edge of the hearth and mentions the uphill edge twice, apparently by a slip of the tongue.

him in the middle and suddenly set upon him.' But however many times they tried to catch him between the two groups, somehow or other the groups always lost touch with each other (?), something went wrong, and he escaped. Failure followed failure, and eventually they arrived down at the house. When they had put down their loads, the mother's younger sister offered them a vessel of water to wash for the meal...They each took a vessel and went to wash. But just as the meal was about to start, Salewaceo said to the mother: 'I'll have the meal in just a moment. First bring me the child. Today I feel like holding him in my lap before I eat.' Well before this, while he was up in the jungle, he had realised that his wife's sisters had killed the child – that's why he asked for it. 'You must be exhausted after your day's work. Have your meal first,' she urged him. 'No, for some reason, today I want to hold the child before eating.' He insisted absolutely. After killing the child they had put him on a winnowing fan in the back end of the house, covered with a banana leaf. Eventually the mother gave him to the father. 'Alas! What was it that led to this anger and enmity between you and your dear in-laws? My sisters have scorched the child to death in the fire.' With these words she gave him the child. Although he had known about the killing all the time, he took the corpse and put it down, looked at it, wept and mourned. Then – I don't know whether he finished the meal – with his heart numbed, I suppose he and his wife buried the child. 'Let us go home, we cannot stay here,' he said. And so he took her back with him to Salewa Lungkhim.

(e) At the same time the Kulung took away the mothers of the waters. The river dried up and the Phuliuku people were almost dead from thirst. They hastened to Salewa's village. Nowadays we talk of brothers according to birth order as Jetha, Mahila, Sahila, Kahila, Kancha, but the old terms were Tongdiu, Khatel, Lindiu, Cindiu and Sibi, or Sibi Rai, from eldest to youngest. They realised that it was Salewaceo the Kulung who had afflicted them like this, and that they were facing starvation and death. So the eldest brother went: 'Oh brother-in-law, we are dying of thirst. You have taken from us the Waters of the Earth, give them back to us. Grant us this mercy, we are dying.' 'No, brother-in-law, I certainly shall not.' The eldest brother came back with nothing accomplished. It was just the same with the next two brothers. In refusing the third brother he recalled the crimes they had committed against him. 'I still have the scars you gave me when you took me up to the bamboo thickets and tried to kill me, even if you failed. And then you killed my child. No, I certainly shall not come.' After the fourth brother too had failed, it was the turn of the youngest. The youngest was just a child and had no part in the crimes. When Salewaceo heard his pleadings, his heart warmed towards him. 'All your elder brothers came and I took no notice of them, but you are the youngest and I cannot bear to see (your sufferings). On the auspicious day I shall come. You go now. I shall need such and such paraphernalia assembled ready for me when I arrive.'

The youngest brother went back and told the others what had been said, that Salewaceo would come on such and such a date when he had assembled his equipment, also that while he made his preparations the water in the springs would be very, very cold; and that they would be able to recognise how far he had got from that fact. When he stepped on the threshold of his house, there would be a sort of frostiness at the spring; the water would almost begin to come, and they would know he was just setting out. When he reached Dharmadhunga and spent the night up there, the water would begin to flow at the spring; but until he had actually arrived, they were on no account to collect or consume any of the water.

But the villagers were completely parched with thirst, almost to the point of death, and when the water came, they cried out with joy. 'Oh Waters of the Earth, where had you gone to? We were dying' – and they drank. By killing their nephew they had created an evil force, and so all the water turned to poison, and they died from its coldness. When Salewaceo arrived, he recognised (?) the action of the curse. If you had not drunk too soon, it would have been all right, but as it is…' It had become poison and the cold killed them. So the territory of his in-laws became deserted, and Salewaceo became the ruler. The family of Thulu died out over in Phuliuku. But we remain Thulung to this day.

Ph   (a) After he came north again, I'm not sure whether or not he got married. One of his daughters, or perhaps it was a younger sister, had a husband called Salewaceo. They had one child, who was roasted alive in this village by the Phuliukuceo people. Whether this Phuliukuceo was Ramli himself or one of his family, or from some other family, I am not quite sure, but they roasted Salewaceo's child. The father had gone off hunting, and the mother was about her business in the fields, or wherever, and the child had been left in his cradle. His mother's brothers roasted him until he was dead, and sat there holding him in the cradle. When the mother returned she saw that the child was dead. In due course the father came back, asked after the child, and found that he was dead. He asked her what had happened, and she told him. 'We must not stay here, what will happen to us? Let us go over to my own village. They clearly cannot tolerate us here, since they have gone and killed our child.'

(e) With these words, Salewaceo took the seeds of the Phuliuku River and went off with them. Thereupon, the river dried up and the inhabitants were entirely without water. 'Salewaceo has played us this dirty trick and taken the seeds of our water supply and stopped it dead. How can we manage without it? He is evidently a magician, we shall have to go and try and fetch him.' The elder brothers went for him, but he took no notice and refused to come. In the end the youngest brother went. 'You have taken the seeds of our water and it has all dried up. We have nothing to drink. Let us go back, the two of us.' 'Now that it is you who have come, I'll agree. But first, you must clean up Phuliuku's source. When I think of setting out there will be a little dampness there, and when I am on my way a little bit of water will come out at the spring. On no account should you drink it. I am coming, but until the curse is exorcised you must not drink.' The brother returned and delivered the message. They agreed, and went off to clean up the spring – you can still see what they did. They built a sort of structure with stones on both sides to tread on and places to put loads. As they were busy with the work, just a little bit of moisture came up, and some time later when Salewaceo set off, the water here began to flow. They were so parched with thirst that they drank it. Before he arrived, he knew that they had done so, and when he came he accused them. 'We had to drink. We were dying of thirst.' 'I told you not to drink before the curse was exorcised. Now it never will be exorcised,' he said. He performed a séance, but to this day the curse has not been lifted. The curse originated by the Phuliuku people still hangs over everybody. One can't say 'It has nothing to do with me'; it affects everybody.

The geographical setting is fairly clear. Karb is the only narrator to state that Salewaceo was a Kulung, but there are other hints to the same effect. Several informants who did not know the story in detail did know of a tradition that the line of descent from Ramli passed through his daughter, and that the uxorilocal son-in-law was from the east. One claimed that the outsider was from Lokhim, but a Kangel informant held that his home was at least beyond the Dharma ridge (referred to by Karb), on which Aisyalukharka is situated. Kam's Payo is probably the Pawe on the Hinku Khola. The ridges mentioned on Salewaceo's return journey form the watershed between the Dudh Kosi and the Arun (cf. 4 III Karb). Laure Ridge is south of Salpa, Bukhur (Kam's Bukrum) somewhat to its north, the latter being the more likely route in the context. The mutilated Sherpas from above Okhaldhunga were probably of Chiawa clan, which predominates in the area. Sherpas have long been established on high ground to the west of the Thulung as well as to their north; Gora is said to have been founded before 1600 (Oppitz 1968: 89).

A minor discrepancy between Karb and Kam concerns the expedition to fetch bamboos. Kam conflates it with the expedition to attack the Sherpas, while Karb – more neatly – treats it as separate and subsequent. In giving no motivation for the killing of the child, Ph's version is surely incomplete. Elsewhere too, there are some unclarities regarding motivation. In particular, since Salewaceo already knows what has been done to his child, why does he delay demanding to see him until he has washed and is ready to begin eating the meal? Aesthetically, the delay heightens the tension, making one wonder how long the bizarre situation will be maintained. It is not only the listener who is lulled into a false sense that the moment of discovery is to be deferred, but also, within the story, his wife and any others who were present and in the know. This raises the question of the wife's role. In the briefest of the versions (Ph), she is explicitly relieved of responsibility for the atrocity since she is not present when it occurs, and it is her brothers who commit it. In the other versions, conceivably she wishes to keep the news from her husband for honourable reasons, but it is odd that, if her heart is really pure, she is not more sharply distinguished from her wicked sisters.

The upshot of the episode is also blurred. In Ph disobedience to Salewaceo's instructions leads merely to the curse being impossible to exorcise, so that it still hangs over the community, while in Kam it leads to the death of all the inhabitants except a few. In Karb it leads to the land becoming desolate and Salewaceo taking over as ruler; however, his final phrase, not to mention his episode VIII, appears to contradict this. The contradiction could be ironed out by supposing that the dispersal of the

Thulung brothers from Mukli had already started at the time of the drought, but Thulung tradition may well contain irreconcilable contradictions.

The motif of the drought recalls the similarly worded event in Ch. 2 II, when it is Khomda who removes the seeds or mothers of the waters. The parallel deserves careful exploration. In both cases (i) the remover of the waters is a male. (ii) His home is distant from the main location of the story. (iii) Khomda comes in response to a summons, and so does Salewaceo in Karb's version. (iv) Khomda is denied the marital relationship for which he has come, while Salewaceo is denied what he thinks is his rightful share in the spoils of the war to which he has been summoned, as well as having his child roasted. (v) The offended party removes the seeds of the waters and causes a drought. (vi) The offended party makes available to those who suffer the drought a supply of unusual water. In the Creation it is urine capable of causing conception, while here it is water that is at once cold and poisonous. Khomda takes steps to ensure that Miyapma will drink the water, while Salewaceo gives clear instructions that it must not be drunk. However, with his clairvoyant powers, he must have foreseen that it would be drunk; and indeed he could have been motivated by a desire for revenge, and have intended the curse to be incurred. (vii) Those who drink suffer or perish as a result. Miyapma nearly commits suicide with her labour pains, and is eventually killed and eaten by her offspring, while the people of Phuliuku either die directly from the poison (Karb),[30] or (apparently more slowly) 'fade away, drop out, become extinct' (*māsinu* N, the word used by Kam). (viii) Even this is not the end of the story. Had not Khomda replaced Rolasila, we human beings might have been splendid, happy and long-lived (2 II Kam). Similarly, in spite of Salewaceo's séance, the curse still hangs over everybody (Ph).

This list of parallels picks out the details from whichever version best fits the case, and ignores many differences between the two stories, but even if one or two of the points are rejected, enough remain to show that they share a common structure. As in previous instances, I suppose that the Creation story is the older, and thus that the Salewaceo episode is a recasting into pseudo-historical terms of what was once frank mythology. If Salewaceo is a reflex of Khomda, his union is a recasting of the primal mating, and his wife Ekli corresponds of Miyapma. This raises the question of whether there is any homology between Ekli's child and Mini. Possibly: for Mini died by losing his skin, while Ekli's child meets his death by

---

30   The coldness of the poison perhaps balances the heat of the roasting.

roasting, a process that chars or destroys the skin; and afterwards, he is covered with a banana leaf both below and above (Kam), or at any rate above (Karb), a covering that might be taken as a substitute skin. There are also echoes of the other primal mating, that of Khakcilik and Wayelungma, whose first-born, Cindiringma, was crushed beneath the central pillar of the primal house. This was purportedly due to the mother's inadvertence, and may parallel the way in which, in some versions, Ekli fails to dissociate herself from the roasting of her own first-born son at her own hearth. Both stories also involve large wedding celebrations and a sequence of emissaries, unsuccessful at first, sent to summon sisters or sister's husbands.

However for more striking parallels we must look outside Thulung mythology and recall the Tibetan Ru-la-skyes discussed in Ch. 2. Born as a lump of steaming and quivering blood, he was placed in the warm horn of a wild yak, rolled in a pair of clean trousers, and 'boiled by the heat'. Similar episodes of baby-boiling were noted from the childhood of Gesar and of the Na-khi Founder. Unlike Ekli's child, all these figures survive their ordeal, so one might think that here too the parallel with the Salewaceo story bears only on details. However, this would be to overlook something that is central to both the Thulung and Tibetan stories.

Whatever the details of the conflict between Salewaceo and his wife's people, the upshot is that the latter die out and are replaced, so the story is essentially about a discontinuity. Undoubtedly, the present-day narrators conceive of the Mukli dynasty as having been normally patrilineal and patrilocal (cf. e.g. VIII Kam). Thus in the normal course of events the Ramli who won Rathongma would have been succeeded by his youngest son, the Ramli who managed to persuade Salewaceo to come. In the present episode however, the elder Ramli is succeeded by his daughter's husband.

In Tibet the supernaturally born Ru-la-skyes appears at what is even more clearly a point of discontinuity in the tradition. Gri-gum was the eighth in the traditional dynastic list. On their death, all his predecessors had faded into the *dmu* cord, a sort of rainbow extending from their heads into heaven, but Gri-gum involved himself in a fight with one Lo-ngam, 'probably a foreigner' (Stein 1972: 49), and cut through the cord, hence becoming the first king to leave a corpse and to need burial. This in itself constitutes a significant discontinuity, 'a revolution in religious ideas', as Tucci (1949: 734) calls it. Moreover in some versions Ru-la-skyes himself becomes king, although he is not the son of Gri-gum; in others, he arranges for the restoration of Gri-gum's line after the period of usurpation by Lo-ngam. In either case, orderly succession is interrupted. Perhaps too, the discrepancy between the two Tibetan versions echoes the contradictions within the Thulung tradition.

It does not seem profitable to compare the two sets of traditions in greater detail, e.g. to relate the Phuliuku brothers sewn up in their leather sacks to Gri-gum's corpse, which has to be rescued from the belly of a water monster. The point is that in both cases, as one moves forwards from the earliest times, one comes to an episode presenting some clear break in continuity. In the Thulung case the similarity between the rupturing episode and the creation is fairly marked. Tibetan creation mythology is altogether more complex, but we argued for other reasons in Ch. 2 that the Gri-gum story had the character of a creation myth. We can now see that not only do both traditions share an episode focusing on dynastic discontinuity, but also that the two 'rupture' episodes are comparable.

As with the Slug-eating Wife, comparison between Thulung and Tibetan material casts doubt on the historicity of the former (or both). Of course the harmony with the salt-supplying Sherpas implied in III may well have been interrupted by individual quarrels, acts of cruelty and mutual hostilities. The Sherpas' reputation as makers of metal weapons may also very well be historically justified. The episode contains a good deal of valuable incidental information about the past, bearing on ritual matters, on kinship (the old birth-order terms), on family organisation (the function of servants), and so on. But as to the main point of the episode, one can hardly accept as historical a Kulung who married a Mukli girl and became king there following the decimation of the local inhabitants. Nor can I easily imagine a drought severe enough to dry up all the springs and rivers of Mukli. Even if the monsoon failed completely, there used to be so much dense forest above the village that a total drought seems unlikely.[31]

VII. The Dispersal

Karb Ramli's family consisted of seven brothers. The eldest was Kharlium, the second Jokma, the third Ramanjo, the fourth Badepsa, the fifth Ninamto, the sixth Jiugba and the last Ramli himself. Within Ramli's line, we are Hanjium, Congkom and Jiugba; we inhabitants of Lokhim and Jubu are the family of Jiugba. It is from him that we originated, with the passage of time and the splitting up of groups – but these are

---

31   [Cf. also references to Salewaceo in Allen 1986: 91 ff.]

not things we have seen or known, just traditions one hears, which may or may not be true.

Kam   Ramli's children by Rathongma were the following: Jiugba the eldest, then Hanjium, Congkom, Hadisep or some name like that, who lived at Necha Phurke, and with the youngest we come to the one whose home was Mukli, who was called Chepa Raja. The eldest was called Jiugba, and his descendants were Putali Pap's people, Gosea Pap's people, Capciuriu, Liumma, Chenda. The descendants of the second brother, Hanjium, were Reamur, Lapla and Həsti. We are the descendants of the third brother, Congkum – we Deamur, Chiwatto, Charipa, Radur. The fourth brother's descendants lived to the south of Benoseobdel, down below Necha Phurke at Cocoku, while the family of the youngest was at Mukli. There were thus five brothers who were kings, some of the fourth brother's descendants being at Tingla on the other side of the Solu Khola, some on this side. In any case, we were three brothers. Congkom's eldest son was Tinma from who we descend. Tinma died inauspiciously from a fall at Bangaun, originating bad deaths for us.

Hadisep is probably for Karb's Badepsa. The first three brothers reappear in later episodes, particularly Kam IX. The names given as their descendants are those of clans in Jubu and/or Lokhim. Putali Pap is another name for the narrator Mj. Cocoku is the village of Kuybhir. The precise significance of the final phrase in unclear.

Ant   (a) From Rathongma there were eight Thulung brothers, one at each of these villages: Jubu-Lokhim, Ribdung, Salle, Kuybhir, Lapka Bidesi, Mukli, Tingla; and the eldest died.
      (b) Of the eight brothers, the three eldest were at Juba and Lokhim between them, there was one at Ribdung and Salle, one at Kuybhir, one at Tingla, and the youngest at Phuliuku, at Mukli Bidesi. All the Thulung have the one father.

Mj   After we men were born, all our various rajas appeared, each in their own kingdoms. There were ten rajas, but the place from which we spread out was Phuliuku ogama – that is where our *həp* raja was. When we came up from the Place of Origin we came via the Solu Khola, and Ramli occupied Phuliuku where our kingdom was located.

Ramli's parents-in-law were at Sungdel. He brought Rathongma from there and at Phuliuku they had eight sons: Jiugba on one side, Hanjium and Congkom on the other; Kharle went off somewhere or other, and Jogma went south. The Khalings came from the north and are not included. Then I suppose there were the Nachiring, Dumi, Ombule and Jeronge. I am not sure where Jogma and Kharle went, but the youngest was Phuliuku.

For the ten rajas compare episode X. *Hǝp* is generally synonymous with *rāja*, and it is not clear whether it here means 'first', 'chief' or, as seems best, both (see further 6 IV iii).

In addition to tape-recorded accounts of the Dispersal, information combined from various sources in Tingla and Mukli gives the following list, working from eldest brother to youngest: Kharlium went to Kuybhir, Luna to Necha, Jokma Kramcile (?) to Necha, Ramanjo or Temlo to Tingla, Khoska to Dewsa, Jiugba or Jiumba to Jubu[32] and Ninamto to Ribdung, while Phuliuku stayed at Mukli.

This list correlates reasonably with Karb's, but it would be wasted effort to comment on all the discrepancies. The main questions that arise are the number of brothers, their names, the villages to be included in the list and the match between the names of brothers and places. As to the number, Mukli, Dewsa and Tingla seemed to agree with both Jubu informants that there were eight brothers. Kam's total of five comes from episode VI. In view of Karb and Kam IX, Hanjium and Congkom seem to belong to a later generation: certainly no weight can be attached to their presence in Mj's list since it also includes subtribes such as the Nachiring, who belong on an altogether different level of segmentation. Taking account of all the lists except Mj, nine villages are mentioned, since Lapka Bidesi (Ant) is a hamlet in Panchen. However, Panchen is usually spoken of as an offshoot from Mukli, and the neatest solution is to assume that the Jogma in the composite list should have gone to Salle. Apparently, Karb omits the brother who goes to Dewsa; his Badepsa was said by one informant to have gone to Jubu.

Possibly the birth order of the different brothers preserves a shadowy historical record of the order in which the Thulung villages after Mukli were in fact founded. However, I have no means of checking this, and there

---

32 Cf. AS *jiumjiumceo* = 'inhabitant of Jubu'.

may never have been a time when a single list would have been accepted by all Thulung.

Whether or not the order has any historical significance, it is worth noting the position of the episode within this chapter. If the previous episode was a sort of replay of the Creation, and if the Creation ended (more or less) with the dispersal of Miyapma's children, then it is appropriate that this too should be an episode of dispersal. However, one must be cautious here since, as Table I shows, none of the narrators moved from the Salewaceo episode into this one without a break. On the other hand, the present order of episodes seemed to me the natural one before I realised this particular point. We have already noted that Gri-gum's sons dispersed after his death, even if in some versions one of them was later recalled as king.

VIII. The Six Brothers

This episode was collected in only one version. It has been divided into two subepisodes: (a) The six brothers and Jiugba, (b) The six brothers and Lunam. The first few lines were delivered in a slow and halting manner, as if the narrator were casting around in his memory.

Karb   (a) Salewaceo had become king here, together with his people from Salewa. Having come from Salewa, we his descendants became rulers (?). Salewaceo's six brothers stayed over there at Salewa while he was here. Then their sister came across here to live at Jiugba. As to the livelihood of the six brothers, they possessed magic powers, very strong magic. In the place where they went hunting they turned into tigers, bears, jackals, wild cats, crested hawks, falcons; the place where their magic manifested itself was a lake. Then, when they entered the lake, they became tigers, bears, jackals, pine-martens, crested hawks, hawks; and then they came out. This is how they went hunting. Jiugba was their brother-in-law.

One day they invited him to go hunting with them, but he was afraid.[33] As soon as he saw his wife's brothers he climbed into a tree and waited there, wondering whether they were intending to kill and eat him. He spent the whole day like this in a state of fear. When they returned from hunting, they brought back from the lake all different kinds of game – deer, wild goat, wild boar, pheasant and other types

---

33   The sequel shows that the invitation involved his leaving home and going to live for a while with the brothers.

of bird. When they came out, they returned altogether to human forms. They hailed their brother-in-law, and he shouted back. 'Where are you, come out, let us go home!' They had gone down into the lake, come out again as humans, hailed him and then returned home. Once they were there, they cooked the deer, wild goat and boar that they had caught, and feasted on them. The next day, off they went in the same way. To operate their magic they always had to go to the lake. By calling on their magic they turned into the various animals. In the evening, after making their catches, they returned from the lake – after they came out of the water, they were all of them humans again. Again their brother-in-law had been terrified, and had hidden in a tree in the jungle. As before they hailed him and returned for a meal.

After a while they asked him to return to his own home. He agreed, but it was many days before he finally came to his own house. With him he took a full load of gifts, meat and raksi no doubt, and presents of all sorts from his parents-in-law. He sent or brought it all here to his home in Jubu. 'So here you are home again,' said his wife. 'Here I am.' Meanwhile her brothers talked things over: 'That brother-in-law of ours delayed here for many days. Perhaps he has quarrelled with our sister and beaten her.' They decided this was what must have happened, and sent over the fourth brother, who was the one able to transform himself into a tiger. The couple were talking to each other. 'Oh yes, it's a splendid business; these relatives of yours – one turns into a tiger, another into a jackal, another into a pine-marten, another into a crested hawk.'[34] 'He is speaking the names of our magic powers, this brother-in-law of ours.' So saying, he killed Jiugba with his highly potent tiger-magic. His sister was furious at his coming here and doing that. 'So my brothers have gone and killed my husband – well, now I shall go and destroy their magic powers.' What she did was to put into the lake some sort of poison, some substance or medicine that prevented the manifestation of their magic. The next day when her brothers went hunting, they were in for a shock. They went in, they came out, they went in, they came out (but all to no avail).

(b) 'What will become of us, who will feed us, what shall we live on, now that our magic power has been destroyed?' they wondered. Their

---

34 I am not sure whether the remark is a genuine expression of admiration, or sarcastic.

father's eldest brother was called Kampuwa, and he had one son who also had magic powers. The son's wife was gifted with the Thirty-two qualities. So they decided to kill their cousin and marry his gifted wife, who would be able to look after them. Wondering how to set about it, they decided to go and collect honey from the cliff-bees, over by the Cliff house,[35] using a ladder. They would get him to go up the ladder, and once he had finished scraping away the honey, they would cut the ladder and he would fall down the cliff to his death. Then they could marry his wife.

They invited their victim on their expedition, and eventually he had to agree to go. At the bottom of the cliff he asked who would be going up the ladder. He tried to refuse saying that he was worried about being stung by the queen-bee, but they insisted. At last he gave in, on condition that they gave him their clothes and all the bits of cloth and old material that they had about them. He would put them all about his person to serve as protection. Having done so, he set off on the ladder. As he scraped away the honey, he took off the bits of cloth and clothing and smeared them with it. Then he stored them all away in a niche in the cliff face. So he continued, taking off his clothes one by one and soaking them in honey. A certain amount of honey was left aside, and this he sent up to them, calling to one of them to pull it up. The basket was returned (?)... And he continued as before digging out the honey and storing it on the cloth in the recess of the cliff. When he had finished making his cache, he said to himself: 'Now they are going to try and kill me.' He went into the little cave and shouted to his brothers that he had finished the honey. Immediately they heard this, they hammered through the rope ladder above. It broke easily, and the ladder fell away into space leaving the man himself safely ensconced in the cliff.

Thereafter, day after day, dabbing his fingers in the honey, he lived off what he had smeared on the clothes. He continued like this for a matter of years, until at long last the honey ran out and there was nothing left for him to eat. He got thinner and thinner, and weaker and weaker. 'This is the end for me, I shall die,' he was saying, when just at that moment this saviour appeared. There he sat in the cave, and his saviour – who was what we call a white monkey – dangled his tail within his reach. 'Whatever happens this must be my saviour – either

---

35 Unidentified, presumably a local landmark.

he will kill me or he will get me to safety.' He spat on his hands and seized the tail in a tight grip. 'What's this that has caught hold of me?' exclaimed the monkey, and leaped upwards, carrying the man out onto the open ground. There he left him and went jumping off on his way. Meanwhile, Kampuwa's son, who was called Lunam, returned to his house.

But at home the husband's cousins were talking to his wife. They exchanged greetings. 'Has that cousin of ours turned up?' 'He has not. You invited him to go with you to collect the cliff honey, and I don't know what happened, whether he died, whether you killed and ate him, whether you made him fall down the cliff; anyway he has not come back here.' Then they teased her, each of the six brothers in turn asking the same question. Each time she gave the same reply. Then, one day, at last, her husband returned, on the point of death. She hid him inside the house and prepared him nourishing meals with meat and rice. She gave him everything he needed, milk, buttermilk, ghee, delicately spiced preparations, and slowly his strength returned. One day the fourth of her husband's younger brothers – of her *riw*, as we say – turned up again to ask her whether his cousin had yet returned. 'I don't know what you can have done to him, whether you killed and ate him, whether you threw him down the cliff. He has not come back since the day you took him off with you to collect the honey.' In reality her husband had now fully recovered his strength. 'Among the six brothers this is the one I can't stand (?)', he said. So he came down and killed him.

'Now I've killed one of them, there are five brothers left. Let us flee.' So he took his wife and father, and the three of them blew up a good blaze on the fire (?). As they fled, here and there they scooped up water in plantain leaves when the leaves were so long, and cut the *moasa* when it was black.[36] Meanwhile the others followed their tracks. 'So our cousin got away the other day, and we did not realise. He has cut the plantain when it was so long, he has cut the *moasa* when it was black. He must have fled from his home.' They had fled north, up above Salewa, up to Salpa silippa, and came out at Pangwa, at Panch Pokhari, leaving signs of their passage all along their route.

---

36 The plantain and *moasa* are several times coupled in contexts having to do with journeys through the jungle (4 Kam III and CP IV). Here, as previously, the exact meaning of the idiom is unclear.

When they were up at Panch Pokhari, being a magician, he divided the waters of the lake with his plumed headdress. So he passed through them himself, taking his wife and father with him, and when they emerged on the other side they settled down. 'How did you get across there?' called his pursuers. 'We have been following your traces, weeping because we missed you. It is our affection that had brought us up here to look for you. But how did you get across this lake, this great body of water?' 'You remember when we went to collect the honey, how you gave me all your old bits of cloth. Well, I put them on and wound myself up in them and we came across rolling over and over.' 'That's true, we did give you all our clothes and old bits of cloth.' So they went home and collected a supply and put them all on. Then they jumped into the lake and sank at once. Every one of the five brothers was drowned.

Apart from occasional difficulties in translation, the narrative line and the motivation of the characters are relatively clear. For Karb, both Ramli and Salewaceo are one among sets of seven brothers; the fourth brother, who plays a relatively prominent part in the present episode, would be the middle one of the original seven. Note that both Jiugba and Lunam's wife are worried about the possibility of cannibalism. My commentator stated that thirty-two was the proverbial number of qualities (*gun* N) for a wife (the text actually has thirty-two 'signs' or 'marks' – *lacchin* N). Presumably one of her virtuous qualities is displayed in her faithfulness to the memory of the husband she must suppose to be dead, and in her resistance to the blandishments of his killers. This concept of the ideal wife is expressed in Nepali, and more likely comes direct from the Hindu world, rather than indirectly via Tibet;[37] but the proposed polyandrous marriage with Jiugba's widow more likely reflects Tibetan ideas than Hindu ones. The technique of collecting wild bee's honey from cliff faces by means of rope ladders and poles seems to have been widely practised, in the past at any rate.[38]

---

37 The Buddha's mother was identified by the possession of thirty-two qualities. Incidentally, the Buddha himself also possessed the thirty-two marks of a Great Man, and his conception was accompanied by thirty-two signs (Thomas 1927: 29, 220, 32 respectively).

38 A Bhote from Changa used to collect honey in this way from Brew Broa ('Wild Bees Cliff') near Mukli's Rindepu hamlet. The bees have now departed – presumably for ecological reasons, though local tradition ascribes it to a

As to the geography, among the brothers of Ramli Jiugba is the one associated with Jubu and Lokhim in the Dispersal. Though Pangwa is unidentified, Salpa lies on the Dudh Kosi-Arun watershed east of Lokhim, and Panch Pokhari lies between the Hinku and Hongu rivers roughly on the latitude of Jubing. Thus subepisode (b) is located clearly within Kulung territory, which accords with the fact that the six brothers and Lunam are all patrilineal relatives of the Kulung Salewaceo. It is noteworthy that this very Kulung-centred narrative was recorded only at the tip of the Thulung tract adjacent to Kulung territory.

Subepisode (a) shows a structural similarity to the Salewaceo story, as the following formulaic summary shows.

Salewaceo. Kulung male (A) marries Ekli (B), sister of a group of Thulung brothers (C). A offends C. C roast child of A and B. A poisons water supply of C.

Jiugba. Thulung male (A) marries unnamed female (B), sister of group of Kulung brothers (C). A offends C. Member of C kills A. B poisons magic lake of C.

In both cases the initial offence is given when the individual Kulung or Thulung is residing in the village of his wife's brothers, and in both cases it is the wife-givers who suffer the poisoning. So if the Salewaceo story is a recasting of a Creation myth from the Thulung point of view, the Six Brothers and Jiugba is perhaps a similar recasting from a Kulung point of view. This would make the magic lake equivalent to a primal like. But at the moment nothing is known of Kulung mythology.

Subepisode (b) is also a story of crime and punishment, this time between agnates. We have commented earlier (4 VII) on the frequent references to the tails of animals in ritual and mythological contexts. The trick by which Lunam drowns his brothers has the same sort of transparency as the trick used by Chamling in 4 III. The motif of the division of the waters recalls 2 III Ant.

The most interesting fact about the subepisode is that, according to Chemjong (1966 II: 63f), it forms an important part of Gurung oral tradition.

---

curse. I was once able to see a Sherpa and his friends in action on a cliff above the Likhu Khola just north of the route from Junbesi to Bhandar.

Since Chemjong's work in not widely available, I transcribe the relevant passage in full, making only one comment on the author's English.

> Pachyu Lama is the chief priest of the Ghaley tribe who performs all the religious functions according to the way of Buddhism of Tibet. But Ghyabring Lama is the Chief priest of Gurung tribe who conducts all the religious rites according to the rules of Gurung culture. In fact, Gurung tribe has no independent script of their own, so they recite their tradition orally and teach their children to do so. The Gyabring priest recites the story of their forefather and mother who took trouble and suffered much for the safeguard of their children. They worshipped God and asked help from Him to drive away their enemies, and according to their belief God heard their prayer and saved their forefather who was entangled in the middle of a very big precipice by his enemies. When he was shut in a wayless cave of the precipice, a big monky became his guide and brought him back to his home.[39] When his enemies came to know[40] about his family members, he left the place and crossed a big lake by means of a boat. His enemies followed them up to the shore of that lake. But by the spiritual power of their forefather, his enemies failed to cross the lake so they were saved. This is the gist of the Ghyabringism from which the Gurung tribe extract good lesson of tolerance and its consequences.

If the story has such a fundamental role in the tribal religion of the Gurung it is no doubt much richer in meaning than is suggested by its rather marginal and inconsequential place in Thulung tradition.[41]

IX. The Foundation of Daughter Villages

This blanket title serves to bring together CP's Foundation of Tingla, and Kam's Foundation of Jubu and Lokhim. The two stories have the same general character but lack shared details, and in this case the grouping does not imply that they are different versions of the same episode.

CP   Afterwards Ramli and Patisang quarrelled, and Patisang came down here to Boksama sirangma. Finding that Yoreota was already here, he told him that he could not stay. The two of them quarrelled, and Yoreota was driven off over to Necha and the Bahing territory. Patisang stayed here, while Ramanjo remained at Phuliuku. We nowadays

---

39   Sherbahadur Gurung's version (Chemjong's footnote).
40   The meaning is 'when they came to *enquire*'.
41   [A comparable story is widespread in the Indo-European-speaking world, e.g. *Mahābhārata*, book 11, Ch. 5-6.]

are Ramanjo's descendants – both Patisang and Phuliuku were the children of Ramanjo.

The episode follows immediately after the Foundation of Mukli. CP's uncertainty about the name Ramanjo was noted in 4 VI, and we saw in VII that Ramanjo is usually regarded as founding ancestor of Tingla. Possibly his name is here confused with that of Ramli.

Nothing further is known of Patisang or Yoreota. Boksagaun, here referred to by its ritual name, was where CP himself lived, close to the old *bhume* site. Some informants claimed that Waksikhom was the first settlement in Tingla.

Kam Hanjium and Congkom crossed to Jubu via Sikudip, while Jiugba crossed via Broku Khola and the path down from Dewsa. In those days the Dudh Kosi was a very large river, with *rebusi*, *kəksi* and *ṭera* trees – such as we use nowadays for fodder – standing on either side forming a sort of bridge. The ends of the branches reached from one bank to the other, making as it were a thatched roof over the river. There were no ferrymen and no boats to cross in. Well, two of our ancestors took the route down by Balanga cəkcile and Pitemtar, forcing their way through the jungle and living by hunting. Eventually, they came to Grumdel. Meanwhile Jiugba, the eldest, came from Dewsa and the Broku Khola, and cleared the jungle at Bangaun. As the others worked south, they met at Lugare and greeted each other politely...Each of them built a shack,[42] and they lived for two or three weeks clearing the jungle at Bangaun...A *bhĩguma* bird came with its call *cəcəpu cəcəpu*. Jiugba claimed that the *bhĩguma*, king of the birds, had come to occupy his land as a king, while the other two proposed different interpretations.[43] They quarrelled and pulled down the shack, and each went off by himself, swearing to kill the others... Congkom decided to move across to Delbaya here, while Hanjium and Jiugba lived over in Jubu at Balakci. All of them now looked for wives...

There was a place where a bear used to forage ... Congkom waited for it in hiding all night long with his bow drawn. At dawn the bear appeared snuffling and grunting...and he killed it. It was vast. He

---

42   Or possibly they built a single shack (*yāksā* N, *tho*).
43   Hanjium refers to a priest (*dewa*), Congkom to Sakhle, i.e. a *bhume* site; but I do not understand the passage.

waited a long time to be sure that the animal was really dead. At last he ventured fearfully out from his hideout and threw stones at it, to see if it would move. Reassured, he went down to his house at Delbaya and told his wife... The two of them went and broke up the corpse and piled up the pieces. While the husband was busy cutting them up, his wife carried away load after load of meat. Back at home he told her to cook it. 'Don't worry about doing it too carefully – I have had nothing to eat since yesterday,' he said. In those days there were no metal cooking vessels, just earthenware ones. They did not cut meat into fine portions, but ate it in great big lumps, without salt or chilli, just boiled in water.

There was so much meat that they realised they could never eat it all, and the husband decided to take some as a present to his two brothers over in Jubu. He made up a load of it and took also a vessel of garnishing made with the blood. He gave some to his second brother, who lived the nearer of the two, and then went on to his eldest brother. Before he went, Hanjium gave him a decent-sized earthenware bowl (*ploka*) of the sort you can still see occasionally in some households. When Jiugba saw the gift, he exploded with indignation: 'Somebody has already had his fill of this, and I am to be given the left-overs!' He seized the plate and threw it on the ground where it broke, and spilled all the meat. Both of them now swore to kill the other, and an evil force was created.

One day Jiugba approached Hanjium and proposed that they should go and visit Congkom. Hanjium understood his wicked intention, which was to set fire to Congkom's house and burn him inside it. He wondered how to warn his younger brother... and lied to Jiugba, pretending that he had a stomach ache. 'I am not well enough to go. You go by yourself.' He also made Jiugba blow him up a fire of huge proportions. The other went off downhill... Congkom understood the message (of the large fire) and left his house and fled. By the time Jiugba set fire to the house, Congkom had already left. Now they were real enemies. Congkom went up to Ngomphar by the jungle edge, which was named after Congkom's child Ngom. The other two brothers remained over in Jubu, performing their own *ḍiumla* and increasing in numbers, while our ancestors stayed here.

The episode is most interesting for its incidental asides. Other informants confirmed that it was once possible to cross the Dudh Kosi using the large trees on its banks. The detailed topography of the episode was not elucidated, but it is nearly certain that the original settlement was at Jubu. Thus the episode essentially recounts the splitting off of Lokhim from Jubu. It also provides a sample of the quarrelling so often mentioned by CP as occurring during the migrations of the ancestors, but never described by him in any detail. The motif of two founding parties coming by different routes to the same original settlement is discussed in the next section.

Up to this point we have tried to present the Thulung narratives in an order which would gain the approval of a Thulung who himself set out to collate his people's traditions and weave them into a continuous whole. The two remaining episodes stand outside this main sequence. There has been no good point at which to introduce them earlier, and they merit inclusion somewhere.

X. The Das Kirant

Das merely means 'ten', but it is not translated in the title since the phrase is so firmly established that it rates as a name.

Ant (Miyapma's son) passed up towards Bhot and brought down a Sherpa wife. From her there were five brothers; Thulung, Kulung, Khaling, Nachiring, Dumi – we are all from the Sherpa wife. Then he passed towards the plains and took a Danuwar wife, and from her too there were five brothers: Chamling, Bontawa, Yakkha, Bahing, Tilunge. These were from the plainswoman, but all of them had the one father – ten brothers, two mothers. They took wives from wherever they could find them, from any tribe, and produced children. Later they could not find wives outside – we had become the Das Kirant – and we took to marrying among ourselves. Afterwards the languages of all the Das Kirant became different from each other. All these various languages, Thulung, Khaling, Kulung, Nachiring, Dumi and so on, were given us by Syan Raja when we sought wives and made marital alliances.

We may start by distinguishing in the episode three separate ideas: that the Kiranti consist of ten groups; that half the Kiranti are affiliated to the north and half to the south; and that in the course of time an original unity was lost and the groups become more differentiated.

We have already noted in Ch. 1 the vagueness of the term Kiranti. The phrase Das Kirant is very widely known and is often brought up when one comments on the differences between one subtribe and another; it is implicit in the 'ten rajas' of Mj VII. There is no generally recognised canon of names to be included, nor any particular order in which they should be given (except that the Nachiring are regularly named immediately before the Dumi – they are in fact neighbours). An ethnographer who raises the question of subtribes other than those given by a particular informant, is likely to be told that they originated later. In spite of the precision of the list that Ant here provides, he himself also used the term Kiranti in one of its broader and less definite senses, remarking that 'there are all sorts of Kiranti – Mech, Koch, Rajbangsi, and others down in Assam'. The three names he mentions refer to peoples living in the south-east of Nepal and adjacent parts of India (see Bista 1972: 134ff).

Ant's division of the Kiranti into two groups is interesting. The 'Sherpa' wife from Bhot should be understood as coming from a population of Tibetan affinities, rather than as being specifically a Sherpa in the present-day sense. The Danuwar are now one of the smaller ethnic groups among the traditional inhabitants of the Terai (Bista 1972: 128ff), and I take it that they here represent the inhabitants of the Plains. Although by no means a complete listing of the Rai subtribes, Ant's list is geographically realistic in distinguishing a northern and southern group (the Tilunge live around Udaipur to the south of the Bahing). Although Ant makes no reference to the Lasagotra/Kasigotra distinction, he probably had it in mind since, as we saw in II 4, these are the terms by which the Thulung regularly distinguish subtribes of northern and southern affinities. The Limbu do likewise, for they too are often said to descend from ten brothers. All ten were once living at Benares, but five of them reached Limbuwan via Lhasa, thus founding the Lasagotra, and five of them went direct from Benares, founding the Kanshi or Kasigotra (Ministry of Defence 1965: 99f).[44] The association with Benares has been touched on earlier, and the more important point here is the equal division of the ten into northern and southern groups. If Ant in fact conceived of the Thulung as Lasagotra, he differed from all the other Thulung I met who had opinions on the issue: the general view was that the Thulung belonged to the southern group and the Khaling to the northern (cf. 4 VI Karb (b)).

---

44   In addition to the ten brothers, some accounts mention three ritual officiants (*bijuwā*).

The last part of the episode refers to two processes, namely a shift from Kiranti exogamy to Kiranti endogamy and the linguistic differentiation of the subtribes. The former is a projection onto a large scale of a process known to occur within the subtribe. Macdougal (1973: 212ff) describes how a Kulung clan is strictly exogamous for seven generations beginning with that of the clan founder's sons, but in the eighth generation, or at any time thereafter, a marriage may take place between members of two subdivisions of the clan. Such a marriage is expected to occur eventually, and leads to the fission of the original single clan into two new clans. The union that precipitates the split is known as a *hāḍphora* marriage, from Nepali *hāḍ* 'bone' and *phornu* 'break, smash, open'. Although clan organisation among the Thulung is in some disarray, the former existence of the custom was recognised, and Ant uses the same expression, *hāḍphorikana bihā* N *bomu*, literally 'to marry bone-breakingly', here translated 'to marry among ourselves'.

As to the linguistic differentiation, we are presumably to understand that the original ten brothers spoke either one language, corresponding to their single father, or two, corresponding to their mothers. I know nothing about Syan Raja.[45]

From several points of view, the episode gives the impression of being Hindu or Nepalese, rather than Thulung or Bodic. Consider the following expressions: Das Kirant, Lasagotra, Kasigotra, *hāḍphora* marriages, Syan Raja. All of them are made up of Nepali elements, and none of them have recognised Thulung equivalents. Thus *prǝciu*, the usual Thulung equivalent for 'Kiranti', is never coupled with a numeral. Secondly, throughout Thulung tradition, as we shall see, it is normal for the line of continuity to pass through the youngest son, whereas here the Thulung are given first among the offspring of the first wife. Thirdly, although Ant locates the episode immediately after the Birth of the Species, it is in no other way integrated with the main body of Thulung tradition.

From one point of view then, the episode might be seen as a product of the interaction between Bodic speakers and Nepalese immigrants. With the appearance of the latter, a sense of Kiranti identity grew up which was expressed in the form of the myth now shared by Limbu and Thulung (and doubtless by other Rai subtribes also). The north-south dichotomy may be

---

45 Syan no doubt = Nepali Sen (from Sk *sena*), an element in proper names, e.g. in those of the rajas who ruled from Makwanpur or Vijaypur in the century or so preceding the unification of Nepal under Prithvi Narayan.

taken either as an observation made by the outsiders about the cultural affiliations of the subtribes, or as a matter of self-identification, or both. In either case its application would be somewhat subjective, and liable to change over time. In the latter respect one might compare it with what has sometimes been called the 'salt line', the division between those who travelled north for the commodity and those who travelled south.

Although there is no doubt about the Nepalese influence recognisable in the episode as we have it, this does not rule out the possibility of a Bodic background. The Kiranti family arises when its progenitor sets out from his home, no doubt located in the middle hills, goes north to collect one wife, then south to collect another. We have met such paired journeys before. (i) Jaw and Khliw parted company and travelled, one north and the other south, only to return with their acquisitions and live together at Jawaji. (ii) In Kam IX, after the three brothers set off from their common home at Mukli, two of them crossed the river somewhere to the north, while the other crossed more or less directly further downstream; but their separation was only temporary, and they met and lived together for a while at Bangaun or Luware. (iii) In the origin story of the Limbu, the two groups of brothers travelled by separate routes from Benares, but met again in Limbuwan. However these parallels are not very close, since the two journeys are made by separate parties and do not involve marriages. A much closer parallel to Ant's story comes from Tibet.

One of the best known traditions about Srong-btsan sgam-po ascribes his introduction of Buddhism to the influence of two of his various wives (the others are far less celebrated). One was a princess from Nepal, later identified with the White Tara, while the other was the princess from China mentioned above in connection with episode II, who is identified with the Green Tara. The symmetry between the two is emphasised in several ways, in addition to their link with Tara: one came from the west, one from the east,[46] both were asked for and taken to Tibet in similar ways, both brought with them sacred images, both founded famous temples in Lhasa, and finally at the king's 'death' (when he dissolved into Avalokiteshvara's statue), the Nepalese wife disappeared into his right shoulder and the Chinese into his left. As the Tibetan historical tradition developed, it tended to magnify far beyond reality the role of Srong-btsan sgam-po as a founding figure of Tibetan Buddhism, and the story of the two wives fitted well with

---

46 Some texts say from the south and east, though Kathmandu is in fact much further to the west than to the south of Lhasa.

the identification of the king with the deity Khasarpana (a form of Avalokiteshvara), accompanied by his two wives. After reviewing these points, Tucci (1962) concludes that there is no reliable historical evidence for the existence of the Nepalese wife, and that in its absence she was most likely concocted out of a desire for symmetry and for essentially hagiographical reasons.

If Tucci is right, the Tibetan story is nearly as mythical as the Thulung one. Whether the story is about the origin of Buddhism in Tibet or the origin of the Kiranti in Nepal, the founder is a man who takes his two significant wives from opposite cardinal points, and in both cases the symmetry of the wives is emphasised (in the Thulung, by their equal number of sons). In Ant's story the Kiranti founder makes the northward and southward journeys himself, whereas in the Tibetan story the journeys to Kathmandu and the Chinese capital are made on behalf of the king by the minister mGar. The difference is the same as in episode II and like that in episode I, where Ramli went to fetch the slugs himself while the Tibetan king merely instructed his wife to send a servant.

In both cases the brides' natal homes point to the competing external cultural influences on the people represented by the central male. Just as the Kiranti are as it were suspended between the dominant cultures of Tibet and the Plains – Lhasa and Benares in the local formulation, so seventh-eighth century Tibet was suspended between Chinese and Indian Buddhism. The religious conflict came to a head at the Council of Lhasa held in *ca* 792, when the decision went in favour of the Indians.

We now have two instances of a Founder who takes his wives from opposite quarters, and one looks for further instances. We saw in Ch. 2 that Khakcilik may originally have married not Wayelungma but a sister. However, no explanation was given for there being *two* sisters, associated respectively with north and south. We can now see that, if Khakcilik did indeed marry two sisters, he was conforming to the same pattern as the founder of Tibetan Buddhism and the ancestor of the Kiranti.

If Ant's story emphasises two wives, the Limbu one emphasises rather the two journeys, oriented towards the neighbouring large-scale cultures. A comparable pattern can be recognised in a tradition about the family of the fifth and greatest of the Dalai Lamas (Tucci 1949: 736). This family claimed descent from a royal prince from Za-hor in Bengal who moved to the area of the Bha-Ta-hor near Lake Baikal, close to the mountain sacred to the family of Genghis Khan. In other words, the progenitor's migration took him from the sacred country of Buddhism to the birth place of an ancestor much revered by the Mongols (the dominant power in Tibetan politics at the time). The traditional home of the Dalai Lama's family was actually at 'Phyong-rgyas' in the Yarlung valley not far from Lhasa, i.e. in between Bengal and Lhasa. This ancestral migration thus resembles that of the Thulung and Khaling ancestors: they too started in the plains, visited or approached a centre of civilisation in the north, and finally settled down in between. It seems that in the Bodic area origins or foundations are commonly associated with paired journeys in opposite directions.

It remains to ask whether Tibetan parallels can be found for the change mentioned by Ant from Kiranti exogamy to endogamy. In discussing the frog-eating queen we saw that, after the first twenty-three or -four queens of the Yarlung dynasty, there occurred what Stein (1972: 50f) calls 'an important constitutional development.' The kings ceased taking as wives the daughters of gods and serpents who left no corpses at death, and began instead to marry among their subjects, 'a state of affairs described by the chronicles as an 'admixture', presumably in the sense of an improper match'. The exact placement of this event is worth noting. The complete sequence of kings who make up the mythological dynasty is divided into five named groups, as discussed at length by Haarh (1969); following one tradition, the numbers in each group are respectively 7, 2, 6, 8, 5. Now the change in royal marriage customs occurs after the group of eight lDe kings, and the figure eight is the same as the total made up by seven generations plus that of the founder in the Kulung exogamic rule.[47] Furthermore, the change in post-mortem fate of the queens recalls the similar change in fate of the kings occurring at the death of Gri-gum. As we saw in VI above, Gri-gum's reign marked a point of discontinuity in the patriline, and it may be more than chance that he was the eighth king in the dynasty. Moreover, according to one of the traditions, the change in the nature of the queens comes after twenty-four reigns, i.e. 3 x 8; and the great Srong-btsan sgam-po comes at number 32 or 33.

Before reaching firm conclusions one should make a thorough comparative examination of notions of descent among the Bodic speakers. As is well known, Tib *rus* or *rus-pa* means both 'patrilineal clan' and 'bone', but I do not know a Tibetan equivalent for the term *hāḍphora*, and it is curious that the Rai term is Nepali in origin. However, even now, it

---

47   Ru-la-skyes too was 'the first of a series of seven wise ministers' (Stein 1972: 49).

seems likely that Ant's reference to the global history of Kiranti marriage has parallels in Tibetan myth.

XI. Daner and Pokner

This is a story of miraculous doings from ancient times. It apparently assumes that the Thulung are already settled at Mukli, but there is otherwise no way of locating it within the general sequence of Thulung traditions.

Ph I don't know the full story of Daner and Pokner, but I have heard people telling bits of it.

(a) Daner and Pokner were the names of two close friends. In those days there was a large lake up at Ghumne Pani – indeed there was real jungle everywhere. The two of them went to the lake and performed their invocations. Then they struck the outlet with the plumes from their headdresses, and all the water flowed away. In the bottom of the lake was a plentiful supply of large frogs. They caught the lot of them and brought them down. Some they killed (?), some they dried, some they cooked whole, and some they ate. The next day, towards evening, the Lord of the Soil came down grieving, searching for then, following their tracks. However, the friends knew that he was coming and flew into their drums and hid there. The Lord of the Soil could not find them and returned home grieving. Thus they had committed an act of wickedness.

(b) In the monsoon season they had to assemble a group of labourers from various places so as to get the work done in their fields. They got them to plant out the rice fields, but made no effort to take any beer or snacks. Instead, for each labourer they cut a bamboo wand and distributed them all round. They told each man to turn and face across the valley to Jubu, and suck on the end of the wand as if from a *tongba*. When they did so, filtered beer flowed steadily from the wands. They drank it and worked at a tremendous rate.

The tongba[48] in (b) is a segment of a large bamboo used as a vessel for beer; one drinks from it, particularly at weddings, by sucking through a

---

48 Tib *dong-po*, one of the few words in Thulung that are probably more or less direct loans from Tibetan, rather than distant cognates reflecting common membership of the Bodic group of languages. The word is also current in Limbu (Chemjong 1961: 119).

small-diameter bamboo tube. The wands mentioned are used by mediums at seances in various ways, and in particular for sucking out from patients putative foreign bodies held to have caused an illness (Allen 1976b, esp. fn 8). The second miracle shows no clear relationship to the first, which bears out the narrator's introductory apology; presumably the story once had a longer sequence of supernatural deeds.

The story of the draining of the Lake at Ghumne Pani was also given by SSJ, who stated that the two friends were mediums (*bijuwā*). This is in any case clear from Ph's version, both because of the shamanic drums and because the use of feathers as cutting weapons is recognised as one of the medium's special skills. Mukli tradition recalls at least one other lake that has disappeared: the lists of place names that occur in many of the priest's chants include Borodin grayongma, in which *boro* means 'frog', *din* 'lake', and the second element probably relates to *graywa* 'crab'. This lake was formerly situated a minute's walk from Ph's house, and some villagers maintained that it had been drained by divine agency. So far as a non-geographer can tell, it is not implausible that small lakes once existed at these two sites.

The 'Lord of the Soil' was rendered by SSJ as *baneskandi* N, a word that is not in the dictionaries. Ph's Thulung term *bayahəp* 'land-lord, earth-lord', is also applied to wealthy human landowners as well as spirits; its meaning seems to be the same as Tib *sa-bdag* 'lord of the soil'. My commentator understood that the Lord of the Soil was angry at the treatment of his realm.

Comparable stories of the drainage of ancient lakes have been reported from many areas.[49] The best known from the Himalayas is no doubt the tradition that Manjushri came from China and carved with his sword the channel for the exit of the waters that once filled the central valley of Nepal (Nepali 1965: 324). It had formerly been the home of innumerable serpents (nagas), of whom one still remains in a certain tank. Secondly, in the eastern Himalayas, tradition relates that when the ancestors of the Apa Tani first arrived from distant lands in the east, they found the valley they now inhabit filled with swamps and stagnant pools, containing lizard-like monsters of enormous size called *buru*. The Apa Tani drained the valley to turn it into arable land, killing the harmless reptiles (Fürer-Haimendorf 1955: 54; 1962: 13). Thirdly, even if it is strictly outside our area, it is interesting to note a Chinese tradition that, when the world began, the middle lands were

---

49   [For fuller treatment see Allen 1997a.]

flooded with vast stretches of water inhabited by serpents and dragons; the humans had nowhere to live. Yu (in another version, assisted by Yi) dug a channel and made the waters flow away, forcing the serpents and dragons into the swamps (Kaltenmark 1959: 461).

From Tibet too, traditions exist both that the whole of the Land of Snows was originally covered by a lake, and that there was originally a small lake in the plain around Lhasa; both lakes subsequently dwindled in size (Stein 1972: 37f). Surprisingly perhaps, none of the extracts cited by Stein state that the lakes were inhabited by any sort of water creature, and no close parallel for the Thulung story has so far been found from Tibet. However, not much emphasis can be laid on the failure of the texts to mention any inhabitants of the lakes. No doubt, for Tibetans, there is no significant quantity of water in nature, whether still or running, that is not assumed to be the home of serpents (*klu*). 'The *Klu* have a special, jealous, proprietary interest in water springs, streams, and lakes,' and their 'ubiquitous presence' strongly affects Tibetan use of natural waters, deterring people from polluting them (Ekvall 1964: 79).

Whether or not the Tibetan primal lake was the home of serpents, we should explore further the frog-serpent relationship suggested by the parallel between the Thulung and Newar stories. A natural link between the two species is that both are cold-blooded water creatures. Both receive fairly elaborate worship from the Newars as controllers of the monsoon rains (Nepali 1965: 323-7). Since the Newar notion of serpents is, so far as I can tell, entirely Sanskritic in character, maybe the frogs were the older and indigenous monsoon-controllers.[50] In Tibet the pre-existing indigenous concept of the *klu* was certainly strongly affected by the Sanskritic concept (e.g. Hoffmann 1950: 158), and the term was also extended from its basic meaning of aquatic and subterranean deities to cover local gods of all the storeys of the world (Stein 1959: 453). But apart from the question of historical changes, one can find in Tibetan mythology a number of links between the various water creatures.

(i) We have already cited serpent creator goddesses, parts of whose bodies give rise to parts of the cosmos (Tucci 1949: 712). Similarly an indigenous (i.e. pre-Buddhist) creation story, summarised in the epic, tells of a blue turquoise frog (or toad – Tib *sbal*[51]): dropping down from heaven,

---

50   Dried frog meat is essential also in offerings to the goddess of smallpox, an important figure in the Newar pantheon (Nepali 1965: 310).

51   Stein regularly refers to a *crapaud,* rather than a *grenouille.* Das gives *sbal* as frog, *sbal-nag* as toad.

it fragments into various parts which give rise to features of the geography and to humans or animals associated with the narrative (Stein 1959: 463). Cosmogonic dismemberment stories are told about other species, notably about a tiger or tigress and a lion (ibid: 514), but not about an indefinite range of species.

(ii) The tortoise in Tibetan is simply a bony frog (*rus-sbal*) and is often used in divination as an image of the whole created world (ibid; Tucci 1949: 722f). The representation actually shows a skinned monster with head and limbs intact, holding impaled frogs in all four members. According to Stein, this monster can probably be identified with the she-demon lying on her back, whose body represents the country of Tibet and who is related to the lake beneath the Cathedral in Lhasa (cf. the discussion of foundation sacrifices in Ch. 3).[52]

(iii) One Tibetan cosmogony (Tucci 1949: 711) starts with a golden tortoise which begot six eggs, whence came five families of *klu* (one egg being unaccounted for). The *klu* are *par excellence* the spirits from whom help would be sought in a drought (e.g. Nebesky-Wojkowitz 1956: 467ff), but a Tibetan prayer, probably influenced by the Chinese, talks of a *sbal-the* ('blue dragon' – note *sbal* again), which might cause drought (Tucci 1949: 740).

(v) Tibetan iconography is so rich and varied that I have barely been able to dip into it, but it is interesting that of the two frog-headed deities mentioned by Nebesky-Wojkowitz (1956: 261, 280), one, the female companion to the chief of all planetary gods, has as the lower part of her body the coiled tail of a snake. In this last respect she resembles the mistress of the *klu-mo*, whose mount is a black tortoise (ibid: 287).

(vi) Here is part of what is probably a late compilation, translated by Macdonald (1959: 445f) as representative of creation myths relating to the subterranean plane.

> A Creator Being decides to build a Creation Castle or primal World House. Using a bronze arrow and a large thunderbolt, he succeeds in

---

52   But we also compared the she-demon to the Limbu Okwanama, 'a fictitious turtle supposed to have been bearing the earth on its back' (Chemjong 1961: 29). According to Sagant (1973: 69), Okwanama's dwelling is the central pillar of the house. Perhaps, if more were known about Gurung tribal religion, one could relate Okwanama to Wainbarnaje, the central pillar of the world and supporter of the heavens. The latter is said to be represented in the house by two birds (*cha-name* and *pleh-name*), representing respectively long life and good fortune (Pignède 1966: 316, 375f).

shaking free a crystal rock containing or associated with a cave inhabited by a serpent.[53] Dragging it off with the aid of two elephants he throws it into the foundation of his castle. When he has completed the building, an eagle hovers over its summit and a spring begins to flow from one of its sides; in the spring is a golden frog as large as a kid. At this moment the hands of the builder begin to dry up, and subsequently his whole body wastes until after three years he has virtually no flesh on him. The condition is diagnosed as being the revenge taken on him by the serpent. The elephants who assisted him are afflicted similarly.

Here then is another cosmogonic myth that associates frogs and serpents, albeit obscurely. It serves as further evidence that the story of Daner and Pokner is more than just an aetiological myth invented to explain a feature of the landscape in the uninhabited pasture above Mukli and Nele. Given the various parallels, the first part of the story must be recognised as essentially a localised fragment from some creation myth. The sandalwood tree in which Mini sheltered in VII 2 was also located close to Ghumne Pani, and we argued that that episode too was a modified creation myth. It follows that the lake in the present episode is yet another version of the primal lake that we met at the very start of the Creation, and that has since recurred repeatedly.

One further motif in the Tibetan story is interesting, namely the wasting disease caused by the offended serpent. Simply as a disease, it reminds one of the affliction suffered by the slug/frog-eating females when they were deprived of the watery foodstuffs appropriate to their origins. At the end of episode I these wasting diseases were related to the comatose condition of Miyapma after Khomda had removed the grandmothers of the waters and deprived her of that essential element. But all these characters who grow thin or dry are female, while the Builder of the Creation Castle is a male. Given the general emphasis on males in Tibetan Creation stories, the builder's sex is not unexpected, especially perhaps since the myth was supposedly put together relatively late. The problem that arises is rather the relation between the Builder's disease and the leprosy of the frog-eater's husband: according to Hoffmann, the latter too arose as a punishment following dealings with a serpent. Does this mean that the leprosy, as well as the wasting disease, can be paralleled with Miyapma's coma? The idea is hardly convincing. Among other difficulties, leprosy affects the

---

53   Stein (1959: 514) mentions a fragmentary account of a being contemporary with creation who triumphs over evil because he recognises the demon in the form of a frog in the interior of a stone.

extremities rather than causing drying or wasting of the whole body. It is better, though quite speculative, to relate the leprosy that affects the two males shortly before their deaths to early stages in the dismemberment of Miyapma, which could have been a long drawn out process. The Builder's wasting can be compared with Miyapma's coma as being a drying condition affecting a Creator, and it can be compared with leprosy in that it is suffered by a male creator as a consequence of dealings with serpents, but the two comparisons are best kept distinct.

CHAPTER 6

Further Analyses
and Explorations

When a social anthropologist has learned the language and studied the social life of a particular tribe, the usual practice on return has been to write a monograph devoted to the people he or she has lived with. Sometimes an attempt is made to cover the tribe as a whole, searching perhaps for some underlying structural formulation relating one type of institution to another; sometimes the focus will be on one particular problem. If a lot of information has been collected, the findings may fill several books. In any case, the assumption is often made that the tribe is the natural unit of study, that it should be looked at as a whole, and that comparisons with other tribes can be left until later, or remarked on briefly in footnotes.

The present study has preferred the view that the most fruitful unit of study is the Bodic-speaking area, and that the Thulung are just a small sample from it. In this penultimate chapter, as throughout, one of the main questions is what can be learned by such a comparative approach. But there is also a narrower aim. Much of the study has consisted simply of the commented translations of Thulung narratives. From a purely ethnographic viewpoint, the translations are a record of what might otherwise have perished entirely; from a linguistic viewpoint they are the necessary complement to the texts; and for the purposes of this study they have been the starting point for comparison. But insofar as they are accurate, the translations also provide a body of material in which the Thulung express their abstract ideas in a form undistorted by the ethnographer's leading questions. Thus we also need to examine the narratives as expressions of the key notions of the Thulung, insofar as they are a tribe. Naturally, this abstracts from the fact that, much of the time, present-day Thulung think and act in exactly the same terms as native Nepali-speakers.

I. The Concept of *ḍiumla*

The term *ḍiumla* was briefly introduced in Ch. 1 IV-VI as meaning 'religion, tribal lore and custom, especially as transmitted by the tribal priests'. Little space has been given to ritual chants or wedding ceremonial dialogues, but as regards the narrative component of *ḍiumla*, a substantial sample has now been presented and examined. Moreover, the word itself has occurred within the narratives in various contexts, and the preliminary definition can now be amplified.[1]

Sometimes (VI i-ii Kam, VI Karb), it can be translated straightforwardly as 'ceremony, ceremonial' or 'rite, ritual'. Thus Ramli founded (*prə(ŋ)-*) all the Thulung ceremonial and decided to hold a proper ceremony for the wedding of his children. When at the start of the same episode the narrator undertook to tell me how all this happened, he used the word in a sense close to 'myth, story'. When he said that in Thulung *ḍiumla* servants were called *tayu*, he might have been giving part of their ritual name, but more likely he meant 'in Thulung as spoken in the old days', i.e. he was referring to the linguistic component of tribal tradition. The meaning of *ḍiumla* is certainly not limited to the overtly ritual aspects of tribal culture. This is already implicit in AS's definition of *ḍiumla* as *riti* N, which means not only 'ceremony' but also 'custom', as well as, even more generally, 'way, manner'. 'Following their customs' might indeed be a satisfactory rendering of what the Ancestors in Ch. 4 were doing in the Primal Lake, in Khumbu and in Ramanjo (or Rapcha), and perhaps also of what the two brothers did who stayed in Jubu and became its founders. However it would not be adequate for Karb's comments in Ch. 3. When Karb mentions *ḍiumla* in talking of the Kiranti as hunters, he is not simply remarking on what happens to have been their customary mode of subsistence. The background to his comment is Mini, the First Kiranti or First Man, born with a bow in his hand. The Kiranti are hunters not 'by custom', or 'according to oral

---

1   The contexts are: Ch. 3 I Karb and n.1, IV, VII; Ch. 4 I CP, VI (twice); Ch. 5 III Kam, VI (a) (four times), (b), (e), VI Karb, IX Kam.

tradition', but by origin. The point can as well be put synchronically: they are hunters in their essence, or by their nature. Students of mythology often note that myths about origins are understood by their tellers as statements about the ultimate nature of things, and this understanding is lexicalised in the word *ḍiumla*.

As usual in tribal religions, no claim is made to universality: what constitutes the essence of things for one tribe can differ profoundly from what constitutes the essence of things for other peoples. As Kam says (Ch. 5 III), the *ḍiumla* of the Khaling is different from that of the Thulung because the former are Lasagotra, whereas the Place of Origin of the latter is Kasi. Opinions differed as to whether Thulung *ḍiumla* differed from village to village. This is partly because, although there is no objection to women hearing or knowing the stories, *ḍiumla* is primarily the affair of men.[2] Marriage is patrilocal, and men rather seldom have occasion to live for any length of time in other Thulung villages.[3] They thus have little opportunity for learning about the *ḍiumla* of other villages. However CP's account of the Ancestors terminated in the foundation of his own village (5 IX), and this suggests that in principle differences of detail *should* exist between the *ḍiumla* of one village and those of others (as distinct from the differences noted empirically).

Here is one final extract that concerns *ḍiumla*.

Kam. The reason we are called Thulu is because in Nepali the word means 'great'. Kirantsor, our forefather, the Sovereign (*hǝp*), the Lord of the Soil, the Rich, this forefather of ours was great (*ṭhulo* N), and that is how we came to be called Thulung.[4] The caste (*jāt* N) of your friend [the ethnographer] is modest, but his rank (*darjā* N) is great; and it is the same with us. If you look at what we eat, then our standing is low, but our rank is great, our *ḍiumla* is great. It is similar with them

---

2   I think it unlikely that if women could be persuaded to tell the stories, perhaps by a female ethnographer, their versions would differ from mens' in any systematic way.

3   In 64 recorded marriages in Mukli's ward 7, 40% of the brides came from within Mukli, 50% from other Thulung villages, and the rest from other Thulung subtribes, or (one instance) from Limbuwan. When the bride is from another village, men would have visited it to negotiate and celebrate the wedding, and the bride would be expected occasionally to take her children to visit her brother.

4   The Thulung are perfectly aware of the phonemic difference between dental *th-* as in the ethnonym and retroflex *ṭh*.

(laughter). The reason our standing is low is that our people (*thar* N), our caste, eats beef, pork and chicken. The Chetris and Brahmans do not eat these types of meat, so their caste is high. Among trees there is none greater than the *amprasi*, what they call the *shrikhaṇḍa* in Nepali – you people and we Kiranti are like that, like the Sandalwood tree. In the whole world, in the whole of creation there is nothing greater than the Sandalwood tree. The *bhīguma* is the king of birds, the Sandalwood is the king of trees, and in the same way, among the kings of mankind, none is greater than Kirantsor. The other kings are not real ones. We have continued growing ever since the Creation, whereas the kings nowadays are like Nehru. People become kings through violence, theft and deceit. They have no ritual names, no *ḍiumla*, no names.[5] One could sum them up as petty kings.

Some of Kam's views may be idosyncratic. No other narrator mentioned Kirantsor, and I did not otherwise encounter the distinction between 'rank' and position in the caste hierarchy. Most Thulung today would deny that they eat beef. However Kam's folk-etymology for the name Thulung is often given, and the passage illustrates well the centrality of the notion of *ḍiumla* to the Thulung concept of their Kiranti identity. The greatness of the Thulung is part of the same notion as the greatness of *ḍiumla*. In principle, everything that is mentioned in *ḍiumla* in the sense of 'ritual' should have a ritual name, and I have already suggested that this formerly applied to *ḍiumla* in the sense 'myth'. When Ramli celebrated his children's wedding, the ceremony could not be performed properly until the children were given their ritual names (5 VI Kam (b)). Similarly, in the present passage, non-Kiranti kings lack ritual names and have no *ḍiumla*, nor any place in it. This makes them *banāwati* N, 'artificial, imitation, a matter of show or externals', in short, lacking in ultimate reality.

One note of caution is needed. I said in Ch. 1 that Thulung make no distinction between frank mythology and narratives that we more readily call folk-stories. The point is illustrated in Ch. 4 where the Exit from a primeval subterranean realm leads on rapidly in Kam to the story of Prithvi Narayan taking courage from watching a dung-beetle. In other instances too (e.g. regarding the story of Chamling's trickery), we have remarked on the unserious tone of motifs that occur alongside or are incorporated in

---

5   I do not know whether a distinction is intended between names and ritual names.

episodes which seem to express views about the fundamental nature of things. Ramli suing for Rathongma was more or less straight folklore; Ramli rejecting the Slug-eater was, we argued, paralleling the Creation myth in a way that was probably important for understanding the history of kinship systems in the area. Yet the Mukli *ḍiumla,* told by a priest, weaves the two stories into one.

The phenomenon has diachronic aspects that will be discussed later, but it also has synchronic aspects. If the concept of *ḍiumla* is visualised in two dimensions, the central meaning of the term has the seriousness and importance we have claimed for it. Peripherally however, it tails off or fades out in various directions. Some informants felt that the Cetla bird who officiated when Miyapma was ill was the first or original medium, and Thulung mediums much of the time use Thulung ritual language. But the Thulung are perfectly ready to call on the services of non-Thulung mediums, and it is unclear to what extent the realm of the medium nowadays lies within *ḍiumla.*

In much the same way, traditional narratives that were once told in ritual language and were central to Thulung ideology now form a continuum with narratives that I cannot believe were ever told in ritual language and have presumably never been more than entertainment. I have no evidence that contemporary Thulung are sensitive to the difference between the poles of this continuum, but presumably they once were. The passage from Kam is a reminder that we are not talking of some remote tribe isolated in the jungle, but of a people who are thoroughly aware of Hindu ideas and to a large degree take them for granted.

There are other aspects of the tribal culture that no doubt used to stand on the fringes of the concept of *ḍiumla.* Many reports from the Himalayas and surrounding areas mention a type of singing involving two individuals or groups, often of opposite sex, who answer each other back and forth with verses improvised according to a recognised pattern. This type of singing (*risiba, risiuwa*) used to be current among the Thulung, but nowadays any Thulung who sing secular songs do so in Nepali. I was quite unable to collect any examples of tribal folk songs (or for that matter of proverbs or riddles), though I suspect that with more prolonged searching it might still be just possible to find at least some songs.[6]

---

6   Another unsolved question is the relationship of *ḍiumla* not only to *risiwa* but also to the categories *sibe, seomdi* and *kurwa,* all of which are used in talking of officiants and mean something like 'ritual' or 'story'.

Another question is the relation between Thulung concepts of their own *ḍiumla* and their view of the ideology (*dharma* N) associated with the literate religion of the state. This is an aspect of Hinduisation and beyond our present scope. However, they did not feel that the notion of *ḍiumla* was incommensurable with the culture of Nepali-speakers and happily translated *ḍiumla* as *muddum*. Although in his word-list AS translates *ḍiumla* as *riti* N, in his introduction (p.6) he talks of the power of the old Thulung language, which enabled ritual officiants to charm insects and plants with their singing, 'with their *risiba* (*mudyum*)'. Although they are not in the dictionaries, both words seem to be Nepali, certainly the second, which is of some interest.

Chemjong's trilingual dictionary gives *mundhum* as a native Limbu word, rendering it *dharmashāstra* N, scripture.[7] In his book (1966: 21 ff) he gives a longer account of it, starting with a definition: 'The word Mundhum means the power of great strength and the Kirat people of east Nepal believe it to be true, holy and powerful scripture'. Although a Limbu script exists and some of the myths have been written down in it, Chemjong's emphasis on 'scripture' is misleading inasmuch as the traditional culture is in some areas entirely an oral one (as shown by Sagant, among others). For most Limbu, the word no doubt means very much the same as *ḍiumla* does to the Thulung, though the content of the myths is of course not the same.

Among the Tamang the word, in the form *mundum*, is apparently synonymous (or nearly so) with the native *hvai* or *vai* (Macdonald 1966: 34). The latter are invocations or songs performed at weddings or family gatherings; they narrate important tribal or Buddhist traditions concerning, for instance, the Creation and the origins of Tamang clans. The Gurung equivalent for the *hvai* are the *pe*, 'histoires mythiques' (Pignède 1966: 323ff). It is suggested by Stein and Macdonald that both words are related etymologically to Tib *dpe*, 'which combines the meanings of example, metaphor, maxim, tale and book' (Stein 1972: 198). We return below to the importance of such myths of origin (Tib *gtam-dpe*) in the Bodic-speaking area.

---

7   It may be coincidence that *mun-* means 'be created' in Thulung. As to *ḍiumla*, it could be a verbal noun in *-la*, and if so, the verb involved could be *diums-* 'be, become', since *d-* and *ḍ-* often alternate (Allen 1975a: 81, 15f); but in the absence of data on related languages this etymology is speculative.

II. The ancestors

Often the ancestors are personified by a named individual. Thus when Khimci the Sunwar came out of the Primal Lake (CP), he must be understood as representing the ancestors of the subtribe as a whole. When a name is not used, several different general terms appear. When talking of Mapa, ancestor of the Khaling, Ant uses *purkhā* N (5 III). In the same context Kam uses *ŋaw*, a word no doubt related to *ŋāceo/ŋāmi* 'old man/woman', which appears in Ch. 2 VI DB; all these words can apply to elderly and respected individuals who are still alive. Elsewhere, Kam commonly uses the ordinary Thulung or Nepali words for 'grandfather'; these words do not for him necessarily imply 'lineal ascendant' for (among other instances) he uses the feminine *bajai* N to refer to the rejected Slug-eater. When talking of *khuliu*, the Place of Origin, we saw that it too could be used in an expression meaning 'ancestors', and there is yet another term, *khali*, mentioned below (n. 10).

The most problematic of the general terms is *seor* or *seor-reor*, used regularly by CP in Ch. 4. I now amplify what I said there, drawing on Allen (1976a: 508-10), which gives the Nepali words used by informants who tried to translate the concept. In many contexts the translation 'ancestors' is acceptable. It is surely the ancestors who migrate from the Place of Origin; the 'ancestors' stones' stand in the hearth; and in the *sekro* rite, the 'ancestors' rope' (*seorrip*) is passed from the fireplace up through the roof of a house to a tall pole (*tharsəŋ*) planted in the courtyard. But one cannot think of the *seor* as existing only in the past, in external objects or in another world, since in some contexts the Thulung think of the *seor* as internal to the individual; one informant even defined it as 'the god within a person'. A further aspect of the concept is brought out by the translation 'fortune', which can be taken either in the neutral sense 'lot, fate', or in the more positive one of 'strength, courage, prosperity'. The aim of priestly rites is sometimes said to be to 'establish firmly (*thar-*) the *seor* of a person or group'.[8] The best way for an outsider to comprehend the Thulung concept seems to be through some notion such as 'line of continuity'. The ancestors are what constitutes the line of continuity in time and space between the Place of Origin and the here and now, and an individual's fortune inheres in the strength of this continuity. This is why one informant could say that the ancestors' rope simply meant 'life' – without it you were dead.

---

8 The verb *thar-* is the same as in *tharsəŋ* (*səŋ* = tree), the pole set up in the *sekro* and other rituals, including the one held by Chamling in Ch. 4 III.

Two expressions in the myths can now be understood more clearly. At the start of the Migration, down in the Primal Lake, and again near its end, in the Foundation of Mukli, CP talks of the Ancestors (*seor-reor*) 'making or doing all the *seor-reor*'. The translation uses the expression 'following their Destinies', but it may be more accurate, if unnatural in English, to think of them as 'maintaining their continuity'.

The other difficult phrase comes at the end of the Slug-eating wife, where Ph says that henceforth there was to be 'no *seor* between us Thulung and the Bahing', or as DB puts it, 'between Luna and Thulu'. The translation 'intermarriage' is justified by the context, but is too narrow and concrete to convey the full meaning. The implication is that the intermarriage broken off at this point had been an expression of shared *seor*, i.e. of a shared essence deriving from community of origin. Unfortunately, the Thulung traditions I collected say nothing specifically about the origins of the Bahing. However, the Bahing language is very closely related to Sunwar (Shafer 1974: 3); similarly Chemjong (1966 II: 87) states: 'From my research work, I found the language of Sunwar, Rumdali Rai, Bahing Rai, and Nechali Rai tribes are the same.' So quite possibly the Thulung were at one time aware of the close relationship between the Bahing and Sunwar implied by the linguistic facts. But several versions of the Exit explicitly mention the Sunwar. Thus what the Thulung and Bahing had in common before the rupture of intermarriage was perhaps that they shared lines of continuity that merged in the parent of the brothers involved in the Exit.[9]

The Thulung are nowadays perfectly familiar with the notion of a genealogy or pedigree *(bamsāvali* N), consisting of a list of named ancestors stretching from a founder to someone still alive. I was able for instance to copy a '*bamsāvali* of the Dewsa Rai', written by AS and in the possession of his grandson. It started with 'Ramlu or Ramli', Thulu, and Hangkeciu (probably taken by AS as the founder of Dewsa), then progressed through a further nine generations, the last of which included the elder brother of AS himself; the diagram also included collaterals at generations four and eleven, and at the bottom, the descendants of AS.[10] Kam too gave his own

---

9   If it is right to link Bahing and Sunwar in this manner, then it is surely significant that the rupture of intermarriage took place between subtribes who, in some versions of the Exit, were eldest and youngest, i.e. most remote from each other. In similar vein, it might be worth examining closely the mChims, the natal clan of the rejected Tibetan Frog-eater.

10   A complex etymological question is raised by the alternation Ramlu or Ramli, to which can be added the common variant Ramliu. The number of important

pedigree: Ramli, Chepa Raja, Kroksiu, Baginanda (the shaman), Dokole, and his own mother Lacchiratna; he remarked on its relative shortness in view of the western and Nepalese dating system (the Nepalese Bikram era starts in 57 BC). It is possible also to collect fragmentary genealogies which relate clans or groups of clans within a village (cf. 5 VII Kam). However the notion of genealogy appears alien to the concept of *seor*. CP's story of the Ancestors traces a line of continuity back to or forward from the Primal Lake, but if we ignore the Foundation of Tingla, the only time a personal name appears in any part of this line, it is that of Mini, the First Man. But this particular episode (2 VII) stood apart from the rest of CP's account in many respects, and its lack of mention of the *seor* can be added to the list. I conclude that the concept of *seor* has to do not so much with a sequence of generations of ancestors but with something more abstract that exists in or is maintained through them.

The abstract quality of the *seor* no doubt accounts for much of the inconsistency within and between versions as regards the names of ancestors. Of all the names used for the founding ancestor of the Thulung in Ch. 4 and 5, far the commonest is Ramli. However, in his first recording session, Karb used only Phuliukuceo, the 'person or man (*ceo*) from Phuliu River', and at the start of Ch. 5 VI he makes it clear that he does not think of him as one individual belonging to a single generation. The name Ramli is not mentioned until the Dispersal, when he appears as the youngest of the seven village founders. In the Salewaceo story, the youngest of Phuliukuceo's five sons was just called Sibi (= Youngest) Rai. Ph uses Ramli and Phuliukuceo indifferently in Ch. 5 II, but in VI expresses doubt about their

---

words ending in one or other of these syllables seems too great to be due to chance. In the subtribe nomenclature, Thulu is the same as Thulung; cf. the association of the Khaling with Khali (Ch. 5 IV), also the names Chamling and Kulung. AS has the latter pair as Nepali, giving Thulung equivalents as Jeopli and Kuliu (or Chapkuwa). He regards Mupli (sic) as the Nepali for Phuliuku (where *ku* = river). An inhabitant of Mukli is a Muklinge. We also have Phuleli, Luwale (Lowali to some), and *khuliu*, the place of origin. The hearth is *bokoli* (or -*liu*) and its ritual name is *b. neyali*; there is also a word *khali* meaning 'ancestors associated with the hearth or the niche in the wall uphill of it'. The *yungkuli* is the stone on which priests dance as an important part of their duties; a *dengkuli* is a stepping stone, as at the base of a ladder. In some instances a link with *lung* 'stone' may be suspected; one also wonders about the obscure substance *le*, *li* or *liu*. The Nepali suffix -*āli*, as in Dewsali 'inhabitant of Dewsa', is irrelevant. The list is not complete.

relationship. Kam does not use Phuliukuceo, but alternates between Ramli and Thulu. In his version of the Salewaceo story, Ramli's youngest son is also called Ramli, but in VII and in his pedigree the name is Chepa Raja. CP is uncertain about the relationship between Ramli and Ramanjo. AS makes Thulu the son of Ramli. A number of informants believed that Ramli was not only the founder of Mukli village but also ruler there, until the area was taken into the kingdom of Nepal and he was put to flight. One might perhaps explain this confused situation as the result of telescoping and of the general decline of Thulung tribal traditions. But there are many other parts of Thulung mythology that still show considerable uniformity from village to village, and a better explanation is that before the advent of Nepali-speakers with their notions of a *bamsāvali*, the tribal culture was simply not interested in sequences of individualised ancestors.

This conclusion can be supported in another way. We have often noted that any entity mentioned in a ritual normally has a ritual name. The ritual name of the ancestors in the abstract is Seor reor, one of those for Mukli itself is Phuliuku yemerku, that for the reputed site of Ramli's 'Palace' (*oganem*) is Ogama sirangma, and those of several clans are given in Ch. 5 VI Kam ii. But I did not discover ritual names for any of the named ancestors Ramli, Phuliukuceo or Thulu. Since ritual vocabulary is not widely known or used, negative evidence must be treated with caution, but the fact remains that none of the rituals I attended so much as mentioned any of these characters. Although one part of the wedding ritual referred to a good number of individual household heads, using their ritual names, not one of the rituals contained anything like a genealogy stretching backwards or forwards through a number of generations.

As for the relation between generations, one can hardly miss the pervasive emphasis on youngest sons. Mini is the youngest of Miyapma's children. Khakcilik is the youngest of three siblings. The Thulung ancestor, whatever his name, is the youngest member of the quartets that appear in the Exit and immediately succeeding episodes. CP does not mention a quartet, but makes the Ancestors younger than Khimci. In DB's story about the Khaling, Mapa hands on his ritual abilities and visionary powers to the youngest of his three sons, Impi Rai, who then carries him on his last journey.[11] In the Salewaceo story it is the youngest of the five sons who succeeds as emissary where his elders fail; in one version he is called

---

11 Impi is a variant pronunciation of *yumpi*, which may or may not be related to the *yum* treated below in III (i).

Ramli, like his father. In the Dispersal, in spite of the differences in detail between versions, it is always the youngest brother who stays at the original settlement of Mukli. It is the youngest of three brothers who is the founder of the narrator's village of Lokhim (Kam IX). Possibly not all these facts are homogeneous, but the general trend is unmistakable: the line of continuity passes through youngest sons. There are only two apparent exceptions. In the Das Kirant, the Thulung are given first among the brothers who represent the subtribes, and in section I of this chapter Kam attributes supremacy to Kirantsor, who is the eldest in his quartet. However, both these stories showed clear evidence of the influence of Nepali-speakers. It is still the Thulung custom for the youngest son to stay on in the family home, while elder sons move away and set up home independently.

In the genealogies that open so many Tibetan myths of origin, it is again very common (in spite of exceptions) for the line of continuity to pass through youngest sons. In the oft-quoted work called the *rLangs Po-ti bse-ru*, the generation of the First Man Ye-smon and the next two contain only single males; in the following four generations the number of siblings varies (3, 4, 6, 35), but in each case the genealogy passes through the youngest, and it is only in the eighth that the eldest of three brothers provides a link (Macdonald 1959: 429).

It is interesting to compare the picture from more recent Tibet where, when inheritance is related to birth order, primogeniture is the norm. Of the thirty or so references to inheritance in the index to Carrasco (1959), seven mention inheritance by an eldest son, and none indicates ultimogeniture. Stein too (1972: 97f) talks of primogeniture and the principle of seniority among brothers. However, this impression of uniformity is probably misleading. According to Cassinelli and Ekvall (1969: 9) there is no rule of primogeniture in Tibet and in Sa-skya the inheritance in the ruling family often passed through the youngest son. In Khumbu it is regularly the youngest son (or in his absence, daughter) who stays on in the family home, pays for the father's funeral and receives the largest share of the father's property (Fürer-Haimendorf 1964: 78, 98 etc). The position of the youngest son is similar in Helambu (Goldstein 1975: 58), and also among the southern Limbu studied by Caplan (1970: 36). Thus the idea that the youngest son is the one most closely associated with his parents may once have been widespread or even universal in the Bodic-speaking area.

The question arises whether any pattern can be found in the number of elder brothers of the linking youngest son. I noted above that both Mini in the Creation and the Thulung ancestor in some versions of the Exit are the youngest members of quartets. But we have also seen, in connection with Ramli, with Salewaceo, and with the non-Thulung homologues of Wayelungma and Khakcilik, the schema of one sibling who is special (the youngest, the link in a genealogy, the hero of a story) plus *six* others who are older, less individualised and/or less important. One further instance comes in the Tibetan story of the monkey and the rock demon. This often mentions six brothers, the founders of six tribes, sometimes termed 'the six clans of father's (side) subjects'; but 'a seventh tribe, that of the maternal uncle (zhang) is generally added to the list' (Stein 1972: 48, 46). Is there a relationship between the schema 1 + 3, and the schema 1 + 6? Or between the second schema and the sequences of seven generations discussed in connection with Ch. 5 X? The comparative approach raises many such questions.

The concept of *seor* has ramifications in at least one other direction. We noted at the end of Ch. 4 that CP applied the term unambiguously to the female Wayelungma, as well as elsewhere to males. Nowadays, whether they are thinking of clan membership, of inheritance of property or of pedigrees, the Thulung think in patrilineal terms, but Ch. 2 raised the possibility of an earlier predominance of matriliny. In Tibet patrilineal relationship is associated with bones (*rus-pa*), matrilineal with flesh (*sha*), so it would be interesting to know the etymology of Thulung *seor*. The Thulung for 'bone' is usually *ser*, though I heard that in Dewsa the old form was *seser*. However, the vowel is uncertain, since AS gives *cəŋsər* (*cəŋ* = 'back') as *ḍhāḍ* N, i.e. 'backbone, especially lower part';[12] furthermore, Hodgson gives the Thulung for bone as 'sasar'. On the other hand, the Thulung for 'flesh' is *seo*, which contains the same vowel as *seor* but lacks the final consonant. Cognates to *seor* from neighbouring languages might solve the question of whether it is related to one of these, to both or to neither. *Seor* is not a particularly common word in everyday contexts and it may need to be deliberately looked for.[13]

As for Tibet, one can compare the concept of *seor* not only with the notions of bone and flesh, but also with the very complex notion of *dmu* (also spelt *mu, rmu, smu* – Stein 1961: 50ff). We have already met this term

---

12 The Nepali word probably accounts for the Thulung augmentative *ser-dar*, used e.g. by Mj when talking of the remains of Khliw.

13   It may or may not be the same word as, or related to, *seor* 'solid particles in a fluid, sediment'. For the possibility of a semantic link, cf. *mim* in the two senses 'grandmother' and 'insect or spirit living in water, in whose absence waters run dry'.

several times in connection with the *dmu* rope connecting heaven and earth, into which the first Tibetan kings melted at death, until it was cut by Gri-gum; similarly, the nine- (or seven-) stepped ladder for the descent of the First King was called the *smu* ladder. But the word has several other meanings or contexts of use, including a category of supernatural beings who dwell in heaven and are particularly associated with the maternal ancestors of the First King. Thus in one Bon-po version of the Descent, the King's grandfather on the thirteenth storey of heaven was married to a *dmu*, while the King's father, the middle of seven brothers, was expelled to his mother's brother's country (called *sMu*), where he too married a *dmu* (Macdonald 1971: 208ff).[14] The grandfather of gShen-rab was a *dmu* (Hoffmann 1950: 141, Stein 1972: 242). The name appears often in lists of the primitive tribes of Tibet, who were born of the monkey and rock demon in the creation story. In the Epic, three of these brother tribes have a mother of the spirit-category *gnyan*, while the youngest and most important tribe of the four, to which Gesar himself belongs, has as mother a *dmu* (Stein 1959: 201, 205). The term can also apply simply to the sky, i.e. heaven (Stein 1972: 48).[15] Finally, in spite of Gri-gum's act, certain specialists can still make use of the or a *mu* rope, both for their own purposes, e.g. liberation from the world, and for the benefit of clients, especially in divination. Moreover the wording of certain prayers shows that a person's 'vitality' or 'increase of life' is sometimes conceived as a lengthening of the *mu* rope (ibid: 211, 211ff). Thus the Thulung and Tibetan concepts have much in common.

III. Some Other Thulung Concepts

This section discusses three separate concepts which appear in the myths and are sufficiently interesting to justify special treatment.

    (i) *Yum*. The Thulung seldom classify people in terms of their personalities or psychological characteristics, but there is one personal

---

14   When the First King descended to earth with his ten '*dmu*-requisites', he left his heavenly clothes at a *smu-le-gong* tree – an act we compared with Ramli's behaviour during his return from Rathongma's home.

15   The Thulung for 'sky' is *dhamu* or *dhoamu*, though in ritual contexts 'Heaven' is usually *pari*. Ph (2 I) and Kam (4 III) use a ritual or archaic word *wabu*, contrasting it with *subu* 'Earth'. In view of the homology Salewaceo = Khomda (who descends from heaven), it might be significant that *sale* means 'thread'.

attribute that is often mentioned in the myths. The word *yum* has generally been translated 'magical power(s)', occasionally 'clairvoyance'; a *yumceo* is one who possesses such powers, a 'magician', and the corresponding adjective is *yumnuŋma*. The powers are attributed to the following characters: Mini at birth; Ramli the suitor; Ramli, the king who overcomes Mapa; Salewaceo; the six Kulung brothers (so long as they are able to hunt in the lake), and in particular the fourth of them who can transform himself into a tiger; and finally Lunam.[16] Salewaceo, by virtue of possessing the powers, is a priest (*nokcho*) and able to perform seances and *ḍiumla* (Karb); this is his justification for claiming the sword that led to his quarrel with the Phuliuku people. The latter were laymen (*lāṭā mokpa*[17]) and lacked *yum*. Except insofar as Mini was born with his *yum*, the myths leave it unclear how the attribute is acquired. Usually it seems to be inherent in the individual, but in the case of the six brothers it seems rather to exist in the magic lake; the powers were destroyed when the lake was treated with 'medicine' (*dawāi* N) or poison. The particular power of the brothers was to transform themselves into hunting animals. In other cases the power consists in knowing what is occurring in the minds of others or at a distance, or in parting the waters of a lake with a plumed headdress (Lunam). Though it is not stated, the power is probably exemplified by Daner and Pokner when they use their plumed headdress to open the lake at Ghumne Pani. The *yum* of Mini, and of Ramli as warrior, probably consisted in their power to steer and call back weapons that fly through the air (Ramli's sword, Mini's arrows).

The power is never attributed in the myths to females, although they sometimes have other attributes. Nagimo in Ch. 3 VII Kam is a *pasubhāgya* [my or his mistake for *pashubākya* N 'omen'?], one who knows all manner of things, including the languages of animals and the future. Jiugba's wife knows the substances which destroy or nullify *yum*, and Lunam's wife has thirty-two virtues. By no means all the important males in the myths possess *yum*. Khakcilik conspicuously lacks it, and as we noted, the power of Mapa's son is rather that of seeing visions.

---

16 References are: 2 IV Ph; 5 II DB, II Kam, V DB (twice), VI Kam (twice), VI Karb (three times), VIIIa Karb (nearly a dozen times), VIIIb Karb (three times). Baginanda (Allen 1976b) also possessed *yum*.

17 *Lāṭo* means 'dumb, foolish' in Nepali, and *mokpa* can mean the same in Thulung; the composite expression may have been influenced by *lāṭā-murkho* N 'a dumb fellow'.

From Tibet one might compare the concept of *'phrul*, 'capacités intellectuelles surnaturelles', such as were attributed to Chinese emperors and Tibetan kings, and helped explain why their countries were great powers (Macdonald 1971: 386). Stein (1973: 417) defines the term as 'capacités ou vertus magiques, surnaturelles, transformatoires'. His article explores a whole series of concepts bearing a semantic relationship to *'phrul*, and gives some idea of the complexity of the material that would have to be covered in a satisfactory comparative account of notions of power and causality in the Bodic-speaking area.[18]

(ii) *Khlamya*. This again has to do with causality, and has here been variously translated 'evil force or power', 'curse', 'act of wickedness'. It is related to the verb *khlam-* 'spoil, bewitch' and is often coupled with *kuyba* or *kuiuwa*, which was rendered to me as *lodar* N 'affliction, misfortune'.[19]

All three narrators refer to the concept at the end of the Salewaceo story. The roasting of the baby created an evil force that would have to be 'exorcised' (*ri-*) by Salewaceo the magician (the verb also means 'break, destroy'). The Phuliuku people disobey his instructions, and the evil force brings about their destruction, or at least hangs over them ever after. The same type of force arises in the course of the Exit (Kam), no doubt because of the human sacrifice, and also when Tiger kills Miyapma (CP). Another instance is in Ch. 5 when Jiugba spurns Congkom's gift and the two brothers plan to kill each other. Finally, Daner and Pokner give rise to a force of the same kind by their treatment of the Lord of the Soil, or possibly of his frogs. Outside the myths, the concept is often referred to in rituals where the *khlamya* of unspecified individuals, of witches or of mediums occurs among the large number of types of evil that an officiant attempts to ward off (Allen 1976a: 503). It appears that a *khlamya* both results *from* deliberate killing, especially in anger, and may result *in* the death of a victim. It seems to be a more serious and dangerous force than an ordinary curse such as

---

18 There are also other Tibetan terms comparable to Thulung *yum*. For instance, the son of King Ye-smon, the First Man, and his wife Chu-lcag, was dBang-ldan, 'un fils capable de se transformer par magie' (Macdonald 1959: 428); *dbang* means 'power, ability', *ldan* 'possessing'. The First King claimed the capacity to govern by virtue of possessing three things: the force called *mthu* (usually employed in aggressive magic), physical vigour, and magic powers *(rdzu-'phrul)* (Macdonald 1971: 212).

19 The expressions *samsi-kuywa* and *riu* seem to mean much the same as *khlamya-kuywa*.

resulted in Khliw being killed by the owl (Mj and Karb); the term used there was *chiul*, which does not occur in rituals, so far as I know. It was equated with *sarāp* N, used when Rolasila cursed the birds (Ant) after his rejection by Miyapma.

A *khlamya* is conceived of as external both to the person who gives rise to it, and to the person who suffers from it (at least until he does so). However, it is sometimes associated with a notion of sinful thoughts. In the Exit, Chamling, when he finds that he has been deceived into killing his brother, accuses the others of being 'sinners' (Kam), and the Phuliuku people conceive the 'sinful' idea of roasting the baby (Karb). As we saw, a reason advanced for not contracting relationships of ritual brotherhood is the risk of committing the sin of harbouring even a momentary feeling of resentment against the ritual brother. In all these cases the notion of sin as a state internal to the individual is expressed with the Nepali terms *pāp* or *pāpi*, and I am confident that the notion is not part of traditional Thulung culture. Similarly, Fürer-Haimendorf (1974: 547f) suggests that the same word has been borrowed by various tribal peoples in South Asia who previously lacked the concept.

(iii) *Hǝp*. Out of context, this is simply a general term meaning 'owner, master, lord (= *dhani*, *mālik* N)'. The head of the house *(nem)* or household may be called the *nemhǝp;*[20] the tiger can be called *sokmohǝp*, 'lord of the jungle'. The term also applies to spirits, and we have met it in this meaning both in the expression 'Lord of the Soil' (5 XI), in the 'spirits of the niche and seat' invoked by CP in Ch. 4 I, and in the 'spirits of the earth' mentioned in Ch. 2 V Dim. Otherwise it only appears in the myths half a dozen times, in connection with the notion of kingship. Thus the ancestors in the Central Valley 'became *hǝp*, became Rajas'. The only named individuals described as *hǝp* are Ramli and Kirantsor (unless one includes the youngest of the eight brothers in Mj's Dispersal).[21] The notion of Kingship is expressed at least twice as often with the aid of the Nepali term, or of its abstract cognate *rāj*. Non-Thulung characters such as Mapa are never referred to by the Thulung term, nor are any of the characters in Ch. 2 or 3. AS gives *bayahǝpme (baya* = earth) as the equivalent of *rāni* N 'queen', but this rare expression is absent from my corpus.

---

20   The commoner term for this is *boapceo*, which however is not known to have any wider meaning.

21   References are 4 IV CP; 5 II Ph; 5 VII Mj; 6 Kam. I have the impression that *hǝp-rājā*, like *hǝpceo*, is felt to be a compound noun.

We have already noted the similarity between the Thulung Lord of the Soil (*bayahəp*) and the Tibetan *sa-bdag* (*sa* = earth, *bdag-po* = lord, master, owner); the *gzhi-bdag* are possibly of lower rank and more limited domains (Tucci 1949: 722), though the two are usually equated. In spite of their name, *sa-bdag* sometimes dwell in stones, water and trees; there also exist *yul-bdag* ('country masters'), perhaps an old name for *sa-bdag* (Hoffmann 1950: 159f). The word *bdag* is not particularly associated with royalty, but the ordinary Tibetan word for 'king', *rgyal-po*, is also the name of a category of spirit who, like *sa-bdag*, inhabit the lowest (terrestrial) level of the tripartite cosmos (ibid: 12f). Although the term was used of the petty kings who are often mentioned as reigning before the Descent of the First King, it was not applied to the early historic kings of the Yarlung dynasty (Haarh 1969: 342).

The Gurung also provide an interesting comparison (Pignède 1966: 364f). The word *kleh* means 'master, lord, owner' and is used as the nearest native equivalent to Tib *lha* 'god'. It appears in the names of several beings, in particular (i) the spirit *tõh-e kleh* 'maître des bois' (but *tõh* also means 'territoire du village' – ibid: 338), (ii) the Creator Kleh-karuri who descended nine ladders (or passed through nine doors) on his way to level the earth, (iii) the Gurung First King, Karu-kleh, who is perhaps the same as the Creator. Moreover the upper stratum of Gurung society ideally consists of four clans, of which the first in the usual list is associated with the function of royalty; in Nepali they are referred to as Ghale, but the native term is Klemai (Ministry of Defence 1965: 89). This is the same word, for *-mai* is merely a plural suffix and Pignède's -h is an indication of tone.

This summary glance at three groups of Bodic-speakers suggests on the lexical level a general link between the notion of owner or master, and categories of terrestrial spirits. Up to a point, the notion of royalty or human sovereignty belongs to the same complex of ideas. The topic will be taken further in the next section.

IV. General Comparison of Thulung and Tibetan Mythology

This section concentrates on themes emphasised in Tibet but absent or muted among the Thulung. To make the comparison in the converse direction would also be interesting, but would demand a better knowledge of Tibetan narratives than I possess. Of course no claim is being made for the completeness of the Thulung corpus either, but it has been the main focus of the study.

The first point is that the great bulk of Tibetan writing is influenced by Buddhism. This generalisation applies in greater or lesser degree to nearly all Bon-po texts, to the Epic (put together around the fifteenth century), and also to some parts of the Tun-huang manuscripts; but it is usually possible to distinguish between Buddhist and non-Buddhist elements. So far as I can tell, there is no good evidence at all of Buddhist influence on Thulung tradition. The Birth of Mini (Ant) and the Dispute with Chamling showed similarities to stories included in the Buddhist cannon, but there was no reason to think the Thulung stories derived from the Buddhist ones. I suggested that Ph's introduction to the creation myth showed the influence of a literate religion, but Hinduism is at least as likely as Buddhism. None of the Thulung characters shows any interest in so central a Buddhist idea as renouncing the world or becoming an ascetic. Ramli presents himself at the court of Rathongma's father in old clothes and smeared with oil dregs, but it is by no means in order to gain liberation.

Buddhist cosmologies regularly describe Mount Meru in the centre of the world, surrounded by four continents linked with the cardinal points. In view of what we have said, it is not surprising that this schema (no less prominent in Hinduism than Buddhism) is totally absent from Thulung tradition, but it is important that the very notion of four cardinal points is also missing. There are various ways of expressing the opposition of north and south (cf. Allen 1972). In Ch. 2 V Dim the bear went 'uphill to the top (*jiujiu*)' or 'high ground' (*lekh* N), while the monkey went to Wayecapciu. In Ch. 3 II Ph, Jaw went to Luwale (Khaling territory) while Khliw again went 'down to Wayecapciu'; they returned 'from above' and 'from below': Kam in the same place has the opposition 'up' to the Nachiring and Dumi, 'down' to the Chamling. For Karb (3 VII) the opposition is between Mades (N, = The Plains) below, and Dodi (territory of Sherpas and Tibetans) above; Ant (5 X) uses the same terms. Similarly, in talking of east and west the Thulung either refer to named places such as the Central Valley, or use Nepali loan words (as in 2 II Ant, or 4 IV Kam). There is no occasion in the Thulung myths where four directions are listed one after another. The nearest approach comes in Ch. 4 III Karb, when three brothers disperse, leaving the fourth where he is; but the directions in which they go have no obvious link with cardinal points, and the departure of Ombu is clearly separated from the departure of the other two.

If the notion of cardinal points is lacking, so too is the notion of a central sacred mountain. In Tibet we have met Avalokiteshvara surveying Tibet from the summit of a mountain, the First King appearing on the summit of one, the sacred mountain that was the progenitor of Ru-1a-skyes, and cosmogonic mountains which mate with lakes in Na-khi and Lepcha mythology. Much more could be said about such mountains and the cult devoted to them (e.g. Stein 1959: 452 ff. or, as regards the Sherpas, Funke 1969: 70 ff.). In Thulung, it is not even certain that there is a word that can satisfactorily be translated 'mountain'. I was given a rare word *kəŋsa* (= *himāl* N, as in 'Himalayas'), which is no doubt related to *kəŋka* 'calf bone, ridge of mountain', but it seems to apply more to a range than a single peak. In any case the word appears nowhere in the corpus of myths, nor is there any evidence, from ritual or elsewhere, to suggest that in the tribal tradition mountains have ever been personified or regarded as especially sacred or significant. They never receive worship.

The cosmological and religious significance of mountains is bound up with the idea that they link heaven and earth, and it is well recognised that they share this feature with other 'Symbols of the Centre' (Eliade 1961: 37ff); examples are the *dmu* cord and ladder discussed in section II. Although they lack sacred mountains, other symbols of the centre are common enough among the Thulung. We have already mentioned the 'ancestors' rope' and the planting of the *tharsəŋ* in the courtyard during the *sekro* rite. Another obvious instance was the central pillar of the primal house. In discussing the Place of Origin, we had to refer to the concept of the shaman who climbs a cosmic tree, a concept which also appears in the Baginanda story (Allen 1976b). Trees, especially the Sandalwood, figure prominently in the Creation. In Ch. 5 III, we noted the schema of the bowman (Mini or Mapa) who descends from a tree. The Sakhle *bhume* site in Mukli, where Mapa lost his first digit, is marked by a vast Silk Cotton tree, at the base of which pigs' heads are offered at the most important of the priest's annual collective village rites. Although the present-day text contains no hint of this, one suspects a vanished meaning in the fact that Khakcilik's name is that of a species of tree.

As for the vertical dimension then, trees (or poles) seem to form the main image used by Thulung tradition to conceptualise the link between cosmic levels. Even so, the image is muted and fragmented. A sceptic might doubt whether some of the Thulung instances mentioned above really have anything to do with cosmology. When the species of tree is given, it usually differs from instance to instance. The story that most straightforwardly relates heaven and earth is the Creation, and the tree that serves as receptacle for Khomda's seed only has an indirect role in the relation; the link between heaven and earth is ensured at least as much by the bird or birds, and one version (Kam) entirely omits the tree.

Symbols of the centre operate in the horizontal plane as well as vertically. Lhasa, built over the heart of the prostrate she-demon with her radiating limbs, was very consciously conceived as the centre of Tibet. This notion too is muted among the Thulung. Mukli is the original settlement and the *bradikhom* (Mj), the place from which the other village founders dispersed, but is never clearly presented as a centre from which anything radiates, like spokes from a hub or rays from the sun. If anything, in Thulung tradition it is the Khaling settlement of Rapcha that has a stronger claim to be a centre. Ramli had to go there for ritual purposes; it was there that Mapa became a god; and the place was also somewhat associated with the Creation (Ch. 4 VI Karb b) – a claim that was never made for Mukli. I argued in Ch. 5 X that the Thulung, like other Bodic speakers, sometimes think of foundations as associated with paired journeys in opposite directions, in which case the end point can be regarded as a centre of sorts; but the notion is far less clearly defined than the regular oriental conception of the *maṇḍala*.

Societies that stress the symbolism of the centre very commonly associate this body of ideas with the notion of a divine king, whose person represents the Centre and whose activity both conforms to and maintains the cosmic order. Early Tibet fits this pattern. The kings were explicitly sons of gods (*lha-sras*) by virtue of the Descent from Heaven. The descent itself took place at 'the navel of the world' (Stein 1961: 12); sometimes the reason for inviting a King from heaven was that the enemies of the four directions had not been conquered (Macdonald 1971: 208). Thereafter the kings were always conceived as located at the centre; for instance a fragmentary Tun-huang text tells of one who took his four wives from the peoples on 'the four frontiers' (ibid: 195ff). The First King introduced to mankind the system called *gtsug-lag*, and it was by virtue of conforming to this that his successors enjoyed their authority. The *gtsug*, 'the order of the universe', was established by the celestial mountains called the *phyva* when they created the world (ibid: 352f). This pre-Buddhist ideology was not an anarchic amalgam of miscellaneous magico-religious notions, but an integrated system of ideas embracing both politics and religion; it gave the kings their right to impose their authority on the kingdoms of the four directions, i.e. on the rest of the world. The concept is comparable to the early Indian notion of *ṛta* (ibid: 367, 365). Tucci (1955-6b: 279) writes similarly: 'The King, as conceived by the Bon-po religion who (sic) is peremptory on this point, is responsible for the normal course of events; if he fails in this task imposed on him by his very nature, the cosmic order is disturbed'.

The centralised royal dynasty of Tibet collapsed in the middle of the ninth century and Buddhism began its second and more successful period of growth towards the end of the next century. This entailed the disappearance of the notion of *gtsug*, with which Buddhism was incompatible. However, the notion of divine kingship took on a new lease of life in the Epic, dissociated from the actualities of day-to-day government. We have already mentioned Gesar as universal sovereign and god of war when discussing the Contest for Rathongma. Gesar was chosen by the gods to come to earth and overcome the four demon kings ruling on the four frontiers of his country, Gling, which stands for the whole world (Stein 1959: 246, 204).

Among the Thulung we have met only fragmentary hints of the notion of a centre applying to cosmology and geography, and much the same is true with regard to social structure. Ramli is described as a *həp* and a *rājā*, and could also perhaps have been called a *ngaw*; but nothing suggests that he is a god or son of a god. The Thulung were not surrounded by four hostile powers, and even if they were, nothing suggests that they would have had any right, let alone desire, to incorporate them in an empire. Admittedly, Ramli's sons attack and plunder the Sherpas (Ch. 5 V), but only after the Sherpas have attacked them first (Karb) or humiliated them (Kam). The nearest Ramli himself comes to a military undertaking is in Ch. 5 V, when Mapa denies him access to Tibetan salt and cuts off the hand of his porter; in the end Ramli obtains the salt, but nothing more. Nor can it be said that he reigns according to or by virtue of any concept of universal cosmic order like the Tibetan *gtsug-lag*. Ramli 'established' the *ḍiumla*, and presumably conformed to it, but as we have seen, the *ḍiumla*, for all its 'greatness', differs from one subtribe to another. The Thulung have no indigenous equivalent to the notion of *gtsug*, though as Nepali-speakers they have some awareness of the notion of *dharma*, which in turn continues semantically the earlier *ṛta*.

However, one or two hints in Ramli's story suggest a grander conception of sovereignty. He is not a great conqueror, but he does have a named sword with magic powers. Gesar has nine weapons, including a named sword, which appeared spontaneously without being forged by a smith; the same weapons are also mentioned in a creation song in a Tibetan play that describes a primal battle between gods and demons (Stein 1959: 428, 455 and n. 51). Gesar is very closely associated with a winged horse (ibid: 535ff), and one informant thought that when the Thulung area was conquered, Ramli fled on a flying horse. When Ramli won Rathongma, he at the same time won the *le*, which was closely associated with the Hindu supreme godhead, with the king of the birds, and with the light of what was perhaps the supreme star. His change of clothes on his return home resembled that of the First King on his descent to earth. For Kam, Ramli is closely linked to Kirantsor, who among all the kings of mankind, is the only real one (6 I). In short, Ramli has a few of the elements that would make him into a clear divine king, but they are inchoate and unsystematised.

An important part of being a divine king is to be associated with the 'gods' and 'Heaven', and we have yet to discuss what these terms could mean in a Thulung context. Since we have barely taken account of Thulung ritual, the following remarks do not exhaust the question, and as for the rest of the Bodic-speaking area, the issues raised go far beyond my present knowledge. Nevertheless, they are important for an assessment of Thulung myths, and it is worth making a preliminary approach to them in the light of the information assembled in this study.

The tribal language recognises a considerable number of (poorly differentiated) types of spirit, especially in ritual language, but there is no word that could be translated 'god' or (following Hitchcock 1966) 'godling'. These concepts are expressed by the Nepali loan words *deu* or *deutā*. If questioned directly, many Thulung would probably say that their myths were about *deutā,* but when they are narrating spontaneously in the tribal language, the term is very rare. Ph at the end of the Creation says that the Thulung are the descendants of a god. The passage is ambiguous, but apparently refers to Mini; elsewhere however, Mini is invariably and obviously human – mortal, and a begetter of mortals. Dim (ibid) says that Monkey, having returned from exile, is now worshipped as the god Rangkime. Rangkime's name is probably from Nepali Rangke-bhut (see further Allen 1976a: 503f, 534ff); the identification of a figure from the tribal mythology with a being respected by the Nepali-speakers recalls the equation of Mamaciuniu and Bhagavan, and is just what one would expect in a Hinduising environment. Kam (5 VI v) mentions a large rock (*dipluŋ*) as the cult site for some Hindu deities. Otherwise however, the one and only reference to a god is when Mapa turns to stone.[22]

Let us summarise what was said above about the application of certain Bodic expressions to different types of sovereignty.

	term/ root	realm *qua* spirits	ordinary kings	divine kings	First Man	Creators	= 'God'
Thulung	*hap*	household terrestrial, territorial	yes, Raja	concept effectively absent	no	no	no
Gurung	*kleh*	forest, ? village territory	yes, Ghale	applies to First King, (? Creator)	?	yes	approx
Tibetan	*bdag*	terrestrial, territorial	seldom?	no?	yes[23]	seldom	no
	rgyal	terrestrial	yes	seldom or never	yes	yes	no
	lha	celestial	no	yes	rarely	yes	yes

In that the table ignores diachrony, it is a gross over-simplification. The Tibetan terms in particular have more than a millennium of documentable history, and Macdonald (1971: 388) mentions a plan to study the semantic evolution of the 'terme-clef' *lha*. The question-marks point to other possible directions for field or literary research. The grandfather of the *sa-bdag* in one source is Tshangs-pa 'bum-khri (Tshangs-pa = Brahmā). Hoffmann (1950: 194) comments on the resemblance of this name to Sangs-po 'bum-khri, who appears both as First Man and, in later Bon, as King of the Creation-Gods. Ye-smon, another common name for the Tibetan First Man, is commonly called *rgyal-po*, and we have met the root also in the 'heavenly mother Gung-rgyal', who gave birth to gShen-rab and was mentioned in the discussion of creator goddesses akin to dPal-ldan lha-mo.

The Thulung facts are altogether simpler. If we ignore Nepali loanwords, there is just the one term having to do with land ownership, whether by spirits or humans. The term was not applied spontaneously to

---

22 At both his petrifications Mapa becomes, not a *lung*, the ordinary Thulung for 'stone', but a *silā* N, = 'sacred stone' (Turner). When he is 'worshipped' the verb is *pujemu*, from *pujā* N.

23 Tucci (1949: 731) mentions a First Man called 'the master of existence' (Srid-pa'i bdag-po) Yang-dag rgyal-po, who eventually builds the primal house in the story cited in 5 XI.

any of the characters in the Creation mythology, who are in general not conceived of as gods, in the sense of beings who control the course of events and/or expect offerings, worship or respect. The Gurung facts would seem to be transitional in that the indigenous term has been influenced by Tib *lha*; unlike the Thulung, the Gurung studied by Pignède have been strongly influenced by Tibetan Buddhism.

In the Thulung myths the role of heaven is distinctly muted. It is the source of rain in Ch. 2 I Ph, which we argued was unrepresentative of Thulung tradition generally. Any symbol of the centre is, at least implicitly, a point of communication between heaven and earth, and one of the functions of the *tharsəng* in Ch. 4 III was to enable the brothers to call on heaven (even though the emphasis was more on the earth-witness motif). Mj (3 IVc) makes a very cursory remark about Wayelungma being taken to heaven. The only other explicit reference to heaven (ignoring the mention of Venus in Ch. 5 II Kam) is as the home of Khomda in the Creation. In the funeral ritual the village of Kotunje, to which the dead are normally conducted, may be not only a place on the ground but also the take-off point for heaven; but I am not sure of this. These scanty references to heaven contrast with the repeated references to earth and lakes, and to beings who emerge from them. Insofar as heaven and the above are associated with the male, and the below with the female, this underlines again the general Thulung emphasis on the female first noted in Ch. 2. But we can now see more clearly that the contrast with Tibet is a matter of social structure and politics as well as cosmology.

If the relation between heaven and earth is very different for Thulung and Tibetan tradition, the same is true of the relation between the terrestrial and the subterranean. In Ch. 5 XI we looked at part of a Tibetan myth in which a Creator was afflicted with a wasting condition because he offended a serpent. There are many variants on this theme: serpents may be offended (as there) by house-building, but also by ploughing, mining and many of the labours of civilisation (Stein 1972: 243f). The Sherpas similarly tell many stories of springs that run dry when serpents are offended (Funke 1969: 27). Even if the '(grand)mothers of the waters' and the slug-eater are associated with serpents, they do not in Thulung mythology punish humans; the springs run dry, but neither Khomda nor Salewaceo are related to serpents.

One other important contrast exists between the two bodies of tradition. When looking for possible homologues for the Thulung Cetla we mentioned the wise old man contemporary with the creation, who was concerned with the summoning of a ruler from heaven. Another of his acts was to intervene in a cosmic battle: he is aligned with the forces of good, represented by a white yak (or mountain), pitted against the forces of evil represented by a black one. He, and comparable figures, often use bow and arrow (Stein 1959: 290, 446). In discussing Gesar's arms we also mentioned the Tibetan play that refers to a primal battle between gods and demons. Up to a point, one is reminded of Mini in his tree shooting his arrow at Tiger below, for Tiger, the future matricide, can easily be seen as representing evil. But the comparison cannot be taken much further. Mini appears to have been reprimanded, and in any case Tiger was resuscitated. Mini behaves rightly in the disposal of his mother's body, and is referred to by Ph as a god, but he is not presented as a representative of the powers of good. Colour symbolism is not used.[24]

Plenty of other instances of killing or fighting occur in Thulung tradition and sometimes it is clear that right is on one side or the other. But it could not be said that Thulung tradition conceives of the world as a battleground between moral forces. This is as true on the individual as on the cosmic level: just as Thulung has traditionally lacked an equivalent of Tib *sdig-pa* 'sin', so it has lacked an equivalent of Tib *dge-ba* 'virtue'. Similarly, it is difficult to classify Thulung spirits into good and evil. The distinction between so-called 'good' and 'bad' deaths is between normal or natural and abnormal or unnatural, and is not moralistic.

A final contrast may be noted. With reference to Mamaciuniu we cited Tibetan lists of types of birth, including birth from an egg, which is very common in Bon-po mythology. There is nothing to suggest that Miyapma's womb is a cosmic egg and the motif is not represented in our corpus.

V. Typology and Derivation

When one has several versions of the same story from a single village or from neighbouring villages, one sometimes feels confident about their approximate diachronic relationships. No systematic attempt has been

---

24 The Thulung have five primary colour terms and follow a common pattern for such terminologies, lacking an equivalent to the Nepali for 'blue'. The terms are rarely used in everyday life and or in ritual, and never appear in the corpus of myths in their usual form. However, colour symbolism among the Bodic-speakers needs a separate study: the name of the Ombule recalls Thulung *om-om* 'yellow', or the *le pikpuri* killed in the Exit, who is red (*rāto* N) around the anus, thereby resembles the *le* necklace, which was also supposed to be red.

made to try and reconstruct earlier forms of Thulung tradition, but a number of remarks have been made in passing. For instance, it was argued that narrators who claimed that Ramli had two separate wives were preserving a distinction that had been lost in Mukli. Regarding the Exit, it was argued that the different versions showed a process of toning down a motif that had come to offend Thulung sensibilities. However, this section is more concerned with the sorts of question that arise from the comparisons between different episodes.

In studying Tibetan material, one cannot help being struck by the variety of creation stories and the frequency with which they are relevant in a whole range of contexts – drama, ritual (particularly of course non-Buddhist), but also the Epic and the 'historical' writings of Tibetans. Stein (1971: 535ff) assembles references showing the fundamental importance of legends of origin not only in Tibet but also among a few surrounding peoples such as the Nakhi. Except in their schools, the Thulung have no drama (in the sense of formal contexts in which a plurality of individuals take on an altered identity at one time – a medium might be said to be acting out his shamanic journey, but he always officiates alone). They have no knowledge of the Epic, and of course essentially no historical writing, and such rituals as I witnessed contained only cursory references to myths, or extracts from them. But again and again in studying their narratives we have returned to creations, beginnings and origins, and we can now amplify what was said in Ch. 2 about different types of birth.

We are no longer concerned with individual versions, but rather with recognising types of story and the relations between them. However, it seems fair to assume that when two types of story are related, the one that is not explicitly concerned with creations or origins derives from the one that is. Any reader who regards this assumption as too speculative can, in the following remarks, substitute for the notion of 'derivation' some more abstract and non-diachronic notion such as 'transformation'. The classification presented only deals directly with Thulung stories, though it has implications for, and has been influenced by, Tibetan and other parallels. When one type of story is said to be derived from another it is not here implied that the process has necessarily occurred actually among the Thulung. Let us consider then the different types of Thulung creation story and their relationships to stories that do not overtly describe creation or emergence.

The main act of creation in Ch. 2 occurs when a male outsider from heaven descends to mate with a female figure on earth, and the upshot is the origin of species and of death. The Salewaceo story is not explicitly about origins, but it describes how a male outsider comes to the home of a Thulung woman, and the upshot is that he takes over from her people. We suggested that the Salewaceo story derives from the Creation, and also that it is of the same general type as the Six Brothers and Jiugba, which differs in being Kulung-centred. We also recognised a second type of story deriving from the Creation. In the Slug-eater, the outsider was the female, and associated with the watery region of the cosmos; the same type of story was probably to be recognised in the first part of Mapa's journey. Apart from these main types of derivation we have also, with greater or lesser confidence, seen the Creation as contributing to the Introduction of Salt (motif of bowman in tree), the Rathongma episode (Ramli's triumphant return), and finally to the story of Ramli the Victorious, controlling his named sword as Mini did his arrows.

Another group of stories has to do with the emergence from earth or water. The former concept occurs at the start of one version of the Creation, and forms the substance of the Lokhim versions of the Exit. From it perhaps derives the story of the emergence of Lunam from his cave or niche in the rock. The suggestion finds support in the reported importance of the story in Gurung mythology, and also probably in the fact that Lunam emerges by hanging on to a *tail*. A myth of this type might explain the importance of tails both in several Thulung rituals and in the Foundation of Mukli (which would then be seen as the last stage of a long emergence); it would also be relevant that in the Exit Kirantsor cut the bird near its cloaca (avian equivalent to the anus). The beings who emerge from water are Miyapma's mother (via rotting leaves and a lotus in Ph), Wayelungma (via a fishing line in CP), and the Ancestors in the Tingla Exit. This type of emergence too may be associated with a severed tail, as in the Tichurong wife-capture story. These emergence stories make the being who emerges the central character in the narrative, and it is not immediately clear that they could give rise to stories like Daner and Pokner where those who emerge from the drained lake are incidental victims, and the hero who does the cutting is an outsider. The possibility seems less implausible if one takes account of the end of the story of Lunam. On the one hand he parts the waters with his sword-like plume, but on the other he and his family thereby emerge from the lake to safety on the far side.

Emergence from a tree is not a prominent theme, but the comparison of the Mamaciuniu episode with Hermanns' material from north-east Tibet suggests that it has a long history. No doubt the male and female whom

Hermanns so briefly mentioned as emerging from a tree were brother and sister as well as husband and wife. Perhaps therefore, the Mini who emerged from Mamaciuniu once had a sister whom he married, who has been dropped from the tradition – much as (we argued) Khakcilik's marriage with his sisters has been disguised.[25]

Though not exhaustive, the classification presented in the last few paragraphs does include the majority of the narratives in Ch. 5. If the notion of derivation is correct, the classification also adds another level of meaning to the narrators' evident view that these stories come 'later' in Thulung tradition. One further case could be added, if the Dispersal from Mukli is derived from the dispersal in episode V of the Creation. As for the Das Kirant, this complex story also includes an element of dispersal; moreover it is told of Miyapma's unnamed son, and might be regarded as actually being part of the Creation. The story of Congkom, who killed and cut up a vast bear and quarrelled with one of his brothers over the eating of it, may also derive distantly from the narrative type represented by episode V of the Creation.

This classification of Thulung stories may need revision in the light of fuller material, but the analysis can perhaps be taken further even with the material as it stands. In keeping with the majority Thulung view, as I understand it, the title of 'The Creation' was reserved for the story which centred on Miyapma, but the Jaw-Khliw story was also to some extent cosmogonic, and the relation between the two has not been satisfactorily explained. Since the Jaw-Khliw cycle appeared to contain two quite separate marriages, that of Khakcilik and Wayelungma and that of Khakcilik and his two bird sisters, the question arises whether some order can be found in all the types of mating and birth that occur in Thulung traditions. Might there even prove to be precisely four different types of marriage, and

---

25   In addition to the Limbu brother-sister unions mentioned earlier, here are two instances from neighbouring tribes in central Nepal. In a Tamang story, a goddess of the woods, servant to Brahmā (identified with Avalokiteshvara) is encouraged by Bhagavan to marry a monkey who looks like a demon with a mask, and who interferes with her activities. Humanity begins with the marriage of their son Phoḍub and daughter Moḍup. In spite of the differences, the title of the story shows that it is a version of the Tibetan marriage of the monkey and rock demon (Macdonald 1966: 39). One of the types of Gurung officiant conducts a ritual called a *rhi-ce myŏ-ce*, which tells of a sister (*ri*) and brother (*myŏ*) who lived in a state of incest and 'were eaten by the mountain', i.e. fell from it, the former accidentally, the latter voluntarily (Pignède 1966: 330, 370).

eight different types of spouse, related to the four types of origin already considered: heaven, trees, earth and water? But before exploring this hypothesis, one would need to take much further the theory of quadripartition among the Bodic-speakers, a theory that has been alluded to earlier, but not used systematically in this study. Since one of my aims is to show the advantages of a certain type of comparativism, it would be foolish to risk a false start by trying to go too far too fast. If the quadripartition theory should prove fruitful, it might cast new light on the classification of Thulung narratives, and what now appear as minor details within episodes might turn out to be compressed versions of important stories.

VI. Diffusion

When similar stories are found in two different cultural areas, several types of explanation need to be considered. First, the similarities might be superficial and evaporate on closer inspection. Otherwise, (i) the two peoples might both have preserved a story that was told before their common ancestors separated or (not always the same thing) before their languages separated. (ii) The two peoples might have developed along parallel lines a story that was originally shared for one or other of these reasons. (iii) Both peoples might have invented the stories independently, perhaps in response to similar circumstances (which in turn would need explanation). (iv) One people might have learned of the story from the other, either directly through individual travellers or migrants, or indirectly through intermediate peoples. (v) The two peoples might have derived the stories independently from some source external to both of them. Moreover, for each particular similarity, different combinations of these explanations may be relevant.

I shall not go through all the parallels we have found between narratives from different parts of the Bodic-speaking area, but a few general points need to be made, particularly about the relation between Thulung and Tibetan mythology. For all its debatable assumptions, glottochronology may provide some estimate of the likely length of time that has elapsed since the separation of Thulung and Tibetan within the Bodic family: it will be of the order of millennia. I presume that many of the more diffuse similarities we have noted go back to this early period, with or without parallel evolution, but it is evidently difficult in principle to distinguish common inheritance from early diffusion. Independent invention is not an economical hypothesis, though it may be relevant to some of the similarities discussed in Ch. 5 X. Of the two types of diffusionist explanation, it is difficult to say much about the possibility of shared external sources, since this study has been almost entirely confined to the Bodic area. This leaves diffusion from one people to the other (ignoring accidental similarities and combined explanations). Diffusion from the Thulung to Tibet is not worth considering, and it is scarcely more likely that there were direct contacts through travellers.

The obvious diffusionist link between the two peoples is via the Sherpas, in the course of the four centuries or so since they immigrated into Nepal.[26] For earlier periods, or in addition, one could speculate about other possible channels. Thus at the head of the Arun valley stands a pass nearly 3,000 feet lower than the one leading from Khumbu to Tibet – but there is no evidence of this having been an important trade route in recent times (Fürer-Haimendorf 1975: 106ff).

Nowadays, the Thulung have Sherpa settlements not far away to their west and north, as we saw in connection with Salewaceo's hunting expedition, and conceivably the Thulung learned some narratives direct from the Sherpas. However, when the Sherpas first immigrated, it was into Khumbu, in which case they were separated from the Thulung by the Khaling. The Khaling play so prominent a part in the later legends that, if diffusion did occur, it was probably via them.

Since the most detailed parallels between Thulung and Tibetan stories concerned the Frog/slug-eater, this is the strongest candidate for diffusionist explanation. The same story seemed to be current among the Khaling, as well as being part of a Thulung story about a Khaling (5 IV). Macdonald's Tibetan version of the story came from a fourteenth-century source, but she used it specifically as an example of a story that was surely current in the early ninth century when the Tun-Huang chronicle was compiled (apparently from pre-existing writings, whose order the compiler did not understand). Although the Sherpas could have taken the story from written versions, it is perhaps more likely that they transmitted an oral form such as preceded the written versions in Tibet. No doubt the reason that the Thulung took the

---

26 According to their own tradition, the Sherpas originated from Kham in East Tibet, which they no doubt left at the turn of the 15-16th centuries (Oppitz 1968). Stein (1961: 84) also concludes that the migration of populations or families from the north-east contributed greatly to the formation of the ethnic and cultural complex of historical Tibet. But we can ignore questions of migration and diffusion within Tibet.

story from the Khaling is related to their recognition of the Khaling as ritual specialists, as possessors of Rapcha and founders of the *bhume* rites.

Until we know more of Khaling mythology we cannot say how many more of the Thulung stories derive from the north. Of course, it cannot be assumed that all such stories were transmitted by the Khaling from yet further north. The Introduction of Salt is a Khaling story, and the Thulung pretty clearly took it from them; however, there was no close parallel from Tibet, and the plumed bowman in the tree is such a typically Kiranti figure that at least this motif seems unlikely to derive from Tibet.

VII. Evolution of Ideas

Confronted by two comparable systems, one can envisage their relations in terms of transformations, and mean by that term nothing more than logical, reversible operations performed by an analyst. Alternatively, one can suppose that the transformations correspond to historical processes. In discussing the typological relations between the stories we took the second approach, and we can now pose a similar question about the ideas that underlie and are expressed in the stories.

The discussion of Creator deities in Ch. 2 emphasised a contrast between the Thulung stress on the female and chthonic, and the Tibetan stress on the male and celestial. A synchronic approach would see here simply an interesting inversion. But the Tibetologists suggest that the Tibetan picture has been much affected by the Bon and Buddhist religions, and that the further back one goes in Tibetan history, the greater the resemblance to Thulung tradition. Of course recent Thulung tribal ideology was not *identical* with that of preliterate Tibet, but it could have been *representative* of it – i.e., in this respect, of the same general type. Now that we have in section IV identified a number of other contrasts between the two bodies of tradition, we must ask whether here too Thulung tradition gives pointers to earlier periods of history in the Bodic-speaking area.

(i) I suggested in IV that the ultimogeniture so prominent in Thulung mythology represents the older Bodic pattern, which has largely been superseded in Tibet itself by primogeniture. So far as I know, this suggestion is new.

(ii) Thulung tradition puts little weight on any straightforward dualistic opposition between good and evil, such as is prominent in Tibetan culture.

Here is another instance. The builder of the primal house in the Bon-po creation story of Ch. 5 XI was the First Man cited in this chapter n. 23. After his appearance from the void, and before his building, a black ray of light gave rise to a black man, who was the cause of numerous evils, while a white ray of light gave rise to a white man, who undertook all sorts of positive and civilising acts. Commenting on his summary of the story, Tucci (1949: 731) points to 'evident' Iranian parallels, and subtitles that section of his appendix 'The Origin of Mankind and some Iranian Influences'. Moreover, the Bon-po themselves often say that their founder came from Iran. Stein (1972: 236), in discussing external influences on the Bon religion, considers that India may have been the source, as much as Iran (or Gilgit), but in either case moral dualism as a cosmic principle reached Tibet from outside. Here again the Thulung would represent the situation in Tibet before the advent of the outside influences.

(iii) Divine kingship is a conception typical of large-scale early literate empires such as seventh-century Tibet, and much less typical of small-scale tribal societies. Thulung tradition contained only fragmentary hints of it, especially in traditions that on other grounds could be regarded as 'later'. Documentary evidence from China and early Tibet can give us only the most sparse and ambiguous indication of what Tibet was like before it became a great empire, and here too Thulung evidence may be helpful. Stein (1959: 547) recognises that the theme of a Universal King, which is attached to the name of Gesar, came to Tibet from outside.

(iv) Divine kingship is closely linked with the symbolism of the centre. Thulung tradition knows of various trees and poles that may connect heaven and earth, and it knows of various quartets, which we suggested as a focus for future research. But the two conceptions are not put together by the Thulung into anything like the classical schema of the *mandala*, which consists of a centre surrounded by elements related to the four cardinal points. Certainly, the schema did not develop spontaneously in Tibet, but the Thulung picture may again indicate the substratum of beliefs on which the schema was superimposed. Haarh (1969: 271) has similarly suggested that central sacred mountains were not a feature of indigenous Tibetan belief until the advent of Buddhism and the systematisation of Bon.

(v) Divine kingship is also closely associated with the notion of gods, a notion which is absent from the tribal tradition. My own view – hinted at earlier, but not developed – is that a fundamental distinction separates a terrestrial king, who is one component of a fourfold division of society, and a divine king, who is a sort of god. According to Hocart (1927: 7), 'We have no right, in the present state of our knowledge, to assert that the worship of gods preceded that of kings; we do not know. Perhaps there never were any gods without kings, or kings without gods.' If, in the last sentence one substitutes 'divine kings' for 'kings', then the Thulung material supports his view.

(vi) At the end of Ch. 2 we asked whether the Tibetan emphasis on mythic males was associated with patriliny, but it was not possible to show that the Thulung emphasis on mythic females was associated with matriliny. Similarly in section II, we could not relate the Thulung notion of *seor* convincingly to descent in either the male or the female line. My hypothesis here is that unilineality itself was little stressed in early Bodic society. When this problem has been studied systematically, it may help resolve some of the puzzles that arise in the comparative study of Tibeto-Burman kinship terminologies.[27]

---

27   If the evolution of Tibetan ideas included a growing emphasis on patriliny, then the story of the Frog-eater, where the female is an outsider, is perhaps a later derivation from the Descent-from-Heaven type of Creation myth than the Salewaceo type of story, in which the male figure starts off as an outsider, but takes over from the family of the female figure.

CHAPTER 7

Concluding Remarks

In the course of this study, many points have been noted that need further research, but here are a few more.

(i) It would be good to know more about the various species of trees and birds that have been mentioned. Present-day Thulung do not seem to have traditional taxonomies in either of these realms, but I doubt if the occurrence of particular species in particular contexts is random.

(ii) Several Thulung characters are associated with insignia or accoutrements. Apart from the nature of *le*, it might be worth exploring the significance of plumes and satchels, particularly perhaps of satchels containing bones, as did Ramli's at one point.

(iii) The motif of obstructed passage occurs repeatedly. Mini's birth was probably obstructed (Ant). Khomda, for no clear reason, 'scarcely fitted in the doorway' (Mj). The last-comer in the Exit got stuck in the Door (Karb), and so did the Slug-eater, though in a more naturalistic door; the pregnant Bhoteni in the Khaling story (5 IV) got stuck in a narrow place. The Tibetan First King exited through his mother's back, because she would die if he went upwards, and he was frightened of the narrow defile below (Macdonald 1971: 208). The motif needs to be related not only to the constrictions between levels of the cosmos and to their well-known homologues such as the roof-hole in the house, but more generally to the fords, cols, obstacles and pauses that occur on ritual journeys of various types.

(iv) There is much to be said about the complex of ideas embracing water, lakes, serpents, women, milk, medicines, poison and illness. The droughts in the Creation and in Salewaceo are associated with removal of the 'mothers' or 'grandmothers' of the waters. The health of a Khumbu Sherpa household depends upon its serpents, who are typically female and worshipped by females (Fürer-Haimendorf 1964: 266ff). The words *dman* 'woman' and *sman* 'medicine' often alternate in Tibetan texts, and may come from the same root (Stein 1939: 309ff). Róna-Tas (1956: 175) doubts a genuine etymological link, but one notes that of the Thulung references to medicines or poisons (which are confined to the Later Legends) all three involve women: the Slug-eater needs her watery medicine, which poisons her husband's mind against her; Jiugba's wife poisons the Six Brothers' magic lake; and Jiugba's wife's homologue, Ekli, is associated with the poisoning of Mukli's water supply.

(v) Although quartets are a particularly rich subject for future research, triads should not be neglected. One could use the section in Stein (1959: 262f) entitled *Classifications quadripartites et tripartites*. In connection with Ch. 5 X attention was called to the schema of one man plus two wives, but perhaps this should be generalised to include the schema of one central character plus two subordinates, as in Ramli and his two dogs, the Tibetan Creator of Ch. 5 XI vi and his two elephants, Baginanda and his two assistants (Allen 1976c). It may be relevant that Gri-gum could only cut his *dmu* rope because he had rendered impotent his three protector gods, the *mgur-lha* on his head, and the *dgra-lha* and *pho-lha* on his two shoulders (Stein 1972: 222). One thinks also of the three *lingo* of Ch. 4 III, only one of which is effective, and of the three hearth stones, of which the single downhill one is sometimes singled out. In Tibet the three hearth stones are sometimes associated with triads of cosmic mountains (Stein 1939: 351).

Above all, however, I think we need comparative investigation of kinship and social structure among the Bodic-speakers, parallel to the present comparative investigation of myth. In a society such as classical Greece, the relationship between myth and social structure can be tenuous or non-existent, but when a society practises prescriptive alliance, one expects the links to be much closer – van Wouden (1968) is particularly suggestive here. Though much remains to be done, work in progress [Allen 1976c] suggests that early Bodic society practised prescriptive alliance, and once the implications of this are more fully developed, the Thulung narratives may yield new meanings.

This study has had a number of goals. The traditional cultures of Nepal are many, diverse and rich, and I have tried to present a partial record of one aspect of one of them. I hope it will be sufficiently interesting to encourage others – foreign researchers, native Nepali-speakers, or native Bodic-speakers – to collect and record similar samples of the rich cultural heritage of the Himalayan peoples before it is too late. We need further material from the Thulung themselves, from other Rai subtribes, and from other Bodic-speaking peoples.

Hopefully too, the study may be helpful or suggestive to Tibetologists. For instance, Tucci (1955-6a: 203) considers that the Gri-gum legends 'in all probability adumbrate real events marking a turning point or crisis in the history of the religion of Tibet'; Gri-gum himself is 'the symbol of a fracture in the current of ideas'. But several of our comparisons have involved Gri-gum, or the no less complex figure of his son, Ru-la-skyes, and although no final solutions have been proposed, an anthropological approach has suggested a different line of enquiry – one that might not readily occur to a Tibetologist. The Gri-gum story seems to relate to the regular and expected periodical breakdown of clan exogamy.

The study has seldom moved outside the Bodic-speaking area, but one can reasonably expect significant parallels from across the whole Tibeto-Burman speaking area, and then, at the highest level of the linguistic taxonomy, from the Sino-Tibetan area. If the Sino-Tibetan speakers resemble the Indo-European speakers, as envisaged by Dumézil, one might then predict a discontinuity: if the comparison were extended further, isolated motifs would be comparable, but not whole patterns. A western reader will doubtless have been struck from time to time by isolated parallels between Thulung and Hebrew mythology, e.g. the parting of the waters, the introduction of death by a reptile, the departure from a primeval dwelling place; others have noted in Lepcha mythology a striking parallel with the Biblical story of the Tower of Babel. No doubt, similar isolated parallels could be found with the mythology of the Indo-Europeans, though the Bodic area offers nothing closely similar to the systematic trifunctional ideology of the Indo-Europeans (Dumézil 1968: preface; Littleton 1973).[1] But it does not follow from this that the ideologies associated with the speakers of each of the presently recognised language families will prove as distinct from each other as are the language families. Perhaps, for instance, as sporadic soundings have suggested to me, we should distinguish language families in which prescriptive alliance has been practised from those in which such an alliance pattern cannot be demonstrated. Ideologies associated with the former may have more in common with each other than they do with the latter.

Such speculations go far beyond the bounds of the present study. But insofar as social anthropology claims to be a science, it must always be ready to relate any specialised study to broader questions about humanity and its social life. The detailed material assembled and examined here might be used for various purposes. For instance, it bears on the relation between religious and mythic narratives which, for their tellers, are expressions of ultimate realities, and narratives which are classed as epic, folklore, or history. However, rather than relating Bodic mythology to narratology, I have tried here to lay foundations for applying to the Bodic area the type of approach that has proved so fruitful in the Indo-European area. I cannot, so far, offer any simple formula, but I hope some progress has been made in assembling and organising material, establishing general themes and classes of motif, and recognising gaps.

The sort of comparativism practised here is fundamentally historical in inspiration, and Ch. 6 VII put forward a number of hypotheses about the evolution of ideas in this particular area. In using the term 'evolution' to apply to changes that lie largely beyond the range of the historian's traditional methods, I imply no meliorism or value judgements. Nor do I think that, before the advent of Hinduising influences, Thulung conceptions and society had remained wholly unchanged since proto-Bodic times, whenever they were. I do not assume that the Thulung situation is invariably the simpler and more basic, and the Tibetan the more complex and differentiated; for instance, with regard to the concept of *yum*, (6 III i), it is possible – and the question may be soluble – that Tibet has retained old distinctions that the Thulung have conflated and remodelled. Nevertheless, in certain respects, Thulung tradition does seem to be representative of

---

1   [Allen 1978b was an attempt to find something similar in the Bodic area. I now think that Dumézil's scheme is too compressed and insufficiently discriminating: Indo-European ideology contained a fourth function, split into two aspects (Allen 1999).]

conditions before the beginning of Tibetan written history. There are not many areas of the world where a single language family embraces a still enduring civilisation that has been literate for some thirteen centuries, as well as accessible tribal cultures that can still just be described as living. If we are one day to have what Mauss (1948: 28) called *l'histoire de l'abstraction, de la catégorisation*, the Bodic-speaking area may have much to contribute.

APPENDIX 1

Texts and Editing

Narrators

When collecting the narratives, no guarantee of anonymity was given, and it seems right to record the names of those who have helped to preserve the Thulung heritage. As was emphasised in Ch. 1 VI, several narrators made it clear that they did not wish their versions to be regarded as definitive.

In Mukli, the main narrator was Ph (Phure), also known as Karabir or Dalli Pap; it was in his house in Caspu hamlet that I lodged while in Mukli. DB (Dan Bahadur) lived at Gairigaun, five minutes' walk away, and was one of Mukli's three priests, probably the most knowledgeable, certainly the most energetic. SSJ (Shamsher Jang) was unusual in that he had been born of a Chetri mother while his Thulung father was living in India. He never learned to speak Thulung, though he understood it. Because of his background, he had been more influenced by Hinduism than most Thulung, though in this respect he merely stood towards one end of a continuum. Married to a Khaling wife, he was certainly regarded as a Rai. Dim (Dime, Dimajit, Pundi Pap) of Dandagaun was not a priest, but knew a number of rites and chants, and could act as an officiant in certain contexts. G (Ganesh), my schoolmaster assistant from Derepu hamlet, gave a version of the Baginanda story. He was aged 29, while the other Mukli narrators were in their mid or late fifties.

In Lokhim, Karb (Karbari) of ward 2 was a *tālukdār* in the old system of local government, and was aged about 60. My host, the village panchayat representative for the ward, took me one evening to visit his fellow-clansman Kam (Kamanjit), aged about 70, who lived below Waya hamlet. Kam was the most enthusiastic of the narrators, continuing happily until late into the night, while my host nodded off and the batteries ran low in my tape recorder. Unfortunately, his style is particularly prolix and rambling, and I found him the hardest of the narrators to follow. For this reason my editing of his Thulung texts does not stick to the exact wording of the tapes quite so closely as in the other instances. Kam claimed to have heard the stories as a child from his maternal grandfather in Mukli, but I do not know to how much of his narrative this applies.

In Jubu, Ant (Antare) of Lugare hamlet was aged 77. Mj (Mulujit, or Putali Pap) was a priest, aged 64, and from the same hamlet. PB (Padam Bahadur or Karbari) was about 58. Both the latter only narrated under a certain amount of pressure from a Brahman schoolmaster friend and from my host in Jubu (the Captain), and they were very unenthusiastic about doing so.

In Tingla, CP (Chandre Pap), father of the schoolmaster Chandra Bahadur, lived in Boksa hamlet, and was also in his fifties. For many years he had been chief assistant to a priest who had recently died, and he was considered more knowledgeable in tribal lore than the priest's young successor. I was his guest for ten days. TR (Tirtha Raj) of Gairigaun hamlet, lived with me in Mukli as assistant for nearly five months, and several times invited me to stay in Tingla. He was 26.

Organisation and selection of texts

The texts in Appendix 2 could have been arranged in various ways. For instance, each narrator could have received a single section. Alternatively, the arrangement could correspond exactly to the presentation of the translations, in which case the texts of a single narrator would be split up and distributed according to chapter and episode. The arrangement selected is a compromise. Appendix 2 is organised by chapters, but within each chapter the texts of a single narrator are kept together. However, within the subsection devoted to a single narrator the individual episodes are ordered as in the translation. This order does not always correspond to the order in which they were told to me.

Table 1 brings together several different types of information. On the left-hand side appear the episodes in the order in which they have been presented above, but with abbreviated titles. The columns for each narrator are arranged by villages, but there is otherwise no great significance in the order from left to right. Within each column the numbers (which are not used elsewhere in this study) show the order in which the episodes were narrated to me. When the number (say *n*) is followed by a comma, this means that the narrator went straight on to the episode indicated by the number *n* + 1; though the *translations* usually begin a new episode with a new sentence or paragraph, the narrator's flow of taped Thulung discourse may or may not be interrupted by any corresponding break. In other words, the division into episodes is sometimes a matter of editorial decision, and may even fall in mid sentence. A semi-colon after a number indicates a significant interruption in the recording session, e.g. one occupied by general conversation, by a meal, or by questions from myself suggesting other possible subjects for stories. Finally, a full stop marks the end of a recording session. There is probably little significance in the order in which, for instance, Ph on different occasions gave me different stories, but the information is provided.

Brackets round a number indicate that the text is not given in Appendix 2. The reasons for omission vary. DB (1)-(5) and CP (15)-(17) have already been published in Allen (1975). Narratives by TR were typed in Nepali, while those by SSJ were explained or dictated in Nepali. CP (1)-(6) and (18) were told in Thulung, and key words were noted down in the course of the telling, but unfortunately they were not tape-recorded. Dim's version of the Creation was tape-recorded near the start of field work, and a rough transcription was made, but the recording was later deleted by accident. The later episodes from Kam's tape have been omitted here because of their considerable length. I have given a substantial sample of his narrative style.

Apart from the selected episodes, Appendix 2 contains a few brief stretches of text marked **P** or **C**. The labels stand for the 'prologues' or 'codas' with which narrators sometimes began or ended a story. They are briefly discussed in Ch. 1 VI.

Not all the narratives that I collected have been used in this study. Ph '7;' (not in the Table) was the Baginanda story (text in Allen 1975: 140ff, discussion in Allen 1976c). Similarly, Ph '13;', the story of Rajime Leom, was translated in Allen (1976a).

Ph also gave me, half in Nepali, half in Thulung, an untaped story about one Diwli from Dewsa. Diwli, being a *muliumi*, was called in as arbitrator in a quarrel that had broken out in Ribdung. His servant (*ḍiulciu*) was sent ahead with the baggage. On his arrival, finding that the man had been speaking ill of him, Diwli killed him, and returned home without settling the quarrel for which he had come. Because of the *khlamya kuywa* resulting from his act, he went to live for a month in Waksimara Cave. He washed his hands in the nearby stream, and to this day one should not drink from it. While he was living there a woman brought him food. They slept together and their son was called Baratiu.

Finally Ph gave me a fragmentary tale about how the *ibema* bird got its name from crying *ibiw* in its grief when flood waters buried the bones of its grandmother.

The episodes or stretches of text recorded by Kam but not translated here are as follows:

16, Rathongma's Wedding Ceremony
19, Genealogy (summarised in Ch. 6 II)
20, History of Agriculture
21; Relations with the Nepalese State
23; conditions of Life for the Early Thulung
26; Jang Bahadur establishes Law and Order in Majh Kirant (Jang Bahadur was the Rana prime minister who seized power in Nepal in 1846, and did much to consolidate the state).
27; Baginanda

There followed a number of episodes, purporting, at least at the start, to be the *ḍiumla* of Dewsa, and concerning the characters Neothel, an orphan fisherman, Diliya who had four sons and fought in a great battle with the Sherpas at Chaurikharka, and a girl called Gayindra, who was apparently eaten by a tiger while seeking wild vegetables. Kam ended with a story concerning Jang Bahadur's humble beginnings as cowherd to a Brahman, his ordeals and ambitions, his victorious expedition to Limbuwan, and a further adventure with a Jogi which was interrupted when the tape ran out. Diliya is probably the same as Ph's Diwli, who was also from Dewsa, and is perhaps somehow related to Salewaceo. Neothel is distantly reminiscent of Khakcilik. But in view of the absence of parallel versions and the poor quality of the tapes, translations would not be reliable.

Table 1: Narrators and order of episodes

	Mukli				Lokhim		Jubu			Tingla	
	Ph	DB	Dim	SSJ	Kam	Karb	Ant	Mj	PB	CP	TR
Ch. 2											
I. Creator appears	8,	6,	(1),	(1),	1,		1,	1,	1,	(1),	
II. Wooing	9,		(2),	(2),	2,		2,	8,		(2),	
III. Birth	10,	7,	(3),	(3).	3,		3,	9,	2;	(3),	
IV. Mini & Tiger	11,		(4),					10.		(5),	
V. Miyapma dies	12.		(5).							(4),	
VI. Mini dies		8,								(6),	
VII. Sandalwood										11,	
Ch. 3											
I. J & K depart	1,				4,	9,	11,	2,	3,		(1),
II. J & K quarrel	2,				5,	10,		6;			(2),
III. W into lake	3,									(18).	
IV. W captured	4,				6,	11,		3,5;7;	4,7;	(15),	(3),
V. Building	5,				8,	12,			6;	(16),	(4),
VI. Agriculture									5,	(17).	(5),
VII. Reunion	6.				7,	13.	12,		8.		(6).
Ch. 4											
I. Primal lake										7,	
II. Exit					9,	1,				8,	
III. Dispute					10,	2,					
IV. C. Valley					(11),					9,	
V. Eastwards					12,					10,	
VI. The north						6,8;				12,	
VII. Mukli					14,					13,	
Ch. 5											
I. Slug-eater	16,	(2),			13,		5,				
II. Rathongma	15,	(1),			15,		6,8,				
III. Salt		(3),			22,	7,	10;				(7),
IV. Ramli and Mapa		(5).									
V. Bhume rites		(4),		(4).							(8).
VI. Salewaceo	17.				(24),	3.					
VII. Dispersal					17,	4,	7.9;	4;			
VIII. Six brothers						5,					
IX. New villages					(25),					14.	
X. Das Kirant							4,				
XI. Daner & Pokner	14;			(5).							
Ch. 6											
I. The ḍiumla					(18),						

Texts

Chapter 2: The Creation

Ph

I

(aba makem – diliju thamaju –) diridin kam loa – meoram make <u>utapanna</u> diummirilo[1] diliju thamajuka seol khobḍiu; (wabu) wabu khusta caŋma thəstalo diliju thamajuka seol khobḍiu; (wabu) ala wabuka ayu diridin tamḍiuma, diliju thamajuka seol khobḍiuma meo diridinḍa <u>janma</u> biūriu, meo seol. ma diphu meo seol meoguiu jipsta; jipstama meottha wadakhor roāma jem leasta, meo wadakhor roāma jemḍa namprəŋma prəsta; namprəŋma presta, namprəŋma prəstam<u>pachi</u>, namprəŋmaku u minara[2] miyapma munḍa.

II

miyapma munḍa, miyapma munḍama diphu bərrama soalame diustam<u>pachi</u> lali bepa diusta; lali bepa diustama miyapmaka ruwasilala lali biūriu. ruwasilala lali biūriu; meokotima jigeŋmanuŋ heleku kekuwanuŋ lalira thiurstiuci, ruwasilakara – jigeŋma thiurstiu, jigeŋma thiurstiuma ləstalo kekuwa ḍarriuma: lu soalceo, miyapmaka lalira ala ruwasilala go thiurŋirim;

---

1   The grammar is slightly unclear; <u>utpanna</u> is the dictionary form.
2   Probably the missing word is <u>miurium</u>, used when Miyapma gives birth.

guci lōci, biūriuma thayriuma, kekuwanuŋ jigeŋmanuŋ ala ruwasilala lali bebḍa ləkcilo ruwasilaka thāhā biūriuma ruwasila thōlesiḍḍa, khomda parjeolliu. khomda parjeolliu, thama khomdaka: gaci ba ləkpa, bantheo ba tpa bhandakherima roaktalo, miyapmaka lali biūma lalira geccokom roakci jigeŋnuŋ kekuwanuŋka. ma ama a ham loaccima gaci lalira gecci khomdaka roaktalo, jigeŋnuŋ kekuwanuŋka: ruwasila waktam loastiuma lali biūriuma gucuku thiurcikima geccokom roaktalo, ama ne wakpa ne hambo miw; a khomjeol le[3] waktam roaktama khomdaka u khomjeol rembeḍḍiu; meomlo jigeŋnuŋ kekuwanuŋka meo khomda seoccima yokci; khomdama[4] seoccima yokcilone, miyapmaka loastiuma – u khomjeol loastiuma: a buy, go ne hopma ne me-e; hopma khomjeolpa ne me-e, go ne; go ne o khomjeolpa – go ne me ləŋu roaktama, guka meom roaktama thōlesiḍḍa; meomlo khomda u chokco bəktama, khomdaka cōsaku u khopāra – cōsaku u khopāra sarsjeolla. sarsjeolliuma kuku mim ciumḍiuma ləsta; kuku mim ciumḍiuma ləsta, pāderāmi kumi khole saḍḍalone miyapma korasira. korasirama u nə damsta; u nə-theom damstama, u sama-rima damsta, u nə damstama bayralone, (minaka) jigeŋmaka meo khopāram kuḍḍa u lapter pliumḍiuma reḍḍiuma kuka charkiuriulone: āmai, siu na re, gana, akom a krium repa, a kora repa roaktalone jigeŋmaka: mimá go re; ku ḍūna biūriulone, ḍu; akom ku manthi a nə damstalo, ḍu roaktama, jigeŋka ŋosiku blamḍa meo khopāram sarki reḍḍiuma, miyapma theonḍiu.

III

miyapma theonḍiumpachi ne miyapmaku miuriumḍane diphu ne khole sabdiuma munmiri. goŋgerwa coāram gupsiu rāi hūmu rāi o jukpa mini rāi munmiri. munmirima diphu o sabdiuma munmirim goŋgerwa coāram khole, mina gupsiu rāi hūmu rāi mim, o noksiu mi,[5] ormim anu (minatheo lāgediummiri) kubidəksatheo lāgediummiri, jaŋgaltheo lāgediummiri;

IV

mini rāi (u minanuŋma) u yumnuŋma bayra, u phepeakcanuŋma; u yumnuŋma bayra, hama gumi samarat[6] diummirimpachi (āph –) uni toaptoabba boap bepa diummirimpachi, (minaka) gupsiukanuŋ mini rāi nuŋ meorcipka – gupsiuka meo u loak kānchā pomu kam lāgi khole (mina

---

3   For re (= po N), by assimilation.
4   Final -ma is quite often optional, especially in ritual vocabulary. Cf. the alternation jigeŋma/jigeŋnuŋ.
5   Mini's three elder brothers appear to be thought of as in some sense plural.
6   Correct Nepali is samartha.

biūriu rəcha) d̲ā̲u̲ rebḍu; lone: ko chem a phepeakcaka pheakse tpu mim, hanu wa ne, roaktalo u maŋka: ā̲m̲a̲i̲ yimpi r̲ā̲i̲, ham i phepeakcaka re pheansena mim, me bomu seo biūriuma liumla beḍḍiu; hamane ko chem ne gu wo (minara lesta) seokhlira ləsta, gupsiu r̲ā̲i̲ wo seokhlira ləstama oraŋka: a wāka poŋi miŋŋa re ham roaktama r̲u̲k̲h̲ḍa thəstama bayra. ala r̲u̲k̲h̲ḍa thəstama bayralone, meo gupsiu r̲ā̲i̲ ne khole seokhli betto ləstalone, meo r̲u̲k̲h̲ku pharra rokthiḍḍa rəcha; ma oraŋka poŋi miŋŋa re roaktama, aresaka h̲a̲l̲l̲e̲diustalone u pel meoguiu loastiuma u pel le c̲h̲o̲piuriu rəcha, u loak kam; u pel c̲h̲o̲piurium b̲e̲l̲ā̲kane, u phepeakcaka pheakseḍḍiu; mina mama, i wa phepeakcaka pheansena seo biūriuma liumla beḍḍium bayra, meono ko chem ne meomsaka pheakseḍḍiuma seḍḍiu rəcha e. meomsaka seḍḍiu e;

V

ma ŋaddo c̲a̲h̲ī̲ u mam: ma-á go ham goāni ma, bantheo lə̄nama ham pona ma; go ano seokhlira ləŋumim b̲e̲l̲ā̲ka ayu kruŋdo mala ugele malŋi, ugele kruŋdo mala udhali malŋi h̲a̲i̲ roaktam bayra rəcha e, meone; aba u maŋkane[7] bantheo krukta meno-menoŋa ləsta rəcha e. meomlone guka seokhli bomu me loaswa, broal diustama seokhli bom me loaswa; meo b̲e̲l̲ā̲kane u chokco bəktama: e a maŋkane goŋa re (…) roaktama u mam gupsiu r̲ā̲i̲ ka u ceoka seḍḍiu; u ceoka seḍḍiuma: ma mam bantheo ləsta, he diusta b̲h̲a̲n̲d̲a̲k̲h̲e̲r̲i̲ma mam ne l̲u̲ wāka homsaka seḍḍiu roakta e. ma gaci (minanuŋ) o jukpanuŋ – chiuniukepciu roāmi, aba chiuniukepciunuŋ hūmu r̲ā̲inuŋ ləkcima kliumci; gaci athajeom u s̲a̲d̲g̲a̲t̲ beccima rokci h̲a̲i̲, biūriucilone meorcipka ləkcimane pecci rəcha e. u mam ne pecci rəcha e, hamane thamane: mam kliumci re me kliumci re, meo mini r̲ā̲ika biūriulone kliumcoko roakcima: me-e h̲o̲l̲ā̲, gaci me kliumci h̲o̲l̲ā̲, a mam pecci h̲o̲l̲ā̲ roaktalone: mi peccokowa; ba (ici i, a ici liu) ici si ā becci ala biūriu, uci si ā beccilone, hūmu kamne u liuḍḍa u sem ḍe bayra rəcha e. u sem bayrama, (minaka) meo u loak k̲ā̲n̲c̲h̲ā̲ka: l̲u̲ gaci ne mam ne kam s̲a̲d̲g̲a̲t̲ mi becciwa., gaci ne pecci rəcha biūriuma, meorcip ano jaŋardu lolemdu hano meno sokmotheo thirstiucim guka; thiurstiuci, caktheo mini r̲ā̲i̲ kam s̲a̲n̲t̲ā̲n̲ o, s̲a̲n̲t̲ā̲n̲, meorkam s̲a̲n̲t̲ā̲n̲ o h̲ā̲m̲i̲h̲a̲r̲u̲. d̲e̲u̲t̲ā̲ k̲o̲ s̲a̲n̲t̲ā̲n̲ h̲ā̲m̲i̲h̲a̲r̲u̲.

---

7   With the intransitive verb the -k̲a̲ is ungrammatical.

C
tyesma dherai dherai galti bhaeko cha, tara go thettom cahĩ akotiŋa. meotto
bayra holā go thettom cahĩ akotiŋa, ra waŋmim wo kole-nəle cəkpa the pa
mim bumi holā, oramtha gana – waŋmim wo hila bonama ottha ghleosta
mala pheri meoramtha gãsina dika-nəhadda hai.

Bibliography

Allen, N.J. 1972a. The vertical dimension in Thulung classification. *Journal of the Anthropological Society of Oxford* 3: 81-94.

_____. 1972b. Social and economic change among the Thulung Rai. Pp. 114-192 in C. von Fürer-Haimendorf *A study of social change in Nepal*. Report on a Research Project sponsored by the Social Science Research Council.

_____. 1974. The ritual journey: a pattern underlying certain Nepalese rituals. Pp. 6-22 in Fürer-Haimendorf (ed) 1974a.

_____. 1975. *Sketch of Thulung grammar, with three texts and a glossary* (Cornell East Asia Papers 6). Ithaca: Cornell University China-Japan Program.

_____. 1975. Byansi kinship terminology: a study in symmetry. *Man* 10: 80-94.

_____. 1976a. Approaches to illness in the Nepalese hills. Pp. 500-552 in J.B. Loudon (ed) *Social anthropology and medicine* (A.S.A. Monograph 13). London: Academic Press.

_____. 1976b. Shamanism among the Thulung Rai. Pp. 124-140 in J.T. Hitchcock & R.L. Jones (eds) *Spirit possession in the Nepal Himalayas*. Warminster: Aris & Phillips.

_____. 1976c. Sherpa kinship terminology in diachronic perspective. *Man* 11: 569-587.

_____. 1978a. Fourfold classifications of society in the Himalayas. Pp. 7-25 in J.F. Fisher (ed) *Himalayan anthropology: the Indo-Tibetan interface*. The Hague: Mouton.

_____. 1978b. Quadripartition of society in early Tibetan sources. *Journal asiatique* 266: 341-60.

_____. 1978c. Sewala puja bintila puja: notes on Thulung ritual language. *Kailash* 6: 237-256.

_____. 1980. Tibet and the Thulung Rai: towards a comparative mythology of the Bodic speakers. Pp. 1-8 in M. Aris & Aung San Suu Kyi (eds) *Tibetan studies in honour of Hugh Richardson*. Warminster: Aris & Phillips.

_____. 1986. The coming of Macchendranath to Nepal: comments from a comparative point of view. Pp. 75-102 in N.J. Allen, R. Gombrich, T. Raychaudhuri and G. Rizvi (eds) *Oxford University papers on India*, vol. 1 part 1. Delhi: OUP.

_____. 1987. Thulung weddings: the hinduisation of a ritual cycle in East Nepal. *L'Ethnographie* 83(100-1): 15-33.

_____. 1997a. 'And the lake drained away': an essay in Himalayan comparative mythology. Pp. 435-451 in A.W. Macdonald (ed) *Mandala and landscape*. New Delhi: D.K. Printworld.

_____. 1997b. Hinduization: the experience of the Thulung Rai. Pp. 303-323 in D. Gellner, J. Pfaff-Czarnecka & D. Whelpton (eds) *Nationalism and ethnicity in a Hindu kingdom: the politics of culture in contemporary Nepal*. Amsterdam: Harwood.

_____. 1997c. Animal guides and Himalayan foundation myths. Pp. 375-390 in S.G. Karmay & P. Sagant (eds) *Les habitants du toit du monde: études recueillies en hommage à Alexander W. Macdonald*. Nanterre: Société d'Ethnologie.

_____. 1999. Hinduism, structuralism and Dumézil. Pp. 241-260 in E.C. Polomé (ed) *Miscellanea Indo-Europea* (JI-ES Monograph 33). Washington: Institute for the Study of Man.

_____. 2000. The field and the desk: choices and linkages. Pp. 243-57 in P. Dresch, W. James & D. Parkin (eds) *Anthropologists in a wider world: essays on field research*. Oxford: Berghahn.

_____. 2003. From mountains to mythologies. *Ethnos* 68: 271-84.

Baruah, T.K.M. 1960. *The Idu Mishmis*. Shillong: P.C. Dutta.

Bista, D.B. 1972. *People of Nepal* (2nd ed). Kathmandu: Ratna Pustak Bhandar.

Bushell, S.W. 1880. The early history of Tibet from Chinese sources. *Journal of the Royal Asiatic Society* 12: 435-541.

Caplan, Lionel. 1970. *Land and social change in East Nepal: a study of Hindu-tribal relations*. London: Routledge & Kegan Paul.

Carrasco, Pedro. 1959. *Land and polity in Tibet.* Seattle: University of Washington Press.

Cassinelli, C.W. & R.B. Ekvall. 1969. *A Tibetan principality: the political system of Sa sKya.* Ithaca, New York: Cornell University Press.

Chemjong, Iman Sing. 1961. *Limbu-nepāli-āgreji shabda-kosh.* Kathmandu: Nepal Academy.

_____. 1966. *History and culture of the Kirat people* (3rd edn). Phidim, East Nepal: Tumeng Hang.

Das, D.C. 1881. Contributions on the religion, history etc. of Tibet, part I. *Journal of the Asiatic Society of Bengal* 50: 187-251.

_____. 1902. *A Tibetan-English dictionary.* Calcutta: Bengal Secretariat.

Driem, George van. 1998. Neolithic correlates of ancient Tibeto-Burman migrations. Pp. 67-102 in R. Blench and M. Spriggs (eds.) *Archaeology and language II: correlating archaeological and linguistic hypotheses.* London: Routledge.

_____. 2003. Tibeto-Burman vs Sino-Tibetan. Pp. 101-119 in B. Bauer & G.-J. Pinault (eds) *Languages in time and space: a festschrift for Werner Winter.* Berlin: Mouton de Gruyter.

Dumézil, G. 1968. *Mythe et epopée,* vol. I. Paris: Gallimard.

Duncan, M.H. 1955. *Harvest festival dramas of Tibet.* Hong Kong: Orient.

Ebert, Karen H. 2003. Kiranti languages: an overview. Pp 505-517 in G. Thurgood & R. LaPolla (eds) *The Sino-Tibetan languages.* London: Routledge.

_____ & M. Gaenszle. 2008. *Rai mythology: Kiranti oral texts.* Cambridge, MA: Harvard University Press.

Ekvall, R.B. 1964. *Religious observances in Tibet: patterns and function.* Chicago: University of Chicago Press.

Eliade, M. 1961. *Images and symbols: studies in religious symbolism.* London: Harvill.

Fournier, Alain. 1974. Notes préliminaires sur les populations Sunuwar dans l'est du Népal. Pp. 62-84 in Fürer-Haimendorf (ed) 1974a.

Fox, J.J. 1971. Sister's child as plant: metaphors in an idiom of consanguinity. Pp. 219-252 in R. Needham (ed) *Rethinking kinship and marriage* (ASA Monograph 11). London: Tavistock.

Francke, A.H. 1924. gZer-myig, a book of the Tibetan Bonpos. *Asia Major* 1: 243-346.

Fürer-Haimendorf, C. von. 1955. *Himalayan barbary.* London: John Murray.

_____. 1962. *The Apa Tanis and their neighbours: a primitive civilisation of the eastern Himalayas.* London: Routledge & Kegan Paul.

_____. 1964. *The Sherpas of Nepal: Buddhist Highlanders.* London: John Murray.

_____ (ed). 1974a. *Contributions to the anthropology of Nepal.* Warminster: Aris & Phillips.

_____. 1974b. The sense of sin in cross-cultural perspective. *Man n.s* 9: 539-56.

_____. 1975. *Himalayan traders: life in highland Nepal.* London: John Murray.

Funke, F.W. 1969. *Religiöses Leben der Sherpa.* Innsbruck: Universitätsverlag Wagner.

Gaenszle, M. 1991. *Verwandtschaft und Mythologie bei den Mewahang Rai in Ostnepal.* Stuttgart: Steiner.

_____. 2002. *Ancestral voices: oral ritual texts and their social contexts among the Mewahang Rai of East Nepal.* Münster: LIT Verlag.

Goldstein, M.C. 1975. Preliminary notes on marriage and kinship. *Contributions to Nepalese Studies* 2: 57-69.

Gorer, G. 1967. *Himalayan village: an account of the Lepchas of Sikkim* (2nd ed). London: Nelson.

Hardman, Charlotte E. 2000. *Other worlds: notions of self and emotion among the Lohorung Rai.* Oxford: Berg.

Haarh, E. 1969. *The Yarlung dynasty.* Copenhagen: G. Gad.

Hackin, J. 1923. *Guide-catalogue du Musée Guimet.* Paris: G. van Oest.

Hermanns, M. 1946-9. Schöpfungs- und Abstammungsmythen der Tibeter (1) & (2). *Anthropos* 41: 275-98; & 44: 817-47.

Hitchcock, J.T. 1966. *The Magars of Banyan Hill* (Case Studies in Cultural Anthropology). New York: Holt, Rinehart, Winston.

Hocart, A.M. 1927. *Kingship.* London: Oxford University Press.

Höfer, András. 1974. Is the bombo an ecstatic? Some ritual techniques of Tamang shamanism. Pp. 168-182 in Fürer-Haimendorf 1974a.

Hoffmann, H. 1950. *Quellen zur Geschichte der tibetischen Bon-religion.* Wiesbaden: F. Steiner.

Jackson, A. 1971. Kinship, suicide and pictographs among the Na-khi (S. W. China). *Ethnos*: 52-93.

Jest, C. 1971. Onze mois au service du roi, un mois au service de dieu: traditions et croyances religieuses des habitants de la vallée de Tichurong. *L'Ethnographie n.s.* 65: 64-86.

Jones, R.L. 1974. Religious symbolism in Limbu death-by-violence. *Omega* 5: 257-66.

Kaltenmark, M. 1959. *La naissance du monde en Chine.* Pp. 453-68 in *La naissance du monde.* Paris: Editions du Seuil.

Lahaussois, Aimée. 2003. Thulung Rai. *Himalayan linguistics: Archive No. 1.* <http://www.uwm.edu/Dept/CIE/HimalayanLinguistics/Archive_2003/Lahaussois.HLA1.pdf>

Littleton, C.S. 1973. *The new comparative mythology: an anthropological assessment of the theories of Georges Dumézil* (revised ed). Berkeley: University of California Press.

Macdonald, Ariane. 1959. La naissance du monde au Tibet. Pp. 414-452 in *La naissance du monde.* Paris: Editions du Seuil.

_____. 1971. *Une lecture des Pelliot tibétain 1286, 1287, 1038, 1047, et 1290: essai sur la formation et l'emploi des mythes politiques dans la religion royale de Sroñ-bcan sgam-po.* Pp. 190-391 in *Etudes tibétaines dédiées à la mémoire de Marcelle Lalou.* Paris: Maisonneuve.

Macdonald, A.W. 1952. A propos de Prajāpati. *Journal asiatique* 240: 323-338.

_____. 1962. Notes préliminaires sur quelques jhãkri du Muglān. *Journal asiatique* 250: 107-139.

_____. 1966. Les Tamang vus par l'un d'eux. *L'Homme* 6: 27-58.

Macdougal, C. 1973. Structure and division in Kulunge Rai society. *Kailash* 1: 205-224.

Mauss, M. 1948. Discussion. Pp. 25-28 in A. Meillet *Linguistique historique et linguistique générale,* vol. 2. Paris: Champion. (Orig. in *Journal de psychologie normale et pathologique* 1923, 20: 944-7.)

Ministry of Defence. 1965. *Nepal and the Gurkhas.* London: HMSO.

Nebesky-Wojkowitz, René de. 1951. Ancient funeral ceremonies of the Lepchas. *Eastern Anthropologist* 5: 27-40.

_____. 1956. *Oracles and demons of Tibet: the cult and iconography of the Tibetan protective deities.* London: Oxford University Press.

Nepali, G.S. 1965. *The Newars: an ethno-sociological study.* Bombay: United Asia Publications.

O'Flaherty, W.D. 1975. *Hindu myths: a sourcebook translated from the Sanskrit.* Harmondsworth: Penguin.

Onta, Pratyoush. 2004. *Nepal studies in the UK.* Kathmandu: Martin Chautari.

Oppitz, M. 1968. *Geschichte und Sozialordnung der Sherpa.* Innsbruck: Universitätsverlag Wagner.

_____ & E. Hsu 1998. *Naxi and Moso ethnography: kin, rites, pictographs.* Zürich: Völkerkundemuseum.

Pignède, B. 1966. *Les Gurungs: une population himalayenne du Népal.* Paris: Mouton.

Rai, Agam Sĩg Dewsā. 1944. *Āshalacchi shikṣā: thulung rāi bhāṣā.* Darjeeling: the author.

Rock, J.F. 1937. Birth and origin of Dto-mba Shi-lo, the founder of Moso shamanism. *Artibus Asiae* 7: 5-85.

Róna-Tas, A. 1956. Tally stick and divination dice in the iconography of Lha-mo. *Acta Orientalia Hungarica* 6: 163-179.

Sagant, P. 1969. Tâmpungmâ, divinité limbu de la forêt. *Objets et Mondes* 9: 107-124.

_____. 1973. Prêtres Limbu et catégories domestiques. *Kailash* 1: 51-75.

Schultze, Marlene & Dora Bieri. 1971. Chaining and spotlighting: two types of paragraph boundaries in Sunwar. Kirtipur: Tribhuvan University, Summer Institute of Linguistics.

Shafer, R. 1974. *Introduction to Sino-Tibetan.* Wiesbaden: Harrassowitz.

Sharma, B.C. 1962. *Nepāli Shabda Kosh.* Kathmandu: Royal Nepal Academy.

Snellgrove, D.L. 1957. *Buddhist Himalaya: travels and studies in quest of the origins and nature of Tibetan religion.* Oxford: Bruno Cassirer.

_____ & H. Richardson. 1968. *A cultural history of Tibet.* London: Weidenfeld & Nicolson.

Stein, R.A. 1939. Trente-trois fiches de divination tibétaines. *Harvard journal of Asiatic studies* 4: 297-371.

_____. 1957a. Architecture et pensée religieuse en Extrême-Orient. *Arts asiatiques* 4: 164-83.

_____. 1957b. L'habitat, le monde et le corps humain en Extrême-Orient et en Haute Asie. *Journal asiatique* 245: 37-74.

_____. 1957c. Le *linga* des dances masqués lamaïques et la théorie des âmes. *Sino-Indian studies* 5: 200-34.

_____. 1959. *Recherches sur l'épopée et le barde au Tibet.* Paris: Presses Universitaires de France.

_____. 1961. *Les tribus anciennes des marches sino-tibétaines: légendes, classifications, histoire.* Paris: Presses Universitaires de France.

_____. 1971. *Du récit au rituel dans les manuscrits tibétaines de Touen-Houang.* Pp. 479-547 in *Etudes tibétaines dédiées à la mémoire de Marcelle Lalou.* Paris: Maisonneuve.

_____. 1972. *Tibetan civilization* (trans. J.E. Stapleton Driver). London: Faber & Faber.

_____. 1973. Un ensemble sémantique tibétain: créer et procréer, être et devenir, nourrir et guérir. *Bulletin of the School of Oriental and African Studies* 36: 412-23.

Thomas, E.J. 1975 (orig. 1949). *The life of Buddha as legend and history* (3rd edn). London: Kegan Paul.

Thomas, F.W. 1957. *Ancient folk-literature from north-eastern Tibet.* Berlin: Akademie-Verlag.

Thompson, S. & J. Balys. 1958. *The oral tales of India.* Bloomington: Indiana University Press.

Tucci, G. 1949. *Tibetan painted scrolls.* Rome: Libreria dello Stato.

_____. 1955-6a. The sacred character of the kings of ancient Tibet. *East and West* 5: 197-205.

_____. 1955-6b. The symbolism of the temples of bSam-yas. *East and West* 5: 279-281.

_____. 1962. The wives of Sroṅ-btsan sgam-po. *Oriens extremus* 9: 121-26.

Turner, R.L. 1931. *A comparative and etymological dictionary of the Nepali language.* London: Routledge & Kegan Paul.

Waida, M. 1973. Symbolism of descent in Tibetan sacred kingship and some east Asian parallels. *Numen* 22: 60-78.

Wouden, F.A.E. van. 1968. *Types of social structure in Eastern Indonesia* (trans. R. Needham). The Hague: Nijhoff.

Index

1. Phure, my landlord in Mukli, is frilling a bamboo to make a *phurke*, an implement often used in rituals. (See p. 237)

2. During the *tivār* festival, on *gāi pujā* day, Phure, his wife and youngest daughter are garlanding their cattle.

3. Phure's wife is whitewashing the outside of the room I rented in Mukli. It is in preparation for the festival of Dasain.

4. Tirtha Raj, from Tingla village, was my main assistant during the first half of my fieldwork. (See p. 238)

5. Distilling *raksi*
on a verandah

6. Dimajit of Dandagaun hamlet, Mukli, standing by the grave of his wife, built the previous day. (See p. 237)

7. Phure weaving a basket in his courtyard

8. The grandest house in Mukli (seen here at the time of the rice harvest) belonged to a wealthy Gurkha Major.

9. Cattle shelter in the forest above Mukli, looking north-east

10. View of Lokhim village, looking north

11. Local man crossing a three-pole bridge during the monsoon

12. Itinerant showman exhibits his bear in Okhaldhunga. His associate had three monkeys on strings.

13. Celebrating the king's birthday at Mukli Primary School

14. The tribal priest (*deva dhāmi*), Dan Bahadur with his *dhol*, and his assistant,
Kaman Singh with cymbals, are announcing an agricultural ritual (*bhume*, Thul. *tosi*).
(For DB see page 237)

15. Dan Bahadur, in his full priestly garb, with his assistant, is dancing to the music, holding a gourd (Thul. *bom*), containing beer.

16. During a *bhume* ritual the priests are preparing to behead a pig at the base of the silk-cotton tree at Sakhle in Mukli.

17. Silk-cotton tree (*simal*, Thul. *ghruksi*) in Tingla. Such trees mark sites for agricultural (*bhume*) rites.

18. A *sekro,* the largest of the household rituals, is being held at Tingla. A pig is tied to poles set up in the courtyard for the occasion, and shot with bow and arrow.

19. Group of *jhā̃kri*s at Chuiya Bazaar (north-west end of Neche Danda) in late August 1969.

20. On my final day among the Thulung I posed with Ganesh, a teacher at Mukli Primary School. During the second half of my fieldwork he was an excellent assistant – patient and careful. (See p. 237)

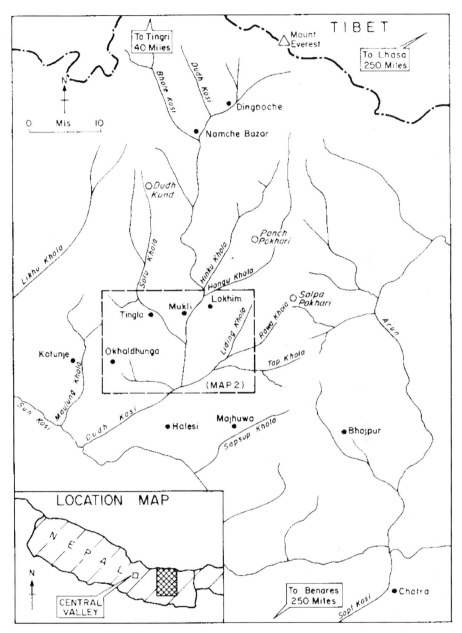

Map 1: Majh (Middle) Kirant

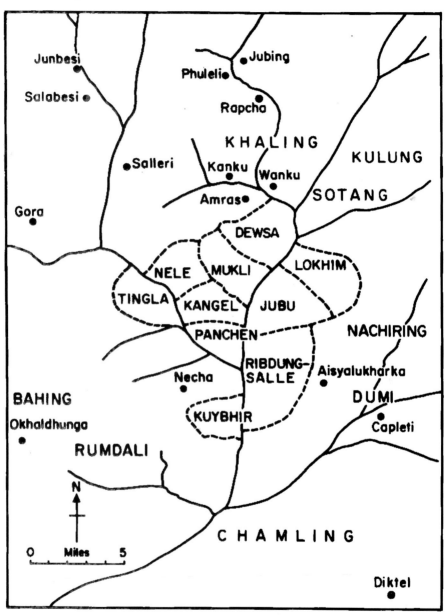

Map 2: The Thulung Area and Neighbouring Subtribes